Shattered Illusions
Albania, Greece and Yugoslavia

SHATTERED ILLUSIONS
Albania, Greece and Yugoslavia

By

NICHOLAS J. COSTA

EAST EUROPEAN MONOGRAPHS, BOULDER
DISTRIBUTED BY COLUMBIA UNIVERSITY PRESS, NEW YORK

1998

EAST EUROPEAN MONOGRAPHS, NO. DXX

This book is dedicated to my wife, Amelia; my children, Keith and Amy Lynn; and my grandchildren, Ryan, Emily, Jacob and Adam Hunter. It also dedicated to Lieutenant Colonel NLD "Billy" McLean; Major David Smiley; and my mother, Dr. Kenneth Winetrout, of American International College.

CONTENTS

ACKNOWLEDGEMENTS

The historical and political events presented in this dimensional, academic study is the product of years of research at major European depositories, the readings of a multitude of biographies and memoirs, together with interviews of those individuals who were directly involved in the events presented herein.

A number of significant, political, diplomatic and military events occurred that served to make the participants aware of the fact that the emerging post-World War I political reality rested upon a series of hopes and illusions. The internal weakness of the foundations upon which the post-World War I world order existed, together with the willingness not to accept the totalitarian challenge because of a loss of never by England and France, could only result in the outbreak of war.

First, I thank my mentor of yesteryear, Dr. Kenneth Winetrout of American International College, for his inspirational words to the effect, "Tell me, Costa, what's going to come first – my demise or your book? Finish it, Nick, for I desire to read it before the grim reaper comes a-knocking." Secondly, I desire to express my gratitude to Sir Julian Amery, the late Lt. Colonel NLS "Billy" McLean and Colonel David Smiley for sharing with me many joyful hours, along with their private papers, photographs, and memories of bygone days. I must also express my gratitude to the late Dr. Milovan Djilas for his encouragement and significant insights relating to the ever-changing Yugoslav political process. Of the changing scene, I am indebted to Dr. Svetozar Stojanovic for the various discussions we had that touched upon the subject of the structural weaknesses of Yugoslav communism in the post-Tito era, together with the potential negative effects of the approaching winds of nationalism before the disintegration of the Yugoslavian nation-state. I am profoundly grateful to Elia Rado and to Guri, who established communications and who served as translators while in Albania.

To my wife, who astutely reviewed, edited and typed the manuscript and concluded, "It reads well", I am deeply grateful. I am also indebted to all of the students and scholars who have worked and are currently working in the complex field of Balkan history. In concluding, I must state that if there are faults within the book, they are mine and mine alone.

PROLOGUE

The manner in which the historical and political events of the 20th century are presented is determined not only by the author, but also by the times in which such words are expressed in book form. The significance of historical study and analysis is to be found in the words of the United States Secretary of State when in a letter to a friend in the year, 1947, James Byrnes remarked:

I read your letter and I recalled the hurdles that we had to overcome after World War I... It is remarkable how history repeats itself.

The 20 year crisis, 1919-1938, among the nations of the European community, in relation to the interwar period, is to be found in the fact that there existed an almost total neglect of the fact of power in diplomatic considerations and relationships. The predatory nature of German Naziism with its apparent ingrained element of pragmatic realism emboldened the Fascist leaders of Italy and Germany and motivated Benito Mussolini and Adolph Hitler to adhere to a brutal policy of conquest and destruction.

The transpiring occurrences in the form of territorial acquisitions of the interwar years, 1919-1938, while illegal, became acceptable in London and Paris. Following the traumatic, psycho-historical bombshell of 1914-1918 and the world economic depression of 1929, there emerged as a reaction, in part to the bloodletting and the tear-gas shells of trench warfare in 1914, the policy of appeasement as the United States of America adhered to a policy of isolationism and later to strict neutrality. Both Berlin and Rome, aware of the prevailing European mind-set in the United Kingdom and France, proceeded through illegal means to acquire adjoining territorial holdings with its German ethnic minority. Despite the invading military Fascist forces and the process of negotiations as in Munich, 1938, over the Sudeten Question, the United Kingdom and the French Republic refused in the words of Albert Camus to accept "The wager of their generation".

The moves and countermoves across the international chess broad served *not* to avoid the awakening of the mythical god of war – Mars, but served to insure what the statesmen of Europe desired to avoid, but could no longer be avoided... It was as Dobrica Cosic had stated in his work entitled *The Believer*, that:

Man, a Sisyphus, only occasionally succeeds in convincing himself that the rock he is rolling to the top of the mountain has fallen back, when in fact, he has only been rocking it back and forth at the foot of the mountain.

Thus, on September 1, 1939, as German military units crossed the German frontier into Poland, World War II was to greet the people of Europe at daybreak as Hitler launched "Case White". The combination of Adolph Hitler's and Benito Mussolini's military conquests and brutal occupation polities gave birth, in part, to the emergence of the resistance movement throughout occupied Europe. Thus, it is to the three European nation-states of the southwestern tier of the Balkan peninsula: to the Land of Eagle-Albania; to the Land of the South Slavs-Yugoslavia; and to Hellas-Greece, that we now turn. It is here that the resistance movement sacrificed its sons and daughters; its mothers, wives and children in its Wars of National Liberation for the emergence of freedom and the false god of Marxist-Leninism.

For the tradition-directed people of the Balkans, the war brought starvation, devastation, and death throughout and land. For the resistance fighters, it brought hope and civil war as brother fought brother and fathers confronted their sons and daughters in the battle for the ashes of the Balkan killing fields and from the burned out villages, the spirit of resistance prevailed as the Yugoslavs, the Albanians, and the Greeks confronted the Italo-German military units and occupation forces, let alone their ideological opposites, in the mountains and valleys of the Balkan peninsula for six years.

CHAPTER ONE

HOPE AND DISILLUSIONMENT

In an attempt to rationalize away the fact that 20th century man with his weapons of destruction and ideological commitments was able to shatter institutions, annihilate the constituted socio-political order and to fracture all relationships which served to maintain a civil society, it has been written that "The tragedy of this century is the tragedy of intelligence gone awry and rebellion run amok". Of the multitude of the negative series of zero experiences which have enveloped the citizens of our Global Village, the former editor of the French resistance newspaper COMBAT, Albert Camus, stated:

> We were born at the beginning of the first World War. As adolescents we had the crisis of 1929; at twenty, Hitler. Then came the Ethiopian War, the Civil War in Spain, and Munich. These were the foundations of our education. Next came the Second World War, the defeat, and Hitler in our homes and cities. Born and bred in such a world, what did we believe in? Nothing. Nothing except the obstinate negation in which we were forced to close from the very beginning. The world in which we were called to exist was an absurd world, and there was no other in which we could take refuge... If the problem had been the bankruptcy of a political ideology, or a system of government, it would have been simple enough. But what happened came from the very root of man and society. There was no doubt about this, and it was confirmed day after day not so much by the behavior of the criminals but by that of the average man...

And yet, as a national tri-dimensional revolutionary actor, this man was to find a meaning to life amid the ruins of an occupied Europe peculiarized by starvation, severe mental and physical persecution and concentration camps as an active participant in a resistance movement that was committed to the sweeping away of the Old Order and to a revolutionary historical process that tragically and unpredictably for many was to unknowingly result in the words of George Orwell "In an age where two plus two will make five when the leader says so".

Of the countless numbers who flocked to the ranks of the pro-communist resistance movements of their respective countries in the southern tier of the Balkans in support of the struggle to bring about a triple revolution in the form of a war of national liberation, civil war and a socio-political and economic revolution, together with the dedicated Marxist-Leninist oriented revolutionaries, the Czechoslovakian philosopher, Milan Kundera, stated:

> *Stay what you will – the Communists were more intelligent. They had a grandiose program, a plan for a brand-new world in which every one would find his place... People have always aspired to an idyll, a garden where nightingales sing, a realm of harmony where the world does not rise up as a stranger against man nor man against other men, where the world and all its people are molded from a single stock and the fire lighting up the heavens is a fire burning in the hearts of men, where every man is a note in a magnificent Bach fugue and anyone who refuses his note is a mere black dot, useless and meaningless, easily caught and squashed between the fingers like an insect.*

> *From the start there were people who realized they lacked the proper temperament for the idyll and wished to leave the country. But since by definition an idyll is one world for all, the people who wished to emigrate were implicitly denying its validity. Instead of going abroad, they went behind bars. They were soon joined by thousands and tens of thousands more... And suddenly those young, intelligent radicals had the strange feeling of having sent something into the world, a deed of their own making, which had taken on a life of its own, lost all resemblance to the original idea. So these young intelligent radicals*

started shouting to their deed, calling it back, chasing it, hunt-
ing it down. If I were to wrote a novel about that generation of
talented radical thinkers, I would call it Stalking a Lost Deed.

To fully understand the cycle of enchantment, disenchantment, contamination and disintegration of the idyll which Milan Kindera spoke of, one must first return to that period of time when in 1914 the "Guns of August" were unleashed and 20th century man was to once again stand at the edge of the historical abyss and to that moment when on the 1930's he refused to accept "The Wager of His Generation".

The world of 20th century Europe opened with an inheritance of a half century of prosperity, universal peace, security and stability. Yet, within that period which many consider to be the watershed mark of European History, 1890 to 1914, man was to witness his dream of universal peace give way to universal war; his sense of certainty break down and evolve into a sense of stark, naked fear; and his dream of universal progress disintegrate into a concern for universal survival.

What numerous forces first combined to spin the hypnotic web of the great illusion and then sweep man forward in a dim and half conscious manner toward that one experience that would not only shake the very foundations of Western Civilization but also force 20th century man to continue to live within the shadow and with the consequences of World War I? What were those forces that would give birth to a universal generation of men that would march to the trenches with a sense of exaltation and return in 1918 with a deep, physical and psychological exhaustion and a sense of universal despair?

By 1914, Europe stood in a relationship to the rest of mankind never before achieved by mankind. She was in the words of Mazzini "the lever of the world". The outstanding characteristics were indeed peace and stability. The period of protracted peace that was inherited from the 19th century brought out man's hopes and expectations. Man felt that war was now abolished or an impossibility. People argued that the high degree of economic integration and cooperation on the international level, together with the natural tendency of man towards programs of scientific interchanges, peace movements and international organizations, served as barriers to the outbreak of any protracted conflict similar to that of the Napoleonic version.

In addition, the ideal of a universal and everlasting peace was fostered by the dominant economic position of Western Europe to the rest of the world. There existed an increasing pressure throughout the world for the products of the modern technological era. The growing demand for new fangled gadgets and raw materials created the basis for world trade. This, in turn, enmeshed the world's economic relationships into one major unit which no one individual or nation desired to disrupt for fear of creating economic chaos and an end to industrial growth that was recorded to be excessively higher than that attained in 1900.

Another economic aspect that contributed to the rationalization that war was impossible, was the practice of investing funds abroad. national investments were scattered throughout the world. Great Britain had invested 18 billion dollars in Latin America, the United States, and India. France had invested 8.7 billion dollars in Russia, North Africa, and Indo-China while Germany had invested 5.6 billion dollars in East Prussia and Russia.

The growing trend on the part of nations to settle their differences by a third party, together with the inability of people to comprehend that such small wars as the Crimean War of 1854-1856, the Russo-Turkish War of 1877, the Austro-Prussian War of 1866, the Franco-Prussian War of 1870 together with the series of Balkan Wars which took place in 1912 and 1913, were creating unsolvable problems and served to evolve a universal image of Peace, Prosperity and Progress.

Times were changing; the year 1905 marked for the first time in a quarter of a century that all of Europe was astir. The Revolution in Russia in 1905 had come as the first major social disturbance since the barricades were stormed during the Paris Communes of 1871. But the other decisive event of 1905, The First Moroccan Crisis, touched off a chain reaction of diplomatic crises which forced the young men of Europe to live and work unknowingly in an environment of impending doom. True, prior to this time, the man on the street from London to Paris to St. Petersburg and from Vienna to Rome to Berlin, had abandoned war as a final solution. Yet, their respective governments had never abandoned WAR – as the means of resolving unresolvable, international disputes.

The recognition of war as the final solution could not escape the mind of those *"elected few"* who were responsible for the security of their respective nations. True, various crises that could have touched off a World War were averted through the process of compromise, such as The Moroccan Crisis of 1905, The Bosnian-Hercegovina Crisis of 1908, The Moroccan Crisis of 1911 and the Balkan Wars of 1912-1913.

The compromise procedure's success reinforced the existing public opinion image that the peace of Europe would be maintained; that a general war was remote and above all, it reinforced man's rationale that any and all situations could and would be solved at the conference table and not on the battlefield. Yet, the Chancellors of Europe were still aware of the growth in international tensions even if the people were not. Out of the fear that war was a possibility, there emerged the Alliance System – yet, it should be noted that the motivating force for the establishment of the Alliance System was the desire to retain national security.

It was only with the brief passage of time that nations who first built the alliance systems out of a desire for security now found that this very system created an inflexibility on the part of a nation's response to any international crisis. Thus, in 1914, following the ultimatum of Austria to Serbia, neither Germany, Russia, nor France would allow the primary parties to go it alone, for this would have resulted in the elimination of the interests of the parties concerned, either directly or indirectly; thus, nations were drawn into conflict situations.

The high degree of inflexibility which determined a nation's action and reaction also served to produce an additional ironic effect. The growing awareness that a European War could emerge forced nations in their concern for national security to increase their military expenditures. In so doing, nations began to question the motives of such action on the part of their neighbor and thus, there emerged an atmosphere of universal suspicion. In such a situation, nations that should have formed or participated in programs of mutual benefit now found themselves in opposing camps. The best example of such a situation is a forgotten aspect of the British-German economic competition in regions long considered to be "private preserves of Great Britain" and upon programs such as the "Berlin to Baghdad Railroad"; the buildup in German merchant and naval fleet as a challenge in military terms, could only fail to realize that Germany had to import food in order to maintain her standard of living. The means of gaining required foodstuffs demanded the development of a favorable trade relationship with any and all nations regardless of their past economic ties.

In the meantime, the Germans, because of British reaction to their programs, considered the British as being concerned only with halting German progress. German failed to realize that England, "The Workshop of the World", was totally dependent upon the resources of its Empire and required a two ocean navy to maintain the sea lanes, for England had to EXPORT. Thus, a nation that must import and a nation that must export failed to correctly evaluate the situation and were pulled into antagonistic positions as they became classified as victims of their times.

When the war broke with its mounting savagery, all young men marched off into oblivion as if they were caught up by some super magnetic force. The unpreparedness on the part of the pre-war generation to fully. The unpreparedness on the part of the pre-war generation to fully understand the harsh reality of war and its consequences is made known to us by Sir Herbert Reed who writes,

> *In 1914, our conception of war was completely unreal. We had vague, childish memories of the Boer War and from these and a general diffusion of Kiplingesque sentiments, we managed to infuse into war a decided elements, we managed to infuse into war a decided element of adventurous romance. War still appealed to the imagination.*

Yet, this should not have existed. The American Civil War clearly demonstrated that the era of the "Gentlemen's War" was over. With the outbreak of World War I, there would now emerge a type of war of a magnitude never before envisioned.

At the start, World War I was indeed an innocent man's war. Few were to understand the full impact of the prophecy of Sir Edward Gray when he stated that evening in Whitehall to a friend, "The lamps are going out all over Europe. We shall never see them light again in our lifetime". To a great degree, it was largely at the outset, regardless of a nation's time of entry, a singing war devoted to polite songs. For Americans who entered in 1918, there were there songs about, "K-K-K-Katy, Beautiful Katy", "Over There", and "Mademoiselle From Armentiers". For the British, there were songs like "There Will Always be an England" and "It's a Long Way to Tipparary", while the German troopers sang "Deutschland Uber Alles", "Die Wacht Am Rhein", and "Heil Dir Im Siegeskranz". Also, the military formations of the French "Poilu" together with their Foreign Legionnaires and mounted Moroccan forces marched off to the front with the highly emotional words and melody of the "Marseillaise" ringing in their hearts and minds.

Yes, the young men of all nations did march off to war as if to soccer match, decked with flowers and kisses and gifts of food. They marched off on the crest of popular enthusiasm with flags flying and bands playing and people shouting, "Vive les Anglais", "Vive les American", and "Lafayette We Are Here". Such a send-off was to produce a sense of Tennysonian idealism and Kiplingesque jingoism as exemplified by Robert Brooke's poem "The Soldier".

> *If I should die, think only this of me*
> *That there's some corner of a foreign field*
> *That is forever England.*
> *There shall be it that rich earth*
> *A richer dust concealed*
> *A dust who England bore shaped made aware.*

Whatever may have been the romantic interpretation of war, it was not to last. Brooke's poem was only a passing mood of the initial stages of the war. The young had not as yet witnessed the full horror and violent deaths of trench warfare. The illusion that existed was to be shattered time and time again at such places as Verdun where the combined name of French and German casualties totaled in excess of 970,000. Tannenberg, Gallipoli, Ypres, The Marne were the battles of World War I which were fought, refought and never won. The only true victor was the "Grim Reaper", for the British, French, and the Germans were to lose a generation of men along a static Western front which extended for 350 miles. For the Russians who manned the broad expanse of an Eastern front, which extended from the Gulf of Finland to the Black Sea, 400,000 inadequately supplied, incompetently led, and demoralized troops were to sacrifice themselves on a monthly basis on behalf of "Mother Russia". For many, the water filled trenches of World War I: Passchendale, Flanders, The Somme, Arras, Bellow Woods, Caparetto, Tannenberg, Masurian Lakes, Chateau Terry and the Qurcq River (where the poet, Joyce Kilmer, died), remain to this day the gravestones of the "Great War".

No, they had not as yet witnessed American and British troops with little but raw courage rushing row after row into German machine gun fire. Nor had they borne witness to the slaughter and the carnage of the Eastern front as Russian troops, many without weapons, disintegrated before the stresses of a major modern war with its final apocalyptic quality. Nor had they seen the bodies pile up with their "red badge of courage" on a field of blue, piled up on each other while more young men advanced and charged forward, ever forward, with bayonets fixed and falling, always falling, before the withering fire, helmetless and in the bright red pantaloons of the French infantry.

It is only after they had written as in one's personal diary,

We all began to run out across the field toward the French lines... just about 50 yards on there lay a dead cow and we threw ourselves down behind it just as a machine-gun began to open fire. As we did so, a dozen rats leaped out of its belly and scurried away over our backs. There we lay for a long time, as shell after shell crashed into the group; there are cries for help all around us and we see men buried be shells one minute and next, all brown up and reburied again. We move forward and fall into the mud, crawling over the dead, the wounded, while the earth trembles and shakes like jelly. Still we crawl into and out of shell holes, while shells are screaming over our heads and the wounded are drowning in the shell holes and 15 feet of mud...

that one can escape from the make-believe into the land of the living dead and write as did Siegfried Sassoons,

> *Our men go steadily on the German front lines Brilliant sunshine and haze of smoke drifting along the landscape.*
> *Some Yorkshire men cheering as if at a football match... the sunlight flashes on the bayonets; shrapnel bursting in small white puffs white puffs with tiny flashes, the birds seem bewildered; I am staring at a sunlit picture of hell.*

or the following muted lines from a sonnet by Sorley,

> *When you see millions of the mouthless dead*
> *Across your dreams in pale battalions go*
> *Say not soft things as other men have said*
> *That you'll remember. For you need not so.*
> *Give them not praise. For deaf how should they know*
> *Is it not curses heaped on each gashed head?*
> *Not tears. Their blind eyes see not your tears flow,*
> *Not honor. It is easy to be dead.*

The war is no longer lost in a drapery of romanticism. Man has finally come into contact with the stark, naked reality of the violence and the horror that man can inflict upon his fellow man.

It is Wilfred Owen who gives in his poem "Dulce Et Decorum East" a lasting expression of man's cold experiences and indignation,

> *Bend double like beggars under sacks,*
> *Knock-kneed, coughing like hags,*
> *We cursed through sludge*
> *Till on the haunting flares we turned our backs*
> *And toward our distant rest began to trudge.*
> *Men marched asleep. Many had lost their boots,*
> *But limped on, blood-shod. All went lame, all blind,*
> *Drunk with fatigue, deaf even to the hoots*
> *Of gas shells dropping softly behind.*

Gas! Gas! Quick boys! An ecstasy of fumbling,
Fitting the clumsy helmets just in time,
But someone still was yelling out and stumbling
And floundering like a man in fire or lime.
Dim through the misty panes and thick green light,
As under a green sea, I saw him drowning.
In all my dreams before my helpless sight
He plunges at me, guttering, choking, drowning.
It in some smothering dreams, you too could pace
Behind the wagon that we flung him in,
And watch the white eyes writing in his face,
His hanging face, like a devil's sick of sin,
If you could hear, at every jolt, the blood
Come gurgling from the froth-corrupted lungs
bitten as the cud
Of vile, incurable sores on innocent tongues –
My friend, you would not tell with such high zest
To children ardent for some desperate glory,
The old lie; Dulce et decorum est
Pro patria mori.
   (It is sweet and becoming to die for one's country)

The total impact which any man experiences when confronted by
the reality of the machine gun, the gas attack, or the personal awareness that he has just killed a man he has not known or even hated, can
never be laid bare for the impartial observer to examine and react to in
the safe environment of a book. Yet, the only insight which an individual can gain, to a degree, in relation to man's reaction to potential
death or the reality of the slogan "Kill or be killed" comes in retro-
spect from the poetry written by the men in action, either at that specific time, or those which were produced a decade or so after the Armistice. Nor can one come to grips with the total impact of the foreboding sense of fatalism which enveloped the wounds and the cries of
mankind as he goes "Over the Top" to meet his destiny without first
becoming familiar with the following verse by Alan Seeger:

I have a rendezvous with death
On some scarred slope of a battered hill
And I to my pledged word am true
I shall not fail that rendezvous.

or of the words of Frederick Manning when the wrote,

Dead are the lips where love laughed or sand,
The hands of youth eager to lay hold of life,
Eyes that have laughed to eyes
And these were begotten
Of love, and lived lightly, and burnt
With the lust of a man's first strength ere they were rent,
Almost at unawareness, savagely, and strewn
In bloody fragments, to be the
Carrion of rats and crows
And the sentry moves not, searching
Night for menace with weary eyes.

Herein lies man's reaction to the Hell we call war. Now, what is the full impact of this experience which history has labeled "The Great War" upon man and the immediate post-war would? Man became aware of the fact that he was no longer the center of the universe, that he was only a speck of dust evolving out there in a meaningless existence completely at the mercy of science and its man-made machines. Man had lost that life-giving substance – hope – for as stated by F. Scott Fitzgerald, "All my beautiful, lovely, safe world blew itself up here with a gust of high explosive". Now, man becomes an artificial part of that which he is to term, the absurd society.

For man's society, one cannot help but note that the old social and political bonds that had worked to hold the old post-war world together, are no longer present. The dike of the 19th century's social structure was broken and the world was confronted with a break with the past.

Wilson had stated that this war was fought to make the world safe for democracy, the war to end all wars. However, France which had lost over one and a half million dead, could not satisfy the psychological attitude of its people by references to a "Noble Dream". The Italians and the British were not able to forget nor forgive. Thus, the flame of idealism had little if no appeal, for HATE now ruled over REASON. The objective of man was now to impose his will upon the vanquished as representanted by the German War Guilt Close #231 and the dictated peace. The issues that served to create that which was prophesied by Ferdinand Foche to be, "Not a peace treaty, but an armistice for 20 years".

The young idealist, victor and vanquished alike, were aware of the great betrayal and thus they cried out in their disillusionment. In a few eloquent lines, T.E. Lawrence sums up the full impact of the younger generation's reaction to that betrayal,

> *We were wrought up with ideas inexpressible and vaporous, but to be fought for. We lived many lives in those whirling campaigns, never sparing ourselves any good or evil; yet when we achieved and the new world dawned, the old men came out again and took from us or victory, and remade it into the likeness of the former world they knew.*
>
> *Youth could win, but had not learned to keep, and was pitifully weak against age. We stammered that we had worked for a new heaven and a new earth, and they thanked us kindly and made their peace.*

Yes, peace comes to tired, war-weary would and man once again seeks to means to security. Yet, the events of World War I and the post-war years, up to the present, clearly demonstrate that Santayana was correct when he stated, "Those who do not remember the past are condemned to relive it".

The awareness of the price for "Europe's Accidental War" or "Danse Macabre" – 10 million dead, 22 million wounded, a cost in excess of 33 billion dollars and over 5 million civilian deaths in areas of actual warfare – created a realization that there could not a return to the values of 19th century Europe. Tragically, Santanya was correct. The war had ended, but man had not changed. He went to the conference table a prisoner of a emotionally charged tide of vengeance and on the basis of the old biblical formula of "An Eye for an Eye", he unknowingly planted the seeds for the new cycle of crisis, accommodation, appeasement, and war.

CHAPTER TWO

SHATTERED PEACE

Each nation and its citizenry can only truly best be understood in terms of its particular experience of life. As a tourist an individual may visit a country and see it only superficially. However, when viewed from the inside, the uniqueness and the majesty of the nation and the people are projected to the individual observer as an entire universe. Thus, as one enters the Balkans, one becomes aware not only of the burden of history on its soul, but also of the despair which emerged with the German and the Italian conquest of their lands together with the stripping away of a nation and an individual's dignity throughout World War II.

One of the psychological consequences which emerges and quickly settles across and land is the action-reaction cycle. At this psycho-historical moment, man is confronted with a crisis of conscience and a conflict of value. The issue confronting him is: should he once again meet the barbarian head on as he did in 1914? Symbolically, the situation that confronts him is similar in many ways to Plato's mythological story of *Phaedrus*. Here, the individual finds Reason holding the reigns of a charion drawn by the white horse of emotion and the black stallion of unbridled desires, as Reason through the usage of his whip, seeks to control the potential destructive force of the two horses and subdue the surging black steed of passion.

Out of the deep sense of despair which did settle across the land and the subsequent conquest and occupation of Europe in the first phase of the conflict situation (with the exception of the Great Britain and neutral Spain, Sweden Portugal and Switzerland), by the forces of Fascist Italy and Nazi Germany, there quietly emerged among a number of the defeated population an expected inner strength. Such inner strength was see among their forefathers throughout the 500 year pro-

tracted occupation of their lands in the Balkan peninsula by the Ottoman Turk together with the nation transformation of a segment of the
country's ethos. Prior to the outbreak of World War II in Europe, the
reader must become aware of the fact that as war clouds appeared on
the horizon, mankind stood on a brink of a catastrophic precipice below which, in a very symbolic manner, existed an absolute black void
of an uncompromising totalitarianism. The catastrophic precipice upon
which mankind's representative in the Western World stood, was in a
figurative manner Spain and the Spanish Civil War of 1936-1939. What
was evolving (as the Spanish Civil War raged) within the individual
and emerging throughout this protracted period of bloodletting, regardless of one's ideological preference, can only be identified as the
rebirth of the indomitable human spirit which gave birth to a willingness to engage in acts of resistance.

Whether in the emerging cycle of action and reaction, be it in China
in 1931; at Mukden, the Italo-Abyssinian War in 1935; Guernica and
Spain in 1936; or Durres and Albania on April 7th, 1939, what was the
ability of a certain segment of the population to say NO? In their reaction to invasion and occupation of their respective countries, they made
their conquerors and the collaborating segment of society aware of the
fact that to the resistance fighter, "No", was non extinguishable. Thus,
as many young men and women took to the forest, the rugged mountainous terrain of the nation and other unsettled regions of the lands of
Albania, Serbia, Montenegro and Greece, they not only confronted
their conquerors, but from a philosophical perspective – they, through
their individual and collective actions on isolated and remote outposts,
painting slogans on houses, carrying out raids on police stations and
disrupting the communication system of a designated region, sought
to make the conqueror and the native collaborator aware of the fact
that their sense of the dignity of the person was not destroyed. Thus,
through their actions, they made the occupation forces and the world
aware of the fact that they could say, "No, therefore I exist". The most
significant word in the above statement is "EXIST".

The quest of a European nation to exist and to maintain its freedom
of action within of Great Britain and France, was difficult to achieve.
Europe at this historical moment was not only caught in a series of
protracted crisis situations that, according to Arthur Koestler, repre-

sented, "... spasms of its death struggle"[1], but according to George Orwell, the 20th century European had, because of the actions and the decisions reached at the Wilhelmstrasse in Berlin and at the Palazzo Venezia and the Palazzo Chigi in Rome, "cast aside" that which Edmund Burke once called the "the decent drapery" of tradition, only to discover that "the thing at the bottom was not a bed of roses after all; it was a cesspool of barbed wire".[2]

The abyss into which the European would first fall into, followed in time by all of the citizens of our "Global Village", possessed much more than just the criteria of devastation, disillusionment, starvation and death. It possessed the environment, of an insane asylum. As Simone Weil put it, *"We seem to have lost the very rudiments of intelligence, the notions of measure, standard and degree; of proportion and relation; of affinity and consequence... we people our political world with monsters and myths; we recognize nothing but entities, absolutes and finalities".[3] It could not have been different for in the world of George Orwell, "We live in a lunatic world in which opposites are constantly changing into one another".[4]

Of this phase of the rush to the abyss, Albert Camus articulated his concerns in two 1939 entries in his *Notebook* of which the following is most powerful,

> *They have all betrayed us, those*
> *who preached resistance and those*
> *who talked peace... Never before*
> *has the individual stood so alone*
> *before the lie-making machine...*
> *We used to wonder where war lived,*
> *what it was that made us so vile.*
> *And now we realize that we know*
> *where it lives, that it is inside*
> *ourselves.[5]*

---

1. Jeffery C. Isaac, *Arenth, Camus and Modern Rebellion* (New Have, Yale University Press, 1992)
2. Jeffery C. Isaac,' *Ibid* p. 26
3. Jeffery C. Isaac, *Ibid* p. 25
4. Jeffery C. Isaac, *Ibid* p. 25
5. Jeffery C. Isaac, *Ibid* p. 31

The psycho-historian and author of *History and Human Survival*, Robert Jay Lifton, calls to mankind's immediate attention that men, "In seeking new beginnings are now haunted by an image of the end of everything".[6] This prevailing sense of the end of everything was also made at an earlier time by Oswell Spengler and Arnold Toynbee let along Mendeleev, who viewed the nation-state and man as possessing, "No more than the life cycle of an organism".[7]

As mankind moved towards its destiny in the early 1930's, in a brief period of time, it was to become a major historical aberration of the 20th century as he moved towards a destiny without appeal that enveloped man with a shroud possessing the criteria of irrationality and extreme nationalism that verged on tribalism. It is at this historical and political moment that there emerged on the stage of history in 1933, in the European heartland and the land of Schiller and Goethe, one Adolph Hitler. Of this person and his rise to power, it has been stated:

> *The West put a modern militaristic, Fascist Germany on the scene... If a 20th century Germany was a monster, by the same token 20th century Western Civilization was the Frankenstain guilty of having been the author of this Germanic monster's being.[8]*

Yet, according to the historian, Alan Bullock, while some many find it difficult to accept Arnold Toynbee's thesis in regards to the rise of Adolph Hitler, it must be noted:

> *As the army officers saw in Hitler the man who promised to restore Germany's military power, so the industrialists came to see in him the man who would defend their interest against the threat of Communism and the claims of the trade unions, giving a free hand to private enterprise and economic exploitation in the name of the principle of "creative individuality".[9]*

---

6. Albert Camus, *Notebook* (New York, Alfred A. Knoph, Inc., 1963) p. 139
7. Arthur Koestler, *The Yogi and the Commissar* (New York, Macmillan and Company, 1946) p. 102
8. Kenneth Winetrout, *Arnold Toynbee: The Ecumenical Vision* (Boston, Twayne Publishers, 1975) p. 45
9. Alan Bullock, *Hitler: A Study In Tyranny* (New York, Bantam Books, 1952) p. 215

In the Germany of the 1930's, it must be noted that the Weimar Republic not only lacked support from the various power centers of German society, but the German Right desired to destroy the hated Republic, reestablish the monarchy, put working class in its place and restore Germany to its rightful place as the power center of Europe. In the pursuit of their ultimate political objectives, they came to believe that Adolph Hitler was not only their man, but one who could be controlled and manipulated as they saw fit. The general public was swept away by the force of nationalism and by the fact that they too desired to do away with the Weimar Republic and nullify the terms of the Treaty of Versailles. The Communists, who saw the Socialist Party as their major barrier to power, were to declare through tier actions and their words against the Social Democrats that they would prefer the Nazis in power than to come to the aid of the Republic which they also equated with the Versailles Treaty.

Of the military's position in 1933, one need only recall what was stated by Adolph Hitler as he addressed representatives of the National Socialist German Workers Party following his appointment as Chancellor of German eight months later:

> *On this day we would particularly*
> *remember the part played by our*
> *Army, for we all know well that if,*
> *in the days of our revolution the*
> *Army had not stood on our side, then*
> *we would not be standing here today.*[10]

On January 30th, 1933, President Hindenburg, acting in accordance to the provisions within the constitution, entrusted the chancellor ship of Germany to Adolph Hitler, the man who led in numbers the largest political party in post-World War I. Germany and who in 1932 had attained only 37% of the vote. If it truly is, as stated by William Appleman Williams in the analytical study entitled *The Free World Colossus: A Critique of American Foreign Policy in the Cold War*, that "History is the record of man's effort to transform the real into the ideal",[11] then

---

10. Alan Bullock, *Ibid* p. 210-211
11. David Horowitz, *The Free World Colossus* (New York, Hill and Wang Publishers, 1965) p. 11

the Second World War becomes the required ingredient and the necessary pre-condition for the emergence of the political Left both in Europe and in Asia. This truism cannot be denied for as stated by Joseph
Stalin to a young resistance fighter and a member of Tito's inner-circle,
Milovan Djilas, at a meeting in the Kremlin towards the closing months
of the war:

> *This war is not as in the past; whoever occupies a territory*
> *also imposes on it his own social system. Everyone imposes his*
> *own system as far as the army can reach. It cannot be otherwise.*[12]

This statement projects Stalin's revolutionary perspective. It also
exposes the deep ingrained Russian psycho-historical sense of fear
and the traditional, national desire to establish a defensive shield in
the West against any potential invasion. This is understandable when
one not only considers and accepts the historical fact that the West has
been and remains in the eyes of the Russian, the arch-aggressor. According the Kenneth Winetrout in his study entitled *Arnold Toynbee,*

> *The Russian experience is easily tabulated.*
> *It is the history most of us know, but rarely put together as*
> *representative of Western aggression. In 1610, Russia was in-*
> *vaded by a Polish army; in 1709 by a Swedish army; in 1812 by*
> *a French military force commanded by Napoleon; in 1915 by a*
> *Germany army followed by an English-American army, and in*
> *1941 by the Germans.*[13]

While this may be limited only to the Russian encounter with the
West, it must be noted that should one elect to expand an analytical
study of the West's impact upon our "Global Village" from the military or the culture frame of reference, one would have to conclude that
the West is the arch-aggressor.

Following the advent to power of Adolph Hitler in Germany in
1933, a series of political and diplomatic events were to transpire on
the European continent that were to result in the Munich Agreements

---

12. Milovan Djilas, *Conversation With Stalin* (New York, Harcourt, Brace and World
INC, 1962) p. 114
13. Kenneth Winetrout, *Op. Cit.* p. 48

of 1938. One must recall that from 1933 to 1939 the Chancellor of Nazi Germany had not only presented demands that were outrageous, but also some that were justified. It must be noted that while both London and Paris granted such outrageous demands in the Munich Agreement, they failed to render to Berlin those that were justified. Thus, the status quo forces, as led by Great Britain and France, shared in the responsibilities for the emerging diplomatic crisis.

Following the remilitarization of the Rhineland by German military forces in 1935, the incorporation of Austria into Hitler's Third Reich in 1938, and the German acquisition of the Czechoslovakian area identified as the Sudetenland, together with the Munich Agreements in 1938, no political realist could at this crucial moment dispute the fact that the relations among the various nation-states of Europe were not only very fluid, but also sufficiently volatile to set Europe ablaze. Yet, because of the rapid series of diplomatic and transpiring political events, the government of Chamberlain of Great Britain and that of Daladier of France, were repeatedly driven to a pattern of reactive diplomacy. Of the sequence of the anxiety-arousing and disruptive political decisions made by Adolph Hitler, one can only conclude that they were the result of processes that occurred concurrently. First, came the willingness of Prime Minister Chamberlain of Great Britain and France's representative, Edouard Daladier, to adhere to a policy of appeasement. Secondly, both representatives accepted not only the terms of the Munich Agreement of 1938, but also the absorption of "Rump Czechoslovakia" six months later into the German Reich. Once again this process, as in the past, confronted the citizens of our "Global Village" (in a single generation) with the horrors of war, at in once again (as in 1914-1918) possessed the potential within a person's lifetime of awakening the God of War – Mars – who would once again extend his long arms to pick certain nations and their people as participants in the Dance of Death.

From the land of Italy in the immediate post-World War I era, there emerged on the political scene a young journalist whose driving force in life was "power for the sake of power". The Young man was Benito Mussolini. It is this former socialist, who upon becoming Prime Minister, stated to a close friend:

What have I achieved up to now? Nothing.

I am a small journalist and a minister for the moment, like so many others; (and he added) but I have a frenzied ambition which burns, gnaws, and consumes me like a physical malady. It is, with my will, to engrave my mark on this age, like a lion and his claw.[14]

The kaleidoscopic attributes of Benito Mussolini's personality profile was to result in his being referred to by his personal friends, members of the Fascist Party, and to a great degree the general public, as "Condottiere" (leader of the militia) and "Duce". Throughout the war, he was labeled by various leading personalities in the Allied camp and among the Western media, as "The Sawdust Caesar". Yet, this former friend of Petro Ninni, disciple of Nietzche, school teacher, journalist, and a World War I veteran of the 11th Bersaglieri Regiment, was to remain a chameleon and a victim rather then the master of his fate. Benito Mussolini was invited to become the Prime Minister of Italy on October 30, 1922.

For the Americans, the bombing of the United States' naval facilities at Pearl Harbor on December 7, 1941, by Japanese navel and air units will remain, as stated by President Roosevelt, "A day which will live in infamy". For the people of Italy, the six thousand dead Italian troopers whose bodies were strewn across the battlefield of Adowa in 1896, rankled the hearts of many and especially Benito Mussolini. Having appropriated unto himself the responsibility for the conceptualization of foreign policy goals, Benito Mussolini undertook a plan of action to transform the real into the ideal as he first sought to wipe out the stain of 1896. In a series of diplomatic moves, the government of Italy first sought the acquiescence of Britain and of France which was to result in a major confrontation at Geneva, the headquarters of the League of Nations. Yet, in spite of the statements that called for collective action against Italy should it elect to invade Abyssinia, Benito Mussolini on October 2, 1935, in an address to the people of Italy, was to state:

---

14. Ivone Kirkpatrick, *Mussolini: A Study In Power* (New York, Hawthorn Book Inc. 1964) p. 176

...With Ethiopa we have been patient for forty years. Now enough!... To sanctions of an economic character we will reply with discipline, with our sobriety and with our spirit of sacrifice. To sanctions of a military character we will reply with acts of war.[15]

The following day, October 3, 1935, Marshall Emilio DeBono with five regular divisions, five Blackshirt divisions, two native divisions and a major force of aircraft, struck across the Abyssinian border.[16]

The Italian invasion of Abyssinia began in 1935. In ended in 1936 following a battle order drawn up by Marshall Badoglio with the capture of the nation's capital city of Addis Ababa and the flight into exile of the King, Haile Selassie. Following a brilliant four month campaign, the representatives of a 1930's technological-military society had not only defeated the representatives of a stone age culture, but had also wiped out the stain of dishonor from its national emblem. On May 9, 1936, Mussolini from a balcony of the Palazzo Venezia, proclaimed victory to a delirious crowd, the annexation of Abyssinia and the assumption by the King of Italy of the title of Emperor of Abyssinia. Yes, he had avenged Adowa, but Mussolini had forgotten the words of the individual-who held the olive leaf crown over the head of the victorious generals of the Roman Empire when they returned jubilant from a campaign, as they proudly rode their chariots before a cheering crowd-whispering, "Glory is fleeting".

As a representative of the Spanish Republic, were he to have placed a call from Madrid to Mellia in Spanish Morocco or to Burgos, Salamanca or Avila on July 18, 1936, he would have been greeted, as was Andre Malraux, with the following exchanges: "Arriba Espana!" "Comment ca va chez vous? Ici la gare." "Va te faire voir, salaud. Vive la Christ-Roi."[17] Civil War now comes to Spain with a sequence of disruptive and violent acts. In keeping with a series of prior agreements reached at the Palazzo Venezia in 1934 between Benito Mussolini and the representatives of the Spanish military, the church and the landed gentry and nobility, the Duce agrees to give the green light for the

15. Ivone Kirkpatrick, *Ibid* p. 319
16. Ivone Kirkpatrick, *Ibid* p. 317
17. Hugh Thomas, *The Spanish Civil War*

movement of the needed military supplies, monies and an Italian military force (under the command of General Rotta) to Spain's right winged revolutionaries. The dictator of Nazi Germany, Adolph Hitler, also rendered aid to the revolt of the generals (who were led by General Francisco Franco) in the form of a half billion marks, a number of aircraft, tanks, technicians and the Condor Legion air squadron which was to obliterate the Spanish town of Guernica. In addition, it must be noted that in Spain, the foreign policy objectives between Italy and Germany clashed while such foreign policy goals between Stalin and Hitler tended to be supportive of one another. This may be attributed to the fact that while Adolph Hitler saw the civil war in Spain as a means of distracting Great Britain and France from focusing their collective attention on the multiplicity of moves by Germany in the European Heartland, it also become the diplomatic technique of creating a conflict situation between Paris and Rome in order to move Rome into a binding relationship with Berlin.

Stalin, ever cautious and a political realist throughout the period of the Popular Front, did render to the Spanish Republic (in the form of the International Brigades) a sufficient amount of military supplies to prolong the conflict, but not to bring victory to the Republic and to the International Communist Movement. To understand the position of the Soviet Union, one must recall that Stalin and Communism were the major challenges to the democracies and capitalism. Thus, Moscow found itself confronted by a dilemma. A Communist victory in Spain together with a Leftist – dominated government, possessed the potential of bringing Great Britain, France, Germany and Italy together in an anti-communist diplomatic and military alliance. However, failure not to assist the legitimate government of Spain would result in a missed opportunity. Stalin was aware that the Italians and the French were antagonistic towards one another and the possibility to turn the battle of words into a probable military conflict was an opportunity which could not be passed over. Thus, the government and the party of the Union of Soviet Socialist Republics, through its agency, the Cominturn, began to recruit individuals and acquire military equipment for the civil war in Spain on the side of the Spanish Republic.

The impact of the Soviet decision to assist the people of Spain in their conflict against the military forces of Francisco Franco, the Catholic Church, and the landed gentry is vividly demonstrated in Robert A. Rosenstone's *Crusade of the Left: The Lincoln Battalion in the Spanish Civil War:*

> *On November 8, 1936, Madrid was in chaos...*
> *The city echoed with shouted slogans, "No pasaran" and "Madrid sera la tumba del fascismo", and everywhere, above the noise and confusion of men preparing for battle, loudspeakers were blaring with the voice of La Pasionaria, the Spanish Communist leader, calling on the Spanish women to resist their enemy to the death, saying: "It is better to be the widow of a hero than the wife of a coward". At 6 : 30 a.m., Madrid's transportation system began to function as usual, and more than one worker on that crisp fall morning kissed his family goodbye and mounted a streetcar as he did every morning. Only on November 8, 1936, he was calmly riding to the front lines and to war.*
> *Daylight on November 8 found rebel artillery battering the buildings of the University of Madrid, just inside the city, and the Moroccan troops and foreign legionnaires of the rebels pushing slowly through the Casa de Campo and into the streets of the city against stubborn resistance, when the first units of foreigners that were to become known to the world as the International Brigades marched through the Spanish capital.*
> *They were tough-looking men, French and Germans, English, Belgians, and Poles, clad in corduroy uniforms wearing steel helmets, their rifles gleaming dully in the light of day. They marched from the railroad station along the tree-lined Paseo de Prado and turned left up to hill to the Gran Via, while the people of the city, thinking the Soviet Union had intervened at last, hung from the balconies and windows overlooking the boulevards, crowded the sidewalks, and cheered until the streets echoed with the cries, "Vivan los rusos!" Past the noisy crowds they swung down the sloping boulevard west to the Plaza de Espana, and then on to the Casa de Campo.*
> *By evening the 2,000 men of the XIth International Brigade were in position, some in University City, most under the trees of the great park, spread out among the militia. The park roared*

*with the sounds of battle that night as the Internationals fought
and died to help hold the enemy back from Madrid. For the first
time in the war, rebel troops met soldiers equipped with good
machine guns, soldiers who entrenched well and fired accu-
rately and would not budge, and by early afternoon on November 9, rebel commanders found that their forces had run into a
stone wall. That evening the Internationals fixed bayonets and
mounted an offensive through the north end of the Casa de
Campo, breaking through the ranks of the Moroccan troops and
foreign legionnaires, taking a heavy toll of casualties as they
pushed the insurgents back until Mount Garabitas was the only
point in the Casa de Campo left to them. By then, one third of
the Internationals were already dead, but the rebel assault
through the park was at an end.*

*Two days later the XIIth International Brigade of Germans,
Frenchmen, and Italians went into action at Madrid, and on
November 15 the foreigners were called into the bloody battle
of University City, where "The marching songs of the German
Communists brought to the crumbling masonry of the laborato-
ries and lecture halls a wild Teutonic sadness", and some men
gave their lives defending a city they had never seen. For a
week the battle raged through the university campus, from building to building, from floor to floor, and in hand-to-hand combat
from room to room. Men built barricades out of library books,
and one young Englishman found that those made out of vol-
umes of Indian metaphysics and German philosophy "were quite
bullet-proof". November 23 saw both exhausted armies digging
trenches and building fortifications. The troops of the rebels
had been halted, and Franco and Mola had been forced to call
off the assault upon Madrid.*[18]

The killings which took place in Spain throughout the Civil War
reflected the ingrained nihilistic tendency which exists in a nation
whenever political authority is being employed for ideological ends.

---

18. Robert A. Rosenstone, *Crusade of the Left: The Lincoln Battalion In the Spanish
Civil War* (New York, Western Publishing Company Inc., 1969) p. 21-24

Under such a political environment, it does become possible for turbulence to take place. Thus, in Spain of the late 1930's, human life is reduced to such a degree that it is extinguished for the achievement of an ideological goal as one's fellow man seeks to destroy another's body and soul. The failure of the individual to recall that man's past sacrifices on behalf of revolutions were, in the words of Albert Camus, "in favor of life, not against it", makes it possible for the justification of the European killing fields to emerge.

The Spanish Civil War ended with a Fascist victory on April 1, 1939. The individuals who had fought against Franco as members of the International Brigades were withdrawn shortly following Prime Minister Juan Negrin's address on the afternoon of September 21, 1938, to the League of Nations that, "... the government was immediately and unilaterally withdrawing all foreign volunteers in its armies".[19] Eight month later many were to find themselves in French concentration camps or in holding areas awaiting assistance, release and a return to their respective countries. Tragically, the realities of Franco's political actions following the close of the Civil War demonstrated that the victorious Fascist forces and its Power Elite were not committed to human life, but to retribution and to death as yesteryear's revolutionaries became both judge and executioner and the nation of Spain became until the 1950's granted recognition to the Fascist government of Francisco Franco because of geo-strategic reasons brought on by Cold War demands.

Italy in the post-World War I era and throughout the decade of the 1930's was the creature of its times. The period when Benito Mussolini was able to bring about the triumph of authoritarian Fascism to King Victor Emmanuel III's kingdom (following his appointment as the Premier of Italy in 1922), is the least admirable Europe has known for many centuries. Yet, one cannot deny that the mood of the active and intense political crisis of the 1930's did produce a nihilistic trend which was to shatter the accepted norms of international diplomacy. Nor can one dismiss the impact of the following: the entry of German military forces into demilitarized Rhineland in 1935; the Italian inva-

---

19. Hugh Thomas, *Op. Cit.* p. 589

sion and conquest of Abyssinia in 1935-1936; and the Munich Agreements of 1938 which was followed six month later by the full absorption of Rump Czechoslovakia into the Third Reich in 1938. Furthermore, the ideological urgency upon the Fascist nation-states of Italy and Germany, together with its concentration of political and military power, was to have a total impact on the forthcoming succession of traumatic and nihilistic political realities which (at certain times) tore away the shroud of the illusionary reality which confronted Benito Mussolini and his Fascist Council. However, neither the King nor the people of Italy were desirous of chasing the Duce's illusionary goal.

In the Ancient World, Rome was able to tale full advantage of its geo-political and military strength to acquire control of the known world. The interplay between Italy's geographical location as a peninsular nation in the center of the Mediterranean Sea and the power of its Roman Legions made it also possible for Rome to extend its political power and culture beyond the Tiber and establish a Pax Romana from Hadrian's Wall in Scotland to the shores of the Caspian Sea in Russia and to the Tigrus and Euphrates River Valley in present day Iraq. Prior to the outbreak of World War II, Benito Mussolini in a private meeting with the members of the Grand Council of February 4, 1939, called to their attention that Italy was a prisoner in an in-land sea, the Mediterranean, with no access to the Atlantic Ocean, the Red Sea and the Indian Ocean if and when war were to break out between the Axis Powers and Great Britain and France. One must recall that both access points, the Suez Canal in Egypt and the Straits of Gibraltar, were British colonial possessions. In addition, Great Britain also controlled the islands of Malta and Cyprus. On the other hand, France held sway over Corsica and the countries of Tunisia, Morocco and Algeria. In Mussolini's view, the alliance with Germany would serve to secure Italy's northern and western frontiers while Italy pursued her vital interests in the Mediterranean and in the Balkans.

CHAPTER THREE

DEATH AND REBIRTH

Throughout in interwar period, 1919-1939, the dictators of Europe, Benito Mussolini of Fascist Italy, Adolph Hitler of Nazi Germany and Joseph Stalin of the Union of Soviet Socialist Republics, engaged in a program of diplomatic conflict and military engagement on behalf of a sanctified ideology possessing the rubric of authoritarian Fascism, Nazi totalitarianism and monolithic revolutionary Communism. As Stalin and the Soviet Union began to emerge from its period of the "Great Purges" of the 1930's Russia found itself being treated as an Orwellian nonentity and was confronted with a very limited degree of commercial and diplomatic intercourse. The two revisionist powers of Fascist Italy and Nazi Germany undertook a program of rectification as applied to the Treaty of Versailles.

In this quest Germany was able to acquire support for actions undertaken on the basis that it was only seeking to acquire lands that were inhabited by Germans. Italy's quest to acquire what she desired under the terms of the 1915 Treaty of London for entering the World War I, is understandable given the denial of such rewards by her Entente comrades. One must not forget that both England and France had agreed in 1915 that the price to be paid to Italy for entering the war on their side, would consist of the South Tyrol, Treste, Gorizia, Gradisca, Istria together with the islands of Cherso and Lussiu. In addition, Italy was also to receive a vast stretch of territory that ran from Dalmatia to Cape Planka plus the port of Vlora in Albania; the island of Rhodes and the Dodecanese group. While Rome was to acquire such lands that were at this time a part of the Ottoman Empire, it must also be noted that she was to receive fifty million pounds and a zone of influence in Asia Minor. Such secret understandings would be made public following the Russian Revolution of 1917 and would have a major impact upon the policies adopted by all nations throughout the interwar period. In addition to the above, one must observe that there were numerous physical confrontations between the Socialists and the Communists on the streets of Berlin, Hamburg, and Munich. Consider also the highly emotional battles between the supporters of the Nazi Party and the Fascists against the Socialists, Communists and the Democratic opposition in Rome, Milan, Bari and which generated and reinforced a political environment in which the voices of reason could not be heard. Thus, estrangement and violence were affirmed by the nihilism of 20th century politics as modern man in 1939 stood on the edge of a psycho-historical and political abyss which could only offer to the European at this historical moment, disillusionment, devastation and death.

That the 20th century was, in Camus' words, "convulsive, nihilistic and absolutely insane"[1] cannot be denied. While history has always known moments of insanity, irrationality and unpredictability, the centralization of power in 1939 brought with it a norm of destruction and 20th century man was not prepared, in the words of Robert Jay Lifton, "... for the sheer velocity of historical developments, the enormity of the consequences of certain public acts and decisions, and most of all, the precariousness of our collective existence".[2] One must be aware of the fact that although Mussolini carried out a "Parallel War" in his quest to demonstrate to the world that both he and Italy were independent of Hitler and Germany, there were no major ideological differences between Hitler and Mussolini in 1939, only conflicting imperial battles that could be satisfied if the bills were paid by their neighbors. Thus, with the benefit of hindsight, one could conclude that the dictators sought to bring about the destruction of the nation-state and the end of the rights of man.

Diplomacy confronts mankind with the reality that every individual life is bound up with the whole of the actions and the reactions of the major nation-states of our Global Village. The individual not only lives within history, but is and remains a prisoner of both historical and political events which envelop him or her. In addition, the person is an

---

1. Albert Camus, *The Plague* (London, Penguin Books, 1947) p. 161
2. Robert Jay Lifton, *History and Human Survival* (New York, Random House, 1961) pp. 3-20

active participant in the psycho-historical drama which impacts on one's outer an inner world. Tragically, the citizens who have only recently begun to move gingerly out of the Great Depression, now found themselves to become actively or inactively involved in an al-embracing Faustian Danse Macabre. In addition, he must also bear witness to man's inhumanity towards his fellow man as the universal threat of a world-shattering conflict situation which confronted man throughout the immediate pre-World War II era, now acquired individual and national attitudinal transformation. The decision-makers began to accept the reality that they may once again be confronted by a major military collision. There exists among the inhabitants of the southwestern tier of the Balkan Peninsula, the following ancient proverb:

> *One country's clan or person's*
> *day of glory is a time of*
> *humiliation for another.*

In the story of Albania, her day of humiliation was Good Friday, April 7, 1939, following the landings of Italian military forces at Santi Giovanni de Medusa (Shengjin), Durazzo (Durres), Valona (Vlore) and Santi Quaranta (Sarande) to begin the drive for the military penetration and occupation of the Land of the Eagle, Albania. The day of glory for the modern day Hellenes of Greece came on the 28th day of October, 1940. On this day, the Italian ambassador delivered the General Metaxis an ultimatum from the "Sawdust Caesar", Benito Mussolini, to surrender Greece's national territory and become a part of the new Roman Empire. Greece's reply to the representative of the King of Italy, Abyssinia and Albania – Emanuele Grazi – was a definitive "NO". Thus, Greece once again as at Thermopylae in 480 B.C., not only checked the Italian forces, but also undertook offensive operations against the military forces of Italy. For the Land of the South Slavs, Yugoslavia, the day of glory was March 27, 1941. It is at this historical moment, following the signing of the Pact of Vienna that resulted in Belgrade's adherence to the Tripartite Pact and which placed Yugoslavia in the Italo-German political and military sphere of influence, that a coup d'état led by Serbian officers, overthrew Prince Paul and the Cevtkonic government. Of this unexpected revolution undertaken by the Serb and a major segment of the people of Yugoslavia, Sir Winston Churchill, while speaking before the Conservative Central Council, remarked:

> *I have great news for you and the whole country. Early this morning the Yugoslav nation found its soul. A revolution has taken place in Belgrade.*[3]

War first came to the people of the southwestern tier of the Balkan peninsula on April 7, 1939, one week following the fall of Madrid and General Francisco Franco's conquest of the Spanish Republic by Fascist military formations. The reader must recall that the Fascist victory in Spain, which had received invaluable support from Italy, was Mussolini's reply in his "Parallel War" to Hitler's Germanic conquest of Czechoslovakia's capital city of Prague. Furthermore, El Duce's quest to demonstrate, in a most symbolic and meaningful manner to Adolph Hitler and the Nazi Party's inner-circle, Italy's separate interests in Europe included not only Albanian lands but also the "unfinished business" of World War I in the Adriatic at the expense of Yugoslavia. Mussolini had no desire to place in a state of potential jeopardy its relationship with Yugoslavia. Thus, on January 15, 1939, Rome informed Belgrade that Italy would be supportive of the Yugoslav quest to increase its frontiers southward and above all, be supportive of Belgrade's hope of acquiring the Greek port of Salonika.[4]

Yet, one must be aware of the historical fact that the Fascist government's major diplomatic objective at this point in time, was to liquidate Albania. That Italy was determined to acquire either direct or indirect control over Albania with its oil and variety of mineral wealth, cannot be denied. In May, 1938, Mussolini instructed his son-in-law, Count Ciano, that he should inform Ribbentrop, the German Prime Minister, that Italy, "... regards Albania as a family matter". In this manner, Benito Mussolini used the same technique and words of Adolph Hitler when he elected to inform El Duce of his desire to absorb Austria and the nation-state of Czechoslovakia into the Third

---

3. Walter R. Roberts, *Tito, Mihailovic and the Allies, 1941-1945* (New Jersey, Rutgers University Press 1973) pp. 14-15
4. Glaezzo, Ciano, *Memoriale di Gabinetto* Perbnna, 1939 (Count Ciano's Diary) p. 12

Reich.[5] The significance of the political intercourse is to be found in the unescapable fact that there existed an artificiality about the political and the ideological bond which existed between Rome and Berlin.

On April 7,1939, with a minimal degree of prior warning and without the usual excuses, a full scale invasion of the Land of the Eagle – Albania – by the Fascist government of Benito Mussolini's Italy, took place along a wide front. Thus, the decision reached on January 8, 1938, according to Count Ciano calling for "... the total liquidation of Albania by agreement with Belgrade"[6] became a reality. The Italian invasion of Albania by a invasion force consisted of one infantry division, four Bersagliari rifle divisions, three tank battalions, and two "Black Shirt" militia units supported by sufficient naval forces and air squadrons and disembarked at four major critical areas: San Giovanni de Medusa (Shengjin), Durazzo (Durres), Valona (Vlore) and Santi Quaranta (Sarande) as it began the drive for the military penetration and the conquest of Albania.[7] This military action by the Sawdust Caesar was not looked upon favorably by King Victor Emmanuel III of Italy. When previously informed of El Duce's plans to invade and conquer Albania, stated: "I am opposed to the policy in Albania since I do not see the point in risking such a venture in order to grab four rocks".[8] This was to set in motion a series of diplomatic, tactical and strategic developments which would in 1940 determine the fate of Greece and in 1941, the destiny of the Land of the South Slavs – Yugoslavia.

The invasion of Albania on Good Friday, April 7, 1939, created no major headlines in the American press and only a ripple in the European media. However, for the intellectual community of Europe, their reactions in a most meaningful manner projected the image that they were in truth ill prepared to shatter once and for all the totalitarian abyss into which European civilization was truly headed. Of the major conflict situation which was to break out on September 1, 1939, Dwight MacDonald reacted in the following manner:

---

5. Ivone Kirkpatrick, *Mussolini: A Study In Power* (New York, Hawthorn Books, Inc., 1964) p 395
6. Glaezzo Ciano, *Op. Cit.*, p. 8
7. Nicholas J. Costa, *Albania: A European Enigma* (New York, East European Monographs Columbia University Press, 1995) p. 37
8. Nicolas J. Costa, *Ibid* p. 34

> *One of the many things I cannot get accustomed to in this*
> *war is the fact that the most ancient, beautiful buildings of Eu-*
> *rope may be blasted to bits in a few hours. Rome, Paris, As-*
> *sisi... who knows when they will join Warsaw, Bath, Coventry,*
> *Nuremburg, Frankfort, Kiev, Cologne, Palermo, Naples, Rot-*
> *terdam, Cracow, London and Berlin? It is like living in a house*
> *with a maniac who may rip up the pictures, burn the books,*
> *slash up the rugs and furniture at any moment.*[9]

For many in Europe and in the United States, it now appeared that the God of War, like a phoenix, had once again risen from the ashes of World War I twenty years later to take on a life of its own and was now determined to produce psychologically shattering inhuman political and military events as well as the "Killing Fields of Europe".

The chain reaction of violence, war and destruction which began in 1914 as the "Accidental War" now set Europe ablaze in September, 1939. Furthermore, World War I had brought into being the elimination of four empires: Austro-Hungarian, German, Russian and the Ottoman Empire. In addition, it was to result in the Balkanization of Europe and the division of Europe into two major and determined political power blocs. The revisionist nations, headed by the Weimar Republic of Germany, sought to evolve major changes in the Treaty of Versailles. The nations who desired to maintain status quo sought to achieve the two following political objectives: restricting Germany and developing the means whereby nations could inoculate Europe from the Bolshevik disease. In this attempt, they were to find only frustration. At this historical moment, we see a political shift to the acceptance of the authoritarian formula, an increase in nationalism as nations adhered to their private agenda in relation to territorial claims, and a willingness not to meet their international, diplomatic obligations whenever a crisis situation arose.

As the 20th century dawned across the political landscape of Europe and at a time when the Russian Socialist Labor Party was in its emerging state of development, Vladimar Illyitch Ulyanov-Lenin be-

---

9. Greg Summers, "Radical Criticisms For A Time of Troubles" Unpublished Manuscript Department of History, Indiana University, pp. 24-25

gan in 1902, to evolve and to acquire supporters for his revolutionary and anti-Marxist theory of the "Doctrine of Elites". Lenin firmly believed, as stated by Franz Borkenau in his analytical study of the international communist movement entitled *European Communism*, that:

> *The broad masses of working men had no understanding of revolution and should have no say in conducting it... Revolution could only be understood and guided by small groups who had mastered the revolutionary doctrine, an elite of intellectuals.*[10]

That the concept of revolutionary elites was anti-Marxist from a theoretical perspective cannot be denied. Yet, given the realities of Russian society, let alone the socio-economic conditions in Eastern Europe at this period of time, it is extremely doubtful if the masses could singularly establish a revolutionary party dedicated to the overthrow of the government and the restructuring of the socio-economic and the political system of either the Russian national state or Eastern Europe.

In discussing war and its impact upon the theory of revolutionary action, Milovan Djilas, Tito's leading tactician and his outstanding dissident, made me aware of the fact that:

> *Were it not for the outbreak of the war the Yugoslav communist would just be one of the various and numerous political parties in Yugoslavia. For us it was World War II which shattered the state's political apparatus and its structure. As in Russia in 1917 it was war that made it possible for us to acquire control over the country and the reigns of power.*[11]

That the war created the situation which made it possible for the communist to acquire power cannot be denied. Of the war and the revolutionary tide which swept across Eastern and Central Europe, Professor Hugh Seton-Watson calls to one's attention the fact that one could identify many types of revolutions within the revolutionary tide that resulted in the emergence of the Communist states throughout

---

10. Franz Borkenau, *European Communism* (New York, Harper and Brothers Publishers, 1953) p. 26
11. Milovan Djilas, Personal Interview, Belgrade, Yugoslavia 1982

Central and Eastern Europe. Of the various types of revolutions, the two which were carried out in Albania and in Yugoslavia, have been identified as "Revolutions by Frontal Assault". The revolutionary pattern in Czechoslovakia has been called "Revolution by Coup d'Etat". As the Soviet military forces swept across Central Europe and the nations of Romania and Bulgaria in their offensive operations to destroy the retreating military forces of Nazi Germany, they were also engaged in bringing about the establishment of a safety shield in which one would find numerous communist nation-states adhering to a pro-Soviet foreign policy.

The revolutionary process which was to result in the establishment of Communist governments such as in Poland, East Germany, Hungary, Bulgaria and Romania, is that of "Revolution by Foreign Conquest". It must also be noted that the attempt to bring about a revolution in Greece while the war continued to rage between the allied military forces and the Axis powers, was unsuccessful due to British military intervention and that of Greek fighting units that were transferred from Egypt to Greece. Thus, while German military force did shatter the old political structures, it was the Red Army together with the establishment of Force of National Liberation that first fragmented and then crushed the old ruling classes of Central and East Europe. It cannot be denied that the Soviet Army played the major role in establishing the "Dictatorship of the Proletariat" in Eastern Europe, but not in Albania and Yugoslavia.

An analytical examination of the diplomatic moves and countermoves of the status quo oriented nations of Europe in the interwar period reveals that with the encouragement of the French Republic, they sought to establish a defensive alliance system dedicated to peace and the preservation of one's national security. Such a security system which came into being in the 1920's was designed to offer mutual protection against a potentially resurgent Germany and to isolate the Union of Soviet Socialist Republics as evident by the inauguration of the Cordon Sanitaire. With the United States of America adhering to a policy of isolationism and Great Britain reverting to her traditional policy of seeking to maintain a balance of power relationship on the European continent, the major burden for maintaining the status quo fell upon France.

The series of defensive treaties that emerged did bind the East European nation-states into a solid defensive bloc against a revisionist Germany once the Nazi Party gained control of Hungary, a major nation, in 1933. Also, following World War I, the majority of territory lost by the nation of Hungary resulted in her becoming a staunch supporter of the Revisionist bloc as headed by Germany and Italy. Thus, approximately nine treaties were concluded of which the 1922 East European Treaty, the Franco-Soviet pact and the Czechoslovakian-Soviet alliance of 1935, were the most significant. The Little Entente, which linked Yugoslavia, Czechoslovakia and Romania, directed its energies against Hungarian revisionism. One must recall that in 1924, Prague had entered into an alliance with Paris and in so doing, it became the connecting link between France and the Little Entente.

In that action begets reaction, the Fascist government of the Sawdust Caesar, Benito Mussolini, sought to evolve a series of diplomatic moves that would grant hegemony in Europe. In 1927, a treaty between Tirana and Rome was established. This treaty became a major force-in-play which served first to transform Albania into a economic province of Italy and eventually transformed Albania into an integral part of the restored Roman Empire of yesteryear in 1939. In 1934, Rome established a set of diplomatic relations with Vienna and Budapest which was directed against the nations of the Little Entente. While Nazi Germany and Fascist Italy did possess a common ideological bond through their adherence to a revisionist perspective, both the German foreign office and the Italian foreign office clashed in relation to their diplomatic objectives in the Balkans, especially in the Land of the south Slavs – Yugoslavia.

It is necessary to recall that at this moment in the diplomatic history of Europe, Hitler desired to maintain the unity of the Yugoslav nation-state. Count Ciano, the Foreign Minister of Italy, a friend of Premier Dr. Milan Stojanovic who in 1937 had signed a friendship treaty with Italy and who had informed his Italian counterpart that "... He would be content to see Czechoslovakia lose most of its territory and reduced to a neutralized Czech rump",[12] pursued a strong pro-

---

12. Hugh Seaton-Watson, *The East European Revolution* (New York, Frederick A. Praeger Publishers 1956) pp. 52-55.

Italian policy. However, due to internal politics, when he was removed from office, the government of Italy reverted to its former anti-Yugoslav position. This was indicated to Belgrade following the Italian invasion of Albania when the Yugoslav request for information on the event was basically disregarded by the Italian government. It was this action-reaction cycle that was to result in Great Britain's unilateral guarantee of protection to Greece, but none was given to Belgrade.

The tragedy of the interwar years should not be limited only to the advent of power of Benito Mussolini and Adolph Hitler. The dilemma confronting the two dictators was to be found in the fact that neither one could transform the nebulous theory of Fascism into an action program which could be understood by the citizens of their respective countries. Furthermore, neither Hitler nor Mussolini, in their quest to reach an illusionary goal, could grasp the fact their actions would result in the destruction of Europe.

Thus, within the context of a maelstrom of psycho-historical forces, 20th century man was to lose his sense of dignity and his sense of reason as Adolph Hitler was to undertake a program in 1939 of the total subjection of the majority and the universal annihilation of the European Jew and the "Inferior" Slavs. Confronted by the abyss of the grave, the political and the moral crisis of the inter-war years and the all-embarrassing emergent power of the nihilistic trend with its multiplicity of psycho-physical forms of suffering, man – in the face of "man's inhumanity towards his fellow man" – refused to be crushed. After all, one must recall that the force of nationalism as exemplified by the study of history, tends to pervert many peoples. Regarding the impact of nationalism upon the individual, Arnold Toynbee calls to our attention in the following statement:

> *The spirit of nationalities is a sour ferment of the new wine of Democracy in the old bottles of Tribalism.*[13]

What began as a solitary reaction against the conqueror of one's nation, became with the passage of time, a community reaction and eventually a nation reaction, as evident by the events in Albania and in Yugoslavia.

---

13. Kenneth Winetrout, *Arnold Toynbee: The Ecumenical View* (Boston, Twayne Publishers, 1952) p. 45

The full fury of war in the Balkans was unleashed on April 6, 1941. It was a total war in which all of society became a battlefield as the young men of the Land of the Eagle (Albania), the Land of the Hellenes (Greece), and the Land of the South Slavs (Yugoslavia), engaged the youth of Fascist Italy and Nazi Germany in a life and death struggle for their nation's soul. Terror and mutual accommodations became the principle means of German and Italian military reaction to the challenge of the resistance movements. The occupation which was to follow the military penetration and conquest of the nations of the southwestern tier of the Balkan peninsula was to surface identity, and magnify the age-old inequities, together with the socio-economic strains and the multitude of political antagonisms, that were to result in a restructuring of the political systems of Albania and Yugoslavia along Marxist-Leninist lines of development and a fundamental reshaping of Greece's political structure.

What (on October 28, 1940) had been a display and an assertion of Italian independence – the invasion of Greece – in order to assure that Greece would remain in Italy's political and economic sphere, was quickly turned into a humiliating military and political fiasco. The modern day Hellenes, under the command of General Ioannis Metaxas, checked the Roman Legions of the "Sawdust Caesar" in the Pindos and Gramos mountains of northern Epirus and then undertook offensive operations that forced the Italian military under the command of Marshal Pietro Badoglio to undertake a "strategic withdrawal" into Albania.

Of the very young men, Ramiz Alia, the successor to Enver Hoxha of Albania, was only a teenager when he joined the resistance. Mehmet Shehu, who had fought in the Spanish Civil War of 1936-1939, was an "old" man of 26 when he took command of the First Partisan Storm Brigade at Vithkuq. Joseph Broz-Tito, the leader of the Yugoslav partisan forces, was only 49, and Milovan Djilas was only 30, whereas Edvard Kardelj was in his early twenties. The reaction which confronted the Italian and the German occupation forces was in the form of the resistance, a movement of youth against youth. After all, according to Dr. Walter Laquer in his study entitled *The Dream That Failed – Reflections on the Soviet Union*, calls to the reader's attention the fact that:

Fascism, like Communism, looked for the support of the younger generation. It was a movement of youth – the Italian Fascist anthem was Giovinezza (Youth). The German government after 1933, like the Soviet government of the 1920's and the 1930's, consisted of people in their thirties.

Goebbels was head of a Nazi organization in Berlin at twenty-eight and Minister of Propaganda and one of the most influential people in the Third Reich at thirty-six. Himmler, a former chicken farmer, became the head of the S.S. at twenty-nine and some of the other key figure were even younger. In Italy, Ciano became foreign minister at thirty-two; Air Marshal Italo Bilbo became a minister at thirty-three; Dino Grandi, who held various positions of importance in the foreign office, was only thirty-four. Others such as Degrelle, Codreanu and Jose Antonio Primo de Rivera became leaders of the Fascist movements in Belgium, Romania and Spain in their twenties.

In the Soviet Union, Tukachevsky was an army general at twenty-six. Viacheslav Molotov, Sergo Ordzhomkidze, Sergi Kirov, Anastas Mikoyan and Lazar Kaganovich, all Stalin's young men, were in their early thirties when they became secretaries of the party Central Committee or government ministers. Gromyko was made ambassador to the United States at thirty-four.[14]

The mid – 1930's in Fascist Italy, Nazi Germany and Communist Russia projected an image of dynamic growth and progress, full employment and nations on the move. In stark contrast the democracies presented their closed factories, a sense of despair, high unemployment figures and a deep sense of despondency. The climate of optimism which pervaded the totality of the societies of the totalitarian states in contrast to the pessimism of the Western democracies of Europe and the United States of America was to cover up, as a result of the revolutionary enthusiasm of Fascist Italy, Nazi Germany and Communist Russia, that which awaited the youth of Europe, America and Asia – the slaughter that was beyond the imagination of the younger generation, the children and the older generation of our "Global Village".

---

14. Walter Laquer, *The Dream That Failed-Reflections On The Soviet Union* (New York, Oxford University Press, 1994) p. 12

Of the Sawdust Caesar – Benito Mussolini – and his role in the unfolding events of the interwar period and of World War II, it can be concluded that, "He was a man who was the victim and not the master of his destiny".[15] After all, this former socialist and journalist was a romantic who sought to emulate and surpass not only the glory of Imperial Rome, but also the Catholic popes with their world-wise sway. His illusionary dream carried its numerous trappings of the Fascist state from the bundles of rods carried by the youth of Italy (as did the lectors of Ancient Rome), to the Roman salute with its Roman parade step. While at times realism was often in conflict with illusionary romanticism, his early military victories, together with his moment of supreme international glory as the "Savior of Europe" at Munich in 1938, were for a time to erode briefly his sense of political and military reality. Of the Fuhrer of Nazi Germany, Adolph Hitler, a man who lived in his own world of illusion and fantasy, all that can be stated of his formative years was that here was a man with a closed mind who since his accession to the chancellorship of Germany in 1933, chased an illusionary dream of power and conquest to the bitter end.

The terrible protracted Balkan nightmare of barbarism and death from which one longed to awake and flee but could not, began as a wave of German bombers flying at roof-top level carried out Hitler's directive entitled "Operation Punishment" following the Yugoslav coup in Belgrade on March 26 and 27, 1941, and in total disregard of General Dusan Simovic's offer to sign a non-aggression pact with Hitlerite Germany.[16] It was Hitler's wish that Yugoslavia be "destroyed militarily and as a nation". The series of terror bombings which began on the Sunday morning of April 5th was to continue until the late evening of April 6th, 1941. With the capital city in ruins and the Yugoslav military overwhelmed by the panzer divisions, the Yugoslavs were forced to capitulate as the Germans were involved in a mopping-up operation that would result in approximately 200,000 officers and men being sent to prisoner-of-war camps in Germany.[17]

---

15. Nicholas J. Costa, *Op. Cit.*, p. 110
16. William L. Shirer, *The Rise and Fall of the Third Reich* (New York, Simon Schuster, 1960) pp. 823-824
17. William L. Shirer, *Ibid* p. 824

The Hellenes, who had humiliated the Italians in 1940, together with British military units who had arrived from fighting in Libya, were no match to Field Marshal List's Twelfth Army of fifteen divisions, four of which were armored. On April 23,1941, General Tsolakogly, on his own initiative, signed the surrender document in Salonika, thus bringing "Operation Marita" to a successful conclusion as the Nazi swastika was hoisted above the Acropolis.[18] It must be noted that the German military machine had swept through and conquered countries with the launching of "Operation Punishment" against Yugoslavia and "Operation Marita" which was to carry the Wehrmacht to Athens and beyond in less than thirty days of actual combat time. For Greece, fate played its hand harshly. It was both tragic and ironic that the modern-day Hellenes, who had driven the Fascist invader of their nation from their nation territory back into Albania and confronted the Italian military forces with a potential Dunkirk in reverse at the Albanian port of Vlore, were forced not only to sign a separate document of surrender with the representatives of Mussolini's Fascist government on the 23rd of April, 1941, but also were forced to endure the Italian occupation of their country as German military forces withdrew to take up positions for the forthcoming invasion of the Soviet Union. Furthermore, not only did the people of Greece bear the humiliation, but Field Marshal List and other Wehrmacht officers, who had previously agreed that Italian military forces were not to proceed south from Albania and cross the border into Greece, had to stand aside on orders from Berlin as Mussolini in a public relations coup announced that "the surrender had been tendered to the commander of the Italian Eleventh Army and details would be worked out together with our German allies".[19]

From defeat to a war of national resistance in Albania, the fate of Yugoslavia and Greece was to be determined by the interactions of numerous internal and external variables. For the tradition-directed peoples of Albania, whose nation-state was first an economic colony of Fascist Italy, it was politically transformed into a occupied country

---

18. Mark Mazower, *Inside Hitlers Greece: The Experience Of Occupation 1941-1945* (New Haven, Yale University Press, 1993) p. 17
19. Mark Mazower, *Ibid* p. 17

(following the Good Friday invasion of the country on April 7, 1939), and absorbed into the new Roman Empire of Benito Mussolini. Prior to the outbreak of the Balkan Wars of 1912-1913, the Austro-Hungarian Empire, Serbia-Montenegro, Greece and Italy were the four nation-states that had demonstrated, through public and private statements, an interest in acquiring either a zone of influence or the establishment of a protectorate over the Albanian lands which ran from Novivaroshi (in the north) south to Janina and beyond. At this period in the history of Europe, the Austro-Hungarian Empire possessed the necessary diplomatic, political and military power in the Balkans. However, it was being challenged by an idea. This idea that came into being in the 1860's was the brain-child of Croation bishop. Bishop Strossmayer, a scholar and a statesman, desired to bring into being theoretically a viable nation consisting of Serbs, Croats and Slovens. This desire to create a unified Slavic state corresponded with Serbia's desire to play the role of the Italian city-state of Piedmont. One must recall that this northern Italian state played a most vital role in the formation of Italy as a free, independent and united nation-state in 1870. Belgrade desired to transform an idea into a political reality at a time when all of Europe was in a potential state of political turmoil.

Of the ebb-tide of Ottoman Power and the protracted conflict situation which was to bring a variety of foreign military forces into the Albanian settlements, the grand dame of my family's clan, my aunt "Mamanice", once made me aware of the fact that whenever various foreign military contingents acquired control of the southeastern city of Korce and the surrounding villages such as Vithkuq, the inhabitants would remove the national standard of the invading force from under the pile of heavy, woolen blankets (valense) and display the national insignia of the invading strike force in hope of avoiding reprisals in the form of hostages and the destruction of their homes.

As a result of research concerning Italian and German military actions engaged in Albania, together with the multitude of activities involving men of the British command identified as Special Operations Executive under the command of Lt. Colonel Billy McLean, I became aware of an isolated episode which took place in 1943 in the village of Vithkuq. At this moment a German patrol undertook a bid to uncover a cache of military weapons and supplies buried under a carpet of human skulls in the back of the village church by the members of the First Storm Brigade, commanded by Mehmet Shehu and members of S.O.E. under the direction of Major David Smiley. This action resulted not only in an extension of the prior destruction rendered the village by the Italian forces of occupation, but also in the following encounter between an elder inhabitant of the community and the commanding officer of the German detachment. A peasant warrior with his weather-beaten face which projected the trials and tribulation of his native land and his village, confronted the German officer who had served previously in Albania with the Austro-Hungarian armies during the Serbian retreat to Corfu and to Saloniki in 1915. In the meantime, as the two confronted one another, the members of the patrol were busy rounding up the aged and the remaining women and children of the village. "Where are the partisan houses?" he was asked. "They are all partisan houses", was the reply. "And my sons and my grandsons are with the partisans for there is not a household which has not lost a son or a daughter fighting you". The German then asked, "Where are the people of the village?" The old man with his head erect answered, "On the heights of the hills which surround you and our village and along mountain passes waiting only to drive you from our country". The German officer who had led the patrol into the previously devastated village of Vithkuq, now ordered the burning of the few remaining structures which had previously provided shelter for the inhabitants. In a gesture of chivalry born out of respect for this noble "Son of Skanderbeg" who, through his actions, had honorably informed the oppressor that there existed a portion of the population which would not buy peace at any price, the officer placed a sentry to guard his humble hovel. Such actions were rare on the part of the Germans, but common on the part of the Albanian.

The full story of the economic penetration of the Albanian lands within the Ottoman Empire requires one to recall that in 1897, following a series of negotiations with Russia, the representatives of the Austro-Hungarian Empire were able to conclude an agreement which acknowledged that Albanian inhabited territory should constitute an independent national entity. This agreement between the two European powers was to result in a 1902 pact between Vienna and Rome which granted to Austria and Italy "Priority rights in Albania". The Austro-Hungarian penetration and investments in this specific Islamic region did not go unnoticed in Constantinople. Of the various moves and countermoves which were transpiring, Hilmi Pasha, the Turkish ambassador to Vienna in 1912 and the former Inspector General of Macedonia, sought to make Vienna aware of the fact that the region was truly incapable of existing on its own resources and that it would require a prolonged period in investments. This prediction coincided with that held by Berlin which (following a study) had come to believe that, "A minimal investment of 15 million gold francs annually would be required over an undetermined protracted period of time". Given the economic realities, the Austro-Hungarian government elected to disregard the negatives in what appeared to be a course of action designed to isolate her major antagonists, Serbia and Montenegro, and then proceeded to establish a major political and economic sphere of influence. This interpretation of Vienna's hidden agenda is supported by statements from Dr. Freiheer Von Mussulin, the director of the Austrian foreign ministry from 1910 to 1916. In his analytical study entitled Das Haus am Ballplatz, her reflects upon the Austro-Hungarian interest in the Albanian geo-political region and states:

> *With a complete disinterestedness, the Austro-Hungarian monarchy maintained throughout the whole area of Catholic Albania a network of churches and schools to train a cadre of teachers... Our only purpose was to raise the cultural and the material level of the Albanian and to train it for self-administration and independence... If we did have a political objective, for which we expended so much effort and so much monies, it consisted of preventing any other foreign power from establishing herself in the Albanian region and becoming the mistress of the Albanian coastal region...*

Dr. Von Mussulin completes his study and analysis of Vienna's interest in the multiplicity of Albanian settled regions throughout the Balkan peninsula with the following forceful, concluding statement, "... our political and economic objectives can only be accomplished by the establishment of a real protectorate."

While the various diplomatic and economic moves, together with raids by their neighboring Serbian and Montenegrin clans in the northern region and the Greeks in the southern areas, contributed to the high degree of turmoil and instability, it also served to reinforce the existing sense of Albanian national consciousness and the acceptance of the idea by various European powers that their interest would best be served if there evolved an independent Albanian nation-state. However, in relation to Austro-Hungarian involvement in Balkan affairs and specifically in Albania, it came to an end on November 11, 1918, following the World War I Armistice.

An historical and political analysis of the moves and the counter-moves of the Italian foreign office leads the observer of the Balkan scene to the conclusion that Italian policy is, has been, and will always be determined by the concept of Realpolitik. Italy, a nation which became a viable member of the international community in 1870, and a member of the victorious Entente Cordiale forty-five years later, has always adhered to an expansionist foreign policy and has possessed since the days of the Roman Empire, a major interest in the political and economic transactions that were evolving in Albania. Her objective has been, since time immemorial, to transform the Land of the Eagle (Albania) into a protectorate or "Italy's Fifth Share". Thus, prior to agreeing to join the Entente Cordiale in 1915, Italy sought and acquired an acknowledgment of her interests in Albania together with her preference to establish herself as the major power in Albania.

The various twists and turns of the Italian Fascist government now under the direction of Benito Mussolini, following the "March on Rome" on October 31, 1922, are most interesting. Of the transpiring series of events, Dr. Frederick A. Ogg's article which appeared in a 1927 *Current History* edition entitled "Italian Penetration of the Balkans", points out to the reader the following significant items:

1. Italy seeks to acquire the dominant position in the Mediterranean and hegemony over the Balkan peninsula.

2. The Italian foreign minister at Tirana, Baron Aliosi, sought through the offer of a 50,000,000 lire of personal gratuity to President Ahmed Zod together with a variety of military stores in exchange for the right to establish a protectorate over Albania.

3. The government of Italy was granted the right to establish a National Bank of Albania in Rome with 53% participation of Italian capital.

4. The Italian State Railroad's investment in the exploration of oil deposits in southern Albania was extensive.

5. The November 23, 1927, revolt in northern Albania was to result in a Pact of Friendship between Italy and Albania which possessed the following significant clause: any disturbance threatening the political, legal and the territorial status quo of Albania would be considered as being contrary to the interests of Italy and Albania.

As one reflects upon the Treaty of Friendship and all prior treaties and understandings between President Ahmed Zog and the government of the Kingdom of Italy, one can conclude that M.H.H. Macartney is more than correct when he concludes, "That the relations which developed was not one of exploitation of Albania by Italy, but of Italy by King Zog". That the Italian economic penetration and thus the conquest of Albania's governmental infra-structure took place must be attributed to Rome's adherence to a policy of Realpolitik and King Zog's greed. Yet, it must be noted that King Zog did undertake attempts in the early 1930's to reduce and eventually eliminate Italy's dominant status in relation to the internal affairs of his kingdom. Thus, in 1932, King Zog rejected the Sawdust Caesar's request for the establishment of a Custom's Union between Tirana and Rome. In 1934 this move was followed by the Albanian government's removal of all Italian officers and mili-

tary instructors from their respective and numerous positions within the military structure and that of the internal security apparatus which was under the control of British advisors. However, it must be noted that whenever King Zog sought to adopt an independent course of action, the Italian Fascist government would project its military power by the usage of their version of "Gunboat Diplomacy".

Throughout the mid – 1920's and the decade of the 1930's, Albania was and has remained until the present time, a nation in crisis. During this period and until its military conquest and occupation by Fascist Italy, it was confronted by a deteriorating economic structure and a critical, unstable political situation. Following the overthrow of the government of Bishop Fan S. Noli in 1924, through the revolutionary technique of Frontal Assault, Ahmed Zod undertook the tasks of consolidation and stabilization. However, prior to accomplishing this task, he first, in exchange for Yugoslav economic and military aid to his revolutionary attempt of 1924, gave the Albanian lands in the region of Saint Naoum and in the Vermoshe area to Belgrade. This decision was to result in the reinforcement of an emerging attitude in Belgrade that President Zog was their man in Tirana. Yet, it must be pointed out that the reaction among various segments of the Albanian society, especially in the southern regions which were inhabited by members of the Easter Orthodox religion, tended to be anti-Zog.

The quest for financial assistance and political maneuverability required of President Ahmed Zog to dump Belgrade for Rome and also to eliminate his political opposition. Both Zia Dibera and Bajram Curri were eliminated. Left Nosi was also physically removed from the political scene. Lugi Gurakuqi met his death at the hands of an assassin in a cafe in Bari. Fan S. Noli's relationship with President Ahmed Zog was normalized following a letter to Zog informing him of the fact that he was no longer involved in political affairs and was going to dedicate his life to the development of an Albania Orthodox Church in North America.

In an analytical study of President Zog's evolving relationship with Benito Mussolini's Fascist government of Italy, Dr. Bernd J. Fisher's academic work *King Zog and the Struggle for Stability in Albania*, presents the reader with an insight into President Zog's attitudinal disposition as related to the purge of the individuals opposed to his actions together with the pacification of the southern areas of the nation which is a Christian Orthodox region as opposed to a Moslem inhabited area. In addition to Dr. Fischer's insights, Dr. Robert Lee Wolff's conclusive study entitled *The Balkans in our Times*, illuminates the reader to the fact that at this critical moment of Albania's high illiteracy rate combined with the nation's economic underdevelopment and (from a West European perspective) social backwardness, it all served to project, Albania was seen as Europe's poor, little country-bumpkin from a remote province of the former Ottoman Empire. Given this characterization of the land and its people which is marked by a strong mixture of a tradition of Gjak mare (blood feud), en mite duharte or beekshesh (gift given as a bribe), together with its tribal structure, ancient law code of Luk Dukagjin, and a strong Ottoman cultural ethos (let alone the rival claims by Italy, Serbia, Greece and Montenegro), it is no wonder that the Land of the Eagle – Albania – is referred to as a European enigma.

From 1928 to 1939, Italian investments and settlements increased by a greater degree than anticipated by Tirana. In fact, in order to offset the growing criticism regarding Rome's dominant position in the internal affairs of Albania, the Fascist government of Benito Mussolini rendered to King Ahmed Zog an annual subsidy of ten million gold francs, interest free, a "token of friendship". Once oil was discovered and extracted from the land, Italian investments increased by approximately 100%. However, it must be noted that the geo-strategic importance of Albania's location together with numerous geological discoveries of previously unknown deposits of raw materials, was to result in the inclusion of a clause in all treaties between Rome and Tirana which granted, "Fascist Italy the right of intervention in the internal affairs of the Albanian government". Thus, Albania became in theory and in fact, an Italian protectorate.

CHAPTER FOUR

RESISTANCE, REBELLION AND DEATH

The socio-political dualism of the interwar period of 1918-1939, confronted the people of our "Global Village" with failed governments, the repudiation of liberalism, and a massive socio-economic dislocation which led to the world-wide economic depression of 1929. For the citizens of the newly established nation-states of the post-war era, because of an inability to resolve numerous complex internal issues, there emerged a tendency to adopt the authoritarian formula of government in addition to looking upon Italian Fascism and its Germanic imitator as the wave of the future. However, to the observer of the European political scene of the World War I era, the significant ideological challenge came out of Czarist Russia. It is here within a nation of revolutionary activity, civil war and international intervention that one encounters the projected image of man's true spirit of self-sacrifice, selfless devotion to a cause – Marxist Leninist – which espoused the highest world order; thus, Communist Russia emerged. Lenin's willingness to establish a socialist system and to withdraw from the war was to result in the Union of Soviet Socialist Republic being branded as a pariah nation and an Orwellian political nonentity.

For the inhabitants of the lower southwestern tier of the Balkan Peninsula which consisted of Yugoslavia, Albania, and the nation-state of Greece, with their collective historical memories of Ottoman rule and the assimilation of Islamic folkways and mores, the quest to establish an economic and democratic infrastructure was at best uncertain. The existing political dynamics of the region were sufficiently chaotic to reinforce the traditional sense of fatalism which pervaded the tradition-directed person's total being. To understand the impact of such upon the individual and upon the psycho-historical process as it related to the people of the Balkans, one need only to read Milovan Djilas' biographical novel entitled *Land Without Justice*. This man of letters, idealist, and revolutionary of yesteryear, who resided in Belgrade at 8 Palmoticeva, called to my attention (when we first met many years ago) his personal predilection for Albanians. For him, they and the people of Czena Gora possessed similar folkways, mores and a determination to maintain their independence which had no equal in human history. It was during our first meeting that he made me aware of his meeting with Joseph Stalin in 1944 as a representative of the partisan high command to Moscow. To this leader of men during the national war of liberation, Joseph Stalin was more than just a man. For Milovan Djilas, the leader of the Union of Soviet Socialist Republics was as stated in the interview and in *Conversations With Stalin:*

> *The incarnation of an idea, transfigured in Communist minds into pure idea, and thereby into something infallible and sinless. Stalin, to met at our meeting, was the victorious battle of today and the brotherhood of man tomorrow.*[1]

Djilas also made me aware of the fact that when the leader of the Soviet Union raised the question, "Who are the Albanians?" – Djilas replied in the following words, "The Albanians are the most ancient Balkan people, older than the Slavs and even the ancient Greeks. Stalin replied, "I had hoped the Albanians were at least a little Slavic".[2]

Throughout the decades of the 1920's and that of the 1930's the student of history and the citizens of Europe and America bore witness to the end of one psycho-historical epoch and the beginning of another. The negative political contours designated the German entry on March 7, 1936, into the demilitarized Rhineland; the conclusion of the Italo-Abyssinian War as the "New Roman Legions" of Benito Mussolini marched victoriously into Addis Ababa on May 2, 1936; the outbreak of the Spanish Civil War on July 16, 1936, as General Francisco Franco led the "Revolt of the Generals" against the government

---

1. Milovan Djilas, *Conversations With Stalin* (New York, Harcourt, Brace and World Inc. 1962) p. 57
2. Milovan Djilas, *Ibid* pp. 78-79

of Republic Spain; and the Munich Agreement of September 29, 30, 1938. This resulted in the Prime Minister of England, Austin Chamberlin, declaring that there would be "Peace in our times" as Winston Churchill's statement declared that England had to choose between war and peace and that she had chosen peace, but that she would have war. There was to be no pardon from the emerging disorganized insanity called war.

For the general population of Europe, their descent into the hell that is labeled World War II began on September 1, 1939, with the German invasion of Poland and Great Britain and France's decision to honor their treaty obligations following their disgraceful, give-away actions at Munich when Hitler referred to the leaders of England and France as "worms". For the people of the Land of the Eagle-Albania, the Land of the South Slavs-Yugoslavia, and that of Hellas-Greece, and all of Europe's cascade into the most bottomless pit of a hell-on-earth, General sir John Hackett of His Majesty's Forces, who was wounded and taken prisoner on the German side of the line during the Battle of Arnhem (which was immortalized in the book *A Bridge Too Far*) and who was taken to a German medical installation after viewing half a body here, naked buttocks there, and legs and heads scattered throughout, was to make one aware of the horror confronting yesterday's civilian be he German, British, Russian, or American that:

> *There was no comfort here.*
> *It was like being in a strange and terrible nightmare from which you longed to wake and could not.*[3]

Of this side of war one could say as did Paul Fussell in an Atlantic Monthly article entitled "The Real War, 1939-1945", that war's full dimensions are inaccessible to the ideological frameworks and that we, according to Barbara Foley, "have inherited from the liberal era". It has been stated "that it is a much more difficult and formidable task to relate a historical tragedy than to take part in it" and in *Wartime*, Milovan Djilas writes the classic account of partisan war as does David Smiley in *Albanian Assignment*; Sir Julian Amery in *Sons of the Ea-*

---

3. Paul Fussel, "The Real War – 1939-1945" The Atlantic Monthly (August, 1989 p. 36

gle; Sir Fitzroy Maclean in *The Heretic*; and F.W.D. Deakin's *Embattled Mountain* and numerous other texts that have been written by
those members of S.O.E. who served in occupied Albania, Greece and
Yugoslavia during World War II.

Entry into a world of a prolonged state of shattering psychological
and traumatic negative experiences that offered no comfort and only
high anxiety initially began when an Italian invasion force consisting
of one infantry division, four Bersagliari rifle divisions, three tank
battalions and two "Black Shirt" militia units disembarked at San
Giovanni de Medusa (Shengjin), Durazzo (Durres), Valona (Vlore),
and Santi Quaranta (Sarande) and initiated a series of military operations to seal the northern Albanian-Yugoslav border and to prevent
the Albanian tribesmen of Kosovo from joining their fellow country-
men in Albania. This coincided with a rapid sweep of the southern
region of the country in order to occupy the cities of Korce and
Gjirokaster while the military units which landed at Sarande secured
the Greek-Albanian border regions. The Italian military formations
that disembarked at Durazzo following their initial unsuccessful attempt (due to the actions of Abas Kupi), were able in their second
attempt to achieve success and occupy the capital city of Tirana which
was only 20 miles away.[4]

For the inhabitants of the Land of the South Slavs-Yugoslavia and
the citizens of Greece, war began on the 6th of April, 1941, when the
capital city of Belgrade was razed to the ground and when Field Marshall
List's 12th Army struck across the Bulgarian border and shattered the
resistance of Greek military forces which was to result in the capitulation of Greece and the hoisting of the German swastika over the Acropolis and the ending of "Operation Marita".[5] Because of the policies of
King Zog in the Land of the Eagle; General Metaxas in the Land of the
Hellenes; and King Alekandar of the Land of the Serbs, Croats, and
Slovenes; prior to the outbreak of World War Ii and then throughout
the war years, the men and women of the resistance movements in

---

4. Nicholas J. Costa, *Albania: A European Enigma* (Boulder, Colorado East European Monographs 1995) p. 37
5. Mark Mazower, *Inside Hitler's Greece: The Experience of the Occupation – 1941-
1945* (New Haven, Yale University Press, 1933) p. 1-8

Albania, Greece, and Yugoslavia, had to live conspiratorially. Yet, in spite of the existing situation which confronted them, each possessed an ineradicable allegiance to God, country, people (for the Communist, to an ideology), and a desire to establish his/her version of "The city on the hill". One must note that it was Milovan Djilas, who, following the initially successful communist-led peasant uprising against the Italian occupation forces in Montenegro in July, 1941, was to state:

> *We cannot separate ourselves from*
> *the people! We must share everything*
> *with them! It they are mistaken, we*
> *shall teach them and learn ourselves!*
> *Or else we are not their sons![6]*

The communists were not the sole organized military force to challenge the occupation of Yugoslavia by Italian and German military units. Following the capitulation of Yugoslavia on April 17, 1941, Draza Mihailovic, together with seven officers and twenty-four non-commissioned officers and men, made their way to the high mountainous region and plateau of Ravna Gora in the Sumajida region of Serbia.[7] Because of his experience in World War I, Draza Mihailovic, the leader of the Ravna Gora Cetniks and a former officer in the Royal Yugoslav Army, was (in the words of Brigadier Fitzroy Maclean) aware that a program of irregular warfare against the forces of occupation would only provoke reprisals, so Mihailovic became...

> *Determined not to destroy, but to preserve, to keep in being*
> *in Serbia something that could serve as a nucleus from which to*
> *rebuild someday: the old order that was so dear to him: the*
> *monarchy, the church, the army and the Serb way of life... If all*
> *went well, in time perhaps, the Allies would reinvade the Bal-*
> *kans. Then would be the time for a general rising. In the mean-*
> *time his aim must be to keep something in being in Serbia.[8]*

6. Milovan Djilas, *Wartime* (New York, Harcourt, Brace and Jovanovic, Inc. 1977) p. 25
7. Walter R. Roberts, *Tito, Mihailovic and the Allies – 1941-1945* (New Brunswick, New Jersey, Rutgers University Press, 1973) pp. 20-21
8. Fitroy Maclean, *The Heretic* (New York, Harper Brothers Publishers, 1957) p. 115

Joseph Broz-Tito, following his initial mid-summer meeting with Draza Mihailovic in the village of Struganik in 1941, and at the conclusion of his second meeting with the leader of the Cetnik groups under his command, had come to believe that Mihailovic did not desire to engage the occupation forces to the degree which the partisan military units were willing to. Yet, in spite of Tito's suspicion, agreements were reached for cooperation but not for the establishment of a united command. On October 26, 1941, having set up his headquarters at Uzice, which is at the lower end of the Morava Valley, a meeting with Mihailovic took place in the village of Brajici. It was at this meeting that Tito became aware of the fact that Draza Mihailovic had established contact with the outside world as he was introduced to Captain William Hudson of the British military. In addition, Tito, the young revolutionary commander of all partisan forces, discussed with Mihailovic proposals forwarded a few days earlier relating to the following series of significant issues:

1. *The retention of separate high commands*
   with close liaison between them.
2. *Joint or closely linked commands.*
3. *Joint equipment and supplies.*
4. *Voluntary and not compulsory mobilization.*
5. *The formation of a joint operational staff together*
   with joint operations against the enemy.
6. *The joint sharing of booty.*
7. *The substitution of National Liberation Councils*
   for existing machinery of government in liberated areas.[9]

Tito and the members of his inner political circle, which in 1944 consisted primarily of Milovan Djilas, Edvard Kardel, Alexander Rankovic and Dr. Ivan Ribar, were at one and the same time both Yugoslav nationalists and revolutionaries. They and Tito were determined to set up a new order based on the ideological principles of Marxist-Leninist and to bring about the destruction of the Old Order.

---

9. Fitzroy Maclean, *Ibid* p. 115

It appears from the vantage point of history that Tito's proposal for unity of action and command became his strategic and insidious means of acquiring total mastery over existing control devices within the Cetnik movement and thus absorb the Cetnik organization – with its noble warrior tradition of an age-old past – into the National Liberation Front and military structure. [10]

A study of the history of warfare makes the participants in the dance of death aware of the fact that the individual and one's total extended family, let alone one's clan, may be wiped out as a direct result of enemy counter action brought on by orders received, such as that issued to the military command of Field Marshal Keitel on the 16th of December, 1942.

> *The enemy has thrown into bandit warfare fanatic, communist trained fighters who will not stop at any act of violence. The stake here is more than to be or not to be. This fight has nothing to do with a soldier's chivalry nor with the decisions of the Geneva Convention. If this fight against the bands in the East as well as in the Balkans is not carried out with the most brutal means, the forces at our disposal may be in the near future not last out to master this plague.*
>
> *The troops are therefore authorized and ordered in this struggle to take any measure without restriction, even against women and children if these are necessary for success. (Humanitarian) considerations of any kind are a crime against the German nation...*[11]

As a result of such orders and given the fact that a soldier is required to carry out the orders received at Kragujevac, seven thousand people, the entire male population, was physically eliminated. The village of Borove in Albania was razed to the ground as its citizens were driven into the flames of their village church to complete the slaughter of the innocent.

Of the German massacre at Kragujevac, the author of the book *Whirlwind* states:

---

10. Walter R. Roberts, *Op. Cit.* p. 24
11. Mark Mazower, *Op. Cit.* p. 153

> *On October a strong force of German troops blockaded the*
> *approaches to Kragujevac and proceeded to muster all the male*
> *inhabitants of the town. There was nothing particularly sur-*
> *prising about the procedure as it was a customary method of*
> *the Germans for recruiting forced labor. Only this time the meas-*
> *ures taken seemed especially drastic. Workers and shopkeep-*
> *ers, waiters, taxi-cab drivers and newspaper vendors, Jews and*
> *gypsies, priest and doctors, the head-master of the secondary*
> *school with his teaching staff and all pupils of the fifth to eighth*
> *class, the entire personnel of the local law court including the*
> *magistrate, lawyers, clerks, jailers, witnesses and prisoners –*
> *all were herded off by German troops to the number of seven*
> *thousand.*
>   *The next morning the mass executions began.*
>   *The victims were mown down by machine gun fire in batches*
> *of forty. The massacre was only stayed to keep some six hun-*
> *dred as hostages and release another few hundred to their homes*
> *to tell the tale of horror.*[12]

The significance of this zero experience upon Draza Mihailovic on
Razna Gora is to be found in the fact that in 1917 he was sent into German occupied territory to organize a national uprising in the Toplica
region. The failed uprising was to cost the Serbs in this heroic gesture,
35,000 men, women and children. The deep psychological scar was to
result in the emergence of a belief that never again would he lead such
innocent Serbs into such a useless act. Furthermore, he came to the conclusion that "it would be wiser to wait, to prepare and to husband resources for the moment when the enemy, weakened and tottering, could
be overwhelmed by a combined frontal assault from allied regular armies and a well-timed sabotage and guerrilla campaign in his rear".[13]

   In Greece the massacre at Komeno lasted six hours and resulted in
317 deaths and the total destruction of the village of Didtome when a
Waffen-SS unit who visited the village, went wild massacring several
hundred people in their homes and hanging many of the villagers, so

---

12. Stephen Clissold, *Whirlwind* (New York, Philosophical Library, 1949) p. 66
13. Stephen Clissold, *Ibid* pp. 56-57

that when a Red Cross team arrived from Athens a few days later, one could only see bodies dangling from the trees that lined the road into the village. Thus, according to Mark Mazower's study of the occupation, "over a thousand villages had been razed: more than 20,000 civilians had been killed as Greece became a cemetery awashed in blood". Given the every-day reality which engulfed the people of Albania, Greece and Yugoslavia, one can better understand the following exchange between a Yugoslav woman doctor and a member of the S.O.E.

> *When the battle was over and you heroes retired to your mountain fastness, the Germans... shot nine thousand hostages – three hundred for every German you killed. They burned to the ground seventeen villages. In Kraljevo there is not a family which has not lost one of its members, and all the refugees from the north were shot. Your military objectives may, of course, have been worth all this, but I cannot know anything about that. All that I see is suffering among the people – my people.[14]*

Through their own efforts, two countries, Albania and Yugoslavia, had liberated themselves from the yoke of foreign occupation. Each nation had engaged in bringing about a triple revolution consisting of a war of national liberation, civil war, and a social revolution which, in turn, was accepted and reinforced by a pro-communist psycho-attitudinal transformation. Whereas Enver Hoxha of Albania and Joseph Broz-Tito of Yugoslavia emerged in 1945 as victors in their war of national liberation against Italian and German occupation forces, both Benito Mussolini and Adolph Hitler went down to defeat together with their thousand-year Reich and their Fascist dream. Of these two men, it can be stated that each was a true practitioner of the political concept of "Real Politik". That the determination to shatter the institutions of the old order and bring about a triple revolution at one and the same time (in the dark days of 1941) may have appeared impossible, but it became a possibility by 1942 and a reality by 1944.

The quest on the part of Tito and Hoxha to transform a theory into a reality – the establishment of their version of a Marxist-Leninist "City on the Hill" – required a total commitment on the part of the people in

---

14. Fitzroy Maclean, *Op. Cit.* p. 119

a war of national liberation against the Italo-German occupation units. It became a major military confrontation against the collaborationist government and its minions, the Ustase and its supporters; thus, in Yugoslavia, we saw an all-out civii war and a socio-economic revolution. That which transpired in the Land of the Serbs, Croats and Slovenes, also took place in the Land of the Eagle-Albania. It must be noted that the Yugoslav assistance rendered the Albanian revolutionaries throughout the war years and until Albania broke relations at the party level with Yugoslavia in 1948, transcended a dollar and cents figure alone. Both Tito and Hoxha, together with the inner-circle of their command, possessed the courage, the tenacity and the willingness to make the supreme sacrifice and the hard decisions to move the people of their respective nations toward the establishment of their version of the "Communist City on the Hill". Both truly believed in the ultimate victory as they led their revolutionary armies at a price, for neither honor nor victory comes cheaply.

War began in the Land of the Serbs, Croats, and Slovenes in 1941 by a decision reached by Adolph Hitler and it ended in Belgrade four years later. Of the return to Belgrade and the following parade a few days later, Milovan Djilas made me aware of the fact that Tito talked of the war having begun in the capital city of Belgrade would end in Belgrade. This is verified by the opening paragraph of chapter five entitled "Serbian Uprising", in Fitzroy Maclean's *The Heretic*.

> *"What struck me most", an old friend said later of a conversation which he had with Tito in 1937, "was his calm assurance that there was going to be a war; that the Communist party would lead a tremendous fight, would win and would govern the country... He had no doubts – to him it was all clear cut and his confidence was absolute".[15]*

In addition, Milovan Djilas also enlightened me, as we drank our cup of Turkish coffee, that the partisan forces who participated in the review were made aware of the fact the "they who had fallen in battle are now part of the foundations of their country, a country of brotherhood and freedom".[16]

---

15. Fitzroy Maclean, *Op. Cit.* p. 95
16. Milovan Djilas, Personal Interview, Belgrade, Yugoslavia, 1980

One must recall that whenever a major bridge was erected throughout the Ottoman era of occupation, workers were encased within to render the edifice mythical strength. Yet, one must return to 1941 and to the Germanic battle plan designated as "Operation Punishment" and become a participant in the partisan journey which went full circle and was a war of movement marked by individual and collective acts of bravery and pathos. With the German invasion of the Union of Soviet Socialist Republics on June 22, 1941, the revolutionaries of yesteryear were able to pass in Tirana, Belgrade and Athens from the illegal underground world of shadows, intrigue and conspiracy to that which Hugh Seton-Watson identified as "Revolution by Frontal Assault". The state apparatus ceased to function when the Italian national tri-color was hosted in Tirana as King Ahmed Zog and the royal family together with the national treasury, fled across the border into Greece and political limbo. Destiny was not kind to the initial Kingdom of Serbs, Croats and Slovenes which ended in 1921, as the king – due to a series of internal protracted problems – carried out a political coup.

There now emerged a second, more authoritarian Yugoslavia – The Land of the South Slavs, which would end with the Germanic invasion, conquest, partition and the flight of the king to the United Kingdom in 1941. From the ashes of the destruction and Germanic conquest of the Yugoslav nation-state, there would emerge like the mythological Phoenix, a third Yugoslavia headed by the leader of the resistance, Joseph Broz-Tito, and the Communist Party in 1945. Of the kingdom of Hellas-Greece, which on October 28, 1940, was invaded by the "New Romans" of Benito Mussolini's Fascist Italy, it must be noted that the military units of Rome were confronted and expelled from the ancient land of Greece. The would-be conquerors were forced to undertake a withdrawal of their forces as the Evzone military formations liberated the southern Albanian cities of Gjirokaster and Korce, two principle cities in the territory Greece had identified as within Northern Epirus and desired to annex. At this time, the Greek offensive operation forced the Italian forces to be confronted with an untenable position at the Albanian port of Vlora to such a degree that Adolph Hitler was forced to cancel his original date for Operation Barbarossa, the invasion of the Soviet Union set for the month of May, 1941.

The decision to come to the aid of Benito Mussolini was in the final analysis to be a major contributing variable to the eventual defeat of the German forces in Russia. The military units assigned to Field Marshal List's 12th Army group, having moved with a greater rapidity than anticipated through the Metsovo Plains against determined Greek resistance, were able to block the Greek reinforcements together with the 5600 British contingent which was coming up from the south. The German military units had taken control of the city of Yannina so quickly and unexpectedly that when the British tried to contact the commander of the Greek military units at Yannina, the reply was, "Hier ist das Deutsche Heer" (This is the German Army). Confronted by a precarious situation, General Tsolakoglu, after maintaining his defensive line of resistance against the Wehrmacht and exerting additional pressure on the Italian forces in Albania, capitulated on his own initiative and signed the final surrender document in Salonika on the 23rd of April, 1941. It must be noted that, according to Mark Mazower, "From Hitler downwards there was nothing but admiration on the German side for the way the Greeks had fought".[17]

The shock of defeat by Field Marshal Lists's 12th Army was followed by the national famine of 1941, which, according to the International Red Cross, resulted in the deaths of approximately 250,000 men, women and children. Yet, in spite of the tragedy which befell Greece, not only did the people of Hellas rise to confront the occupation forces, but throughout the Land of the Eagle and the Land of the South Slavs, the people once again (as had their forefathers) elected to offer a determined resistance to the Italian and the German military forces in an all-out war of national liberation. The ethno-social mosaic which constitutes the Balkan Peninsula has long been known since time immemorial for its political diversity and its aggressive nationalism. Its one quintessential feature, common to all of the tradition-directed inhabitants and tribal clans of this explosive territory, is the protected struggle for survival. The men of my extended family have fought and have died over a multitude of generations. Fighting occurred not only between Christians and Moslems, but also among those

---

17. Mark Mazower, *Op. Cit.* pp. 18-41

of the same faith due to a blood feud whose origins are lost in time. The Balkans are, have been, and shall always remain the cursd land. Furthermore, while there have always been through the ages quarrels between clans and tribes, and between religions and nations, the Balkan will always remain an active participant in the grand, but tragic narrative of the folk epic of the Balkans.

In that man can fight everything except his own times, the cascade of political and military events which transpired made one aware that in the Land of the Eagle-Albania; the Land of the South Slavs-Yugoslavia; and in the Land of the Hellenes-Greece; man is at all times willing to meet his fate or one's destiny. Inbred with the spirit of human revolt, revolutionary man came to life first as an individual and then as a representative of a collective. When in the face of the tragedy of executions, concentration camps and the death of one's community because of an abstraction, revolt passes into the mind where feeling gives birth to an idea and then the idea gives birth to resistance and revolution.

The year, 1942, marked the beginning of the end for the Axis power in Europe. For the Sawdust Caesar, Benito Mussolini, the series of premises and rationalizations presented to justify the Italian entry into the war had been shattered. The progress of events in Europe rapidly moved forward. By May, 1942, the dictator of Nazi Germany had not only triumphed over the Prussian officer corps, but he was now, to a greater degree than ever, in total control of the levers of political and military power in his capacity as head of state. Hitler was also Minister of War, Supreme Commander of the Armed Forces, and Commander-in-Chief of the Army. In addition, on April 26, 1941, the Reichstag rendered to their Fuhrer, Adolph Hitler, total power over the individual and the law. The German armies, which had anticipated celebrating Christmas and the New Year in Moscow, found that, due to Zukov's counter offensive and high mobility, they had to reestablish their main line of resistance 75 to 200 miles from the Soviet capital, Moscow. Yet, in spite of this ominous sign, it must be noted that the Mediterranean had become an Italian lake to a greater degree than Benito Mussolini ever believed possible. The military units of the Wehrmacht were in striking distance of the Soviet oil fields at Grozny and their fall was anticipated to take place in the immediate future. In addition, in North Africa, Field Marshal Rommel, known on both sides as the "Desert Fox", was about to begin his drive from Alamein from Egypt's capital and the Nile as the swastika flew high over the Caucasus on Mount Elbrus. With the German Wehrmacht and the Italian 8th Army pervading vast regions of the Soviet Union, North Africa, the European continent, and with Berlin dictating to puppet governments and officials throughout Europe while knocking on the gates of Leningrad, Stalingrad, and the city of Cairo in North Africa, the integrity of the German power was subtly eroding and crumbling like the sandcliffs of a battered coastline. Little did they know that symbolically they were representative of "dead men walking" and as one is aware, according to the study of history, unburied things cause trouble.

The act that twisted the course of events in Albania, Greece, and in Yugoslavia was the reemergence of the birth of an active nationalism. The Italo-German effort to contain, repress and negate its covert expression only served to increase the seething activity beneath the lid which by 1941 gave birth to active and total overt resistance. For the Land of the South Slavs, acts of resistance ran the spectrum from: failure to adhere to the curfew; ambushes and the killing of a lone guard; the elimination of a patrol; all were but the sparks to a fire which would consume Montenegro. For the people of Yugoslavia, resistance to the Italian forces of occupation possessed a greater appeal than that of a class war. It is at this time in 1941 that the Ravna Gora (Cetnik) Movement under the command of Draza Mihailovich and Tito's partisan units commanded by Milovan Djilas found themselves jointly engaged in a highly successful combined offensive military operation which resulted in the evacuation of Italian occupation forces for a two week period from Montenegro.

In the succeeding weeks, the Italian military, reinforced by air power and sufficient combat hardened troops, returned to Montenegro and proved the old military axiom that a well trained and experienced military force will be superior to the inadequately organized, poorly equipped and inexperienced opposition force – in this case, of the combined units of Cetniks and Partisans. The reentry of the Italians together with the decision on the part of the Partisan command to with-

draw and to focus on nuisance type operations, resulted in the following exchange between Todor Milutinovic and Milovan Djilas.

> *Why the devil did you stir things up, he explained, if you did
> not want to have the people with you? This is not like distribut-
> ing your leaflets, you know human heads are rolling and the
> nation is on fire! Don't disperse the army now that it is assem-
> bled. Let's hold council and see what we can do now that you
> started the bloody dance!*[18]

In the Land of the Eagle-Albania, as in Yugoslavia, the act of rebellion and resistance appears to the man outside a natural reaction. Resistance began at the individual level. To the sons and the daughters of
Skanderbeg, who since the conquest of their native lands, had borne
the deep sense of humiliation together with the yoke of subjugation,
the oncoming struggle represented only the beginning of the end of
feudalistic servitude and the end of occupation. It also meant the
reestablishment of a free and independent Albania. To the young intellectual, the ensuing conflict against the militia forces of Fascist Italy
until its capitulation in 1943 and the German forces of occupation from
1943 to the end of the war in 1945, was symbolically a new era which
was to be characterized by a clean break with the old forces of resignation, injustice, servitude, and the disintegration of the Albania of feudal lords and peasantry and above all – the entry of the Land of the
Eagle into Europe. To the young communist revolutionary and idealist, who had lived as a marginal man in a state of moral isolation and
extreme potential physical elimination, his sacrifices and his failures,
with the onset of the war of national liberation, now became durable.
To this person and that hard-core minute element of young, dedicated
professional revolutionaries, the emerging period of revolution by frontal assault served to verify their vision that they were the representatives of that avantguarde revolutionary tide that would mold their country's destiny and would justify the sacrifices which they were about to
make. To that element which viewed the emergence of the Army of

---

18. Milovan Djilas, *Op. Cit.* p. 24

National Liberation as a tool of the Comintern and who in time, like Draza Mihailovic, would enter into various degrees of accommodation with the occupying powers in an attempt to offset and destroy the partisan movement, there could be no turning back. Accepting the full consequences of their actions, together with the political ramifications, they believed that history would be the ultimate judge. If they succeeded, then success would serve as its own justification. If they failed, then the future historians of their native land would condemn them.[19]

With the exception of Albania, which had been conquered by Italy in 1939, the socio-political structures of the nation-states of Greece and of Yugoslavia were, by the spring of 1941, to be caught up in a total war as their lands were transformed into a battlefield. Greece, "The Cradle of Western Civilization", was at this historical moment internally divided by the Venezelos debate and the war in Albania. One must recall that on the 28th of October, 1940, the "New Roman Legions" of Benito Mussolini's Fascist Italy struck southward from their bases in Albania in their quest to conquer and absorb Greece into the New Roman Empire. The modern-day Hellenes not only repulsed the invaders, but carried out a series of offensive operations that resulted in the liberation of southern Albania's administrative regions of Gjirokaster, Korce, and the potential entrapment of Italian military at the port of Vlora. The precarious situation which confronted the military formations of Italy forced Mussolini to request German aid which, following the Yugoslav coup d'état on March 27, 1941, resulted in the invasion and the conquest of Yugoslavia and Greece.[20]

The Greece of 1941, following the collapse of its military, was confronted by a combined fiscal and monetary crisis that with the passage of a brief period of time, gave birth to a high rate of inflation that was well in excess of 100%, a vigorous black market, and a famine that was to result in 250,000 deaths.[21] Furthermore, the failure of the occupation government through its actions and its failed programs, gave birth to the emergence of a state within a state that would chal-

---

19. Nicholas J. Costa, *Op. Cit.* p. 24
20. Nicholas J. Costa, *Ibid* pp. 43-48
21. Mark Mazower, *Op. Cit.* pp. 40-41

lenge the legitimacy of the government in Athens. The negative features of the occupation by Italy was viewed by pro-Hellenic Germans as a moral and a political defeat. The inflation, the black market, and the famine of 1941 were to become positive forces in the evolution of a combative mind-set. Yet, that which evolved in relation to the emergence of a movement of national resistance was "blowing in the wind" as a result of individual acts of defiance.

Such acts were seen in the cheering by the citizens of Athens and the offering of food, raki, cigarettes, and bundles of cheese and olives to British prisoners of war as they were being loaded on to a truck to be taken to a prisoner-of-war camp or to a collection point. In addition, according to Kosta Vangeli, a young shoeshine boy yelled, "Aera", at a carbiniere and quickly ran away with the irate Italian in hot pursuit only to stop as the young man turned around with his hands in the air shouting, "Bella Grecia", a very popular term used by the Italians when surrendering to the Greeks in Albania. Furthermore, students would paint a huge V on sidewalks and on buildings "5 minutes to 12". The spirit of resistance was to symbolically rise from the ashes of an occupied Greece. Within one month, following the capitulation of Greece in May, 1941, two boys climbed up the Acropolis and under the noses of the guards, removed the swastika in a most significant and noble act of defiance.[22]

Such acts were to result in the establishment of a negativistic reaction of such ferocity by German occupation troops that by adhering to such a policy not only in Greece, but also in Albania and in Yugoslavia, one would be confronted by the chilling and the silent landscape of death. It is from such "Killing Fields" that out of the blood soaked land of Hellas would emerge in 1942, the Greek communist-led resistance alliance, EAM, and the Greek People's Liberation Army, ELAS. This force of andarts (warriors) was under the command of Nicholas Zakharia and Georgos Sianto. It is this force together with the forces of Napoleon Zervas's Greek National Democratic Army League that would confront the military occupation of their country by Fascist Italy

---

22. Mark Mazower, *Ibid* pp. 92-93

and Nazi Germany. In an ironic twist of events, ELAS would also confront British military units in the streets of Athens for the political soul of Greece as Anglo-American forces confronted the Axis powers in Italy and on the Western Front.

CHAPTER FIVE

THE BARBARIANS

What is true in history is often less important than what people believe to be true. In the midst of the Italo-German occupation of Albania, Greece and Yugoslavia, the people had to acquire a perceptional change and an understanding of the politics of war. Those who engaged in a war of national liberation and at the same historical moment, a civil war, as they sought to bring about an economic and a social-political transformation in accordance to Marxist-Leninist dogma, found themselves confronted by "resistance, rebellion and death" regardless of their status of non-combatants or that of combatants. The protracted conflict between collaborationist, the forces of the status quo and the revolutionary, together with the willingness of the occupation forces to kill 50 to 100 innocent people for every German killed by the Partisans, was totally beyond their comprehension. Tragically, in the Balkans one must be aware of the fact that the legacy of Conflicting memories has always led to the emergence of conflict situations between clans, nations and between Christians and the followers of Allah.

To a major degree the young revolutionary, a tradition-directed person, who was involved in the war of national liberation as a communist or a liberal democrat, had to first recognize his and her claim to authority in some source outside one's self for decisions made and actions undertaken. In addition, the andarts, partisans and the Chetniks had to possess an operative ideological justification. For the resistant person, such was to be found in the success of a movements program in creating common interests and attainable goals together with a leadership's ability to promote and practice the principles proclaimed within the context of a protracted guerrilla warfare or that of a civil war. The nation's revolutionary forces, seeking to respond to the failure of the dominant society or the "Old Order", the Marxist-Leninist movements of the political left attempted to bring about (through to process of "Revolution by Frontal Assault") a dramatic fundamental, structural, political and attitudinal shift in one's mind-set.

In 1941 with the Germanic invasion of Yugoslavia and of Greece at one and the same time, (Albania had previously been economically integrated into the "Sawdust Caesar's Roman Empire" and militarily conquered within a week's time in 1939) one finds that the people of Albania, Greece and Yugoslavia, while seeking life, found only the silence of death. It has been stated that the people of the Balkans are sensitive to one's destiny and that their protest transforms itself into a revolutionary force when needed, even against the Gods themselves. It is at this critical and significant moment as German Panzer units cross the Polish frontier into the Soviet Union, June 22, 1941, that the human condition made up of death, illusion and of hope, propel the men of the "Left" to go forth from their villages to meet their destinies and to engage the enemy in defense of the country and the Citadel of Communism at one and the same time. The reign of the "God of War – Mars" and his playmate, "The Beast", has begun anew and we once more become "The Barbarians".

The conflict situation which broke out in its full fury with the launching of "Operation Punishment" and that of "Operation Marita" simultaneously upon the Land of the South Slavs and the Land of the Hellenes on April 6, 1941, was no less political in its assumptions and disastrous in its consequences for the people of Yugoslavia and of Greece than which had transpired while under the domination of the Ottoman Turk, the Balkan Wars of 1912 and 1913, and World War I. It is at this historical moment that Great Britain and the United States of America, a relative newcomer to the region, pay a great degree of attention in order that future political and strategic interest issues relating to the war and to post-war consideration, be clarified and clearly defined.

It was only in 1943 that the Anglo-American command could finally consider from the soft underbelly of North Africa, following the defeat of Field Marshal Rommel's Africa Corps, to undertake an offensive operational plan of action. On July 10, 1943, Anglo-American forces stormed the beaches of Sicily to begin the initial step that would lead to the liberation of Adolph Hitler's "Fustang Europea" or Western Europe. Tragically, there existed at this moment and throughout the war, a conflict of views between the United States and the British military command relating to the geo-strategic matrix as related to overall military operational battle plans on the invasion of Europe and the Balkans and the post-war status of the Balkan Peninsula. One may recall Churchill's desire to strike through northern Yugoslavia, through the Lyublyana Gap, and then meet and confront the Russians at the Cuzon Line.[1] In so doing the Russians would be prevented from entering and taking over the European heartland through the process of the establishment of "Popular Democracies". As stated by George Dimitrov, former General Secretary of the Comintern,

> *The Soviet regime and the Popular Democratic regime are two forms of one and the same system of government.*[2]

It must be noted that prior to the battle of Stalingrad, Stalin had recommended just such a move to the Anglo-American command. In addition, according to Gabriel Kolko in his analytical and insightful study *The Politics of War*, that the fundamental difference in strategy and concerns over plans for the invasion of France and other irritants, let alone personal resentments, resulted in Churchill angrily informing his Chief of Staff (1943) that he was inclined to tell the Americans:

> *All right, if you will no play with us in the Mediterranean, we won't play with you in the English Channel. And if they say, all right, then we shall direct our main effort in the Pacific – to reply, you are welcome to do so if you wish.*

The high degree of frustration and resentments were to give birth to mutual doubts that would plague the Anglo-American alliance to the very end of World War II.

---

1. Gabriel Kolko, *The Politics of War: United States Foreign Policy* (New York, Vantage Books, Random House, 1968) pp. 14-20

2. Hugs Seaton-Watson, *The East European Revolutions* (New York, Frederick A. Praeger, 1956) p. 167

The protracted and yet tragic psycho-historical variables, together with a sequence of catastrophic, political events since time immemorial, has taught the inhabitants of the Land of the Eagle-Albania, the Land of the South Slavs-Serbia and Montenegro (currently constituting the nation-state of Yugoslavia), Croatia, Slovenia, Macedonia and Bosnia-Hercegrovnia, that their national ethos and their nations' symbolic and non-material culture of the land and its people, has been molded by warfare. With the exception of the Ottoman Turkish conquest of the nations of this region of southeastern Europe and the subsequent 500 year period of occupation by the forces of Islam, the 20th century has been the most dramatic phase as well as the most traumatic of times because of internal conflicts, quests to defend one's lands against the neighboring nation's irredentists' urge. The Balkan Wars of 1912 and 1913, World War I of 1914-18, the period of internal political shifts and conflicts as the shadow of totalitarianism began to engulf Eastern Europe from the outbreak of World War II (1939-1945) to the ensuing Cold War era. Thus, one should not wonder why the people of the Balkans refer to the region as the cursed land – dhe vende mallkoj (Albanian).

As the twilight of a very long and dark night of war and barbarism was descending across the great curving mountainous Balkan range, the tradition-directed clans who "know nor understood any other life pattern than their own and no other customs than those of their ancestors"[3], were unprepared to understand the serpentine movements of the complicated, political world of the twentieth century. As a peasant locked in a daily battle for survival, his outlook was limited to his own interests: family, land, bread, credit, and reduced taxes. Tragically for the Albanians, Greeks and Serbo-Croatians, their Europe was involved in a predatory Danse Macabre. On Palm Sunday, April 6, 1941, the people of Yugoslavia and Greece found their nations being invaded by Germanic and Bulgarian military units; they never had a chance.

The German military under the command of Lieutenant-General Alexander Lohr, which had come into Greece from the brutal and totally negative military environment of past German theaters of opera-

---

3. Nicholas J. Costa, *Albania: A European Enigma* (Boulder, Colorado East European Monographs, 1995)

tion, was a Russian Orthodox by birth, spoke Russian and had a sophisticated understanding of the psycho-historical makeup and mindset of the Greek.[4] Throughout the German tenure in Hellas and from the initial strike, they adhered to a warfare prescribing a maximum type of initiative, high mobility in the field of operation and the usage of superior force possessing more than maximum fire power in the air and on the land. In addition, because of their past combat experience in Yugoslavia, they were the force in readiness who were quick to exploit every opportunity and in so doing, were able to maneuver as the situation required in order to achieve the final Fascist victory.

With the fall of Yugoslavia and Greece, the people were confronted with the moral choice between being a victim or an executioner – and nothing else. Given the traditions of a noble past, the choice of the citizens of the nation-state of Serbs, Croats and Slovenes was predetermined by the forces of history and one's psychological makeup. They once again elected to confront the enemy and become the executioners. For the people of the land of Hellas and of democracy, the tradition of resistance combined with their love of liberty and of freedom, offered the people of Greece no choice but to confront the enemy as their noble and honored forefathers had confronted the Turks and Bulgarians in the 20th century. In relation to the noble Pericles and Aristotle, one must recall that according to Nikos Kazantzakis, there exists within the descendants of Alexander The Great an eternal fire within one's soul and a wild and unending desire for liberty and for freedom whatever the cost. There also exists a willingness to confront the invader to the bottomless pits of HELL in a heroic and tragic manner if need be. The reading of Nikos Kazantzakis' book *Freedom of Death* along with other publications by the author, makes the reader and the historian aware of the fact that the conclusion reached and the above statement present a psycho-historical fact.

In 1941 the Italian and the German forces of occupation became the victims of the fury they had aroused throughout the nations of Europe which they had trampled underfoot. The desire of the conquered peoples to react and to say "No" from the northern reaches of Norway to

---

4. Mark Mazower, *Inside Hitler's Greece: The Experience of the Occupation 1941-1945* (New Haven, Yale University Press, 1993) p. 155

the Greek islands of Cyprus and Crete, from occupied France to the Volga river and beyond in the Soviet Union may be attributed to an inner psycho-historical reflex to the tyranny of the occupation, the application of modern techniques of extermination of one's fellow man in the death camps, and a revolt against the past. Yet, their conqueror achieved military successes in Russia, North Africa and in the Balkans. It must be noted that the victor was confronted by an historical paradox. Its uninterrupted string of conquests led to the dissolvement of Nazism and totalitarianism as it spread. It destroyed itself through its victories.

Throughout the interwar period, 1918-1939, many individuals who were involved in illegal and clandestine revolutionary activities in Albania, Greece and in Yugoslavia, were to find (were they to reflect upon past actions as professional revolutionaries) that they had backed into the future. Individuals such as Georgi Dimitrov of Bulgaria; Gottwald of Germany; Longo and Togliatti of Italy; Thorez of France; Zakhariadis and Sianto of Greece; Ali Kelmendi and Enver Hoxha of Albania; and Josip Broz-Tito of the Land of the South Slavs represented an historical communist-oriented, tri-dimensional revolutionary wave of reaction which was sweeping across Southeastern Europe.

For the peoples of Albania, Greece and Yugoslavia, there existed in the multitude of villages and in the cities, a gathering place of those peasants who were to seek their fortunes in a land across the sea of "behind the Moon" where it was said, "that even the streets were paved with gold". That faraway country was America. Of the many who stood at the gathering place in the Croatian village of Kumrovec in 1907, a father turned to his son to make him aware of the fact that it was his intention to send his son to America to seek his fortune. The name of the 15 year old boy was Josip Broz. Due to an inability to acquire the needed funding, the young adolescent was not to undertake the journey, but if one were to "read" the remaining residue of the muddy-like Turkish coffee in his cup, the reader would find that his journey would take him to the battlefields of the Eastern front, the conspiratorial world of the revolutionary, and that of the head of the Yugoslav Communist Party. Also, the remaining grains in that coffee cup would reveal that

---

5. Franz Borkenau, *European Communism* (New Haven, Harper and Brothers Publishers, 1953) p. 108

he would play a most vital role in the process of recruitment and dispatch of 1500 Yugoslav volunteers (of whom 750 were killed in action, 300 were wounded, and the remaining number interned in a French holding camp) to the Spanish Republic as members of the International Brigades to fight against Franco. While his life, prior to the outbreak of World War II, was a protracted game of cat and mouse, he would rise to become the Secretary General of the Communist Party of Yugoslavia in 1937 and following the German bombing of Belgrade on April 6, 1941, the leader of the partisan formations in the war of national liberation.

Amidst the years of the "Great Terror", the young, faithful servant from Yugoslavia had been summoned to Moscow. An examination of his Comintern dossier would possess references to his work on behalf of the international communist movement. In addition, it would have included within the file several notations relating to his 1928 trial which projected in words and deeds his dedication to the revolutionary struggle. Of the events of 1928, one finds a reference to the right-wing newspaper *Novosti* which stated:

> *Josip Broz was brought in next. His undoubtedly the most interesting personality in this trial. His face makes you think of steel. His light gray eyes behind his spectacles are cold but alert and calm. In his case, his attitude in court is perhaps more than a mere pose, for he has been prosecuted before and has already served several sentences for his political beliefs. Many of those present were doubtless aware of the stubbornness with which he maintains his views, and his cross examination was listened to attentively and in complete silence.*[6]

Of this episode, Richard West, in his study of the revolutionary of yesteryear, calls one's attention to the November 15, 1928 *Novosti* article which stated the following:

> *The Communist trial which has become known as the bomb thrower's trial was concluded yesterday, with its dominant tone struck once more at the end by Josip Broz. After the large audi-*

---

6. Fitzroy Maclean, *The Heretic* (New York, Harper Brothers Publishers, 1957) p. 8, 70

ence which was already rising to leave to courtroom, (he)
shouted three times, "Long live the Communist Party! Long live
the Third International!"... Thus it was that this unyielding Com-
munist disappeared behind prison walls, for all the world like
the captain of a ship who shouts when the ship is sinking.[7]

Approximately two decades ago while discussing this event and
Tito's actions and words, Milovan Djilas called to my attention that
"given Tito's dedication and belief, one could only send a strong message to the people of Yugoslavia, of whom many were illiterate, and
to the membership of the Communist Party of Yugoslavia. That devotion to the cause, in the revolutionary struggle, required of one to, if
need be, sacrifice one's self. In many instances we led and educated
by example".[8]

In the summer of 1937 as the "Great Terror" was greedily devour-
ing the "Old Bolsheviks" and the children of the revolution, it must be
noted that Stalin's quest for total and complete power also required the
elimination of the Soviet Union's military high command. This leads
one to suspect that Stalin was fearful of a Bonapartist Coup d'état.
Given the political environment together with Stalin's suspicious mind-
set at this significant, psycho-historical moment, the Deputy People's
Commissar for Defense, Marshal Tukhachevsky, and the totality of the
Soviet Union's High Command were arrested, tried and executed. A
few years later the members of their respective families were also eliminated after having served a sentence in a labor camp in Siberia. Stalin
had kept his word to the accused. He had permitted the families of
those whom the prosecutor, Andrei Vyshinsky, referred to in the most
negative terms, to live, but only for a year or two. Those who fell victims of the purge did so as a result of a belief in the revolution. Thus for
many, the act of repentance which demanded one's life is difficult to
understand. However, this was the Stalinist era. At this time, if the
party demanded one's confession, then he would confess. Yet, one must
be aware that the quest for a confession as stated by the interrogator

7. Richard West, *Tito and the Rise and Fall of Yugoslavia* (New York, Carroll and
Graf Publishers, 1994) p. 57
8. Milovan Djilas, Personal Interview, Belgrade, Yugoslavia, 1981

was not automatically obeyed. One need only to review the record of Bukharin's trial. At this critical moment, Bukharin did not confess in the accepted manner following a protracted period of interrogation. While this revolutionary of yesteryear and personal friend of Lenin did confess in order to render one last service to the party, it must be noted that the manner in which he did so made it obvious to all in attendance in the courtroom that the charges against him were false.[9]

In addition, such luminaries as Kamenev, Zinoviev and Kirov, the old Bolsheviks of yesteryear and the creators of the revolution, were also arrested and executed. Given the environment into which Tito was entering, one can understand his statement following his invitation to return to Moscow in 1937.

When I went to Moscow I never knew whether I should come back alive. And while I was there I never knew that I would not wake in the middle of the night to hear the fatal knocking at my door.[10]

He was not to suffer liquidation in a cell in Lubianka prison nor was he to beg for punishment as did Gorkic and a majority of the other Yugoslav who had been summoned to the Red Citadel. Instead, the "Red Gods of the Kremlin" smiled on this young and dedicated communist revolutionary who received from Dimitrov the responsibilities of the office of the post of "General Secretary" – "provisionally". He was to return to Yugoslavia, develop cadres throughout the country, develop revolutionary elites and rid the party of factionalists, sectarians, nepotists, deviationists and regional nationalists. It would be interesting to speculate at this moment on the question in relation to how Tito would have reacted if he had been arrested and stood trial? Would he have confronted his tormentors, such as the lead prosecutor, Andrei Cyshinsky, with a repeat performance of his 1928 trial in Belgrade? According to Vukmanovic-Temp, "Tito would, at that time, do nothing to harm the movement".[11] Milovan Djilas also believed that as a

---

9. Robert Conquest, *The Great Terror: A Reassessment* (New York, Oxford University Press, 1990) p. 74-75
10. Fitzroy Maclean, *Op. Cit.* pp. 74-75
11. S. Vukmanovic Tempo Personal Interview Belgrade, Yugoslavia, 1

young, dedicated revolutionary, he also would have rendered one last service to the revolution; he would have sacrificed himself.[12]

The year is now 1939. Over Europe the storm clouds of war are gathering and Mars, the God of War, brings about a series of political and diplomatic events that can only guarantee that the curse of mankind – war – would break out momentarily. In Spain, 1936, the "Revolt of the Generals" resulted in a vicious civil war as the forces of Fascism (1939) were to gain the ultimate victory over the Spanish Republic. The hot blasts of war could be noticed by all as Hitler moved into his native Austria and the summer months brought Munich and the temporary, political, but not military capitulation of France and England due to a loss of nerve. Prior to September 1, 1939, Mussolini, in order to boost his faltering ego and the reemphasize that the Mediterranean was an Italian Lake and that the Balkan Peninsula fell within the Italian sphere of influence, transformed an economic colony, Albania, into a military conquest (Good Friday, April 7, 1939) within a matter of days. Following a series of discussion between Ribbentrop and Molotov, there emerged on August 23, 1939, the German-Soviet Nonaggression Pact. On September 1st three major German armies consisting of 190 divisions crossed the German Polish border. The Second World War has begun.

Karl Von Clausewitz, a 19th century Prussian student of war and of military matters, has made the world aware of the significant fact that, "War is the continuation of politics with other means". As one delves into the difficult and complex morass of the political environment of the nation-states of the Balkan peninsula throughout the interwar phase of our previous 30 Year War, 1914-1945, the historian and the reader alike cannot help but note that the annotation, when applied to the pathos of Balkan politics, is totally valid. Tragically, the mythological Gods who lived, played and who controlled the lives of the people of Greece on Mount Olympus, did not have a sufficient period of time to permit the people of the Balkan countries to solve their multitude of political, economic, and social problems nor to work out their destinies.

---

12. Milovan Djilas, Personal Interview, Belgrade, Yugoslavia, 1976

It must also be noted that in the newly established independent nation-states which emerged in the Balkan Peninsular, the diversified collage of native ethno-national countries with their unique cultural attributes and hidden national agendas, created throughout the inter-war period of national political and economic consolidation, an explosive situation. Unlike Turkey under the leadership of its president, Mustapha Kemal – "Ataturk", a county which underwent a radical tridimensional and revolutionary structural, cultural, and attitudinal transformation, the kaleidoscopic changes in Albania and in Greece, in the words of Doctor Peter Sugar, were "only surface changes". Both the nations of Hellas and the land of the Eagle-Albania, since the ending of the Balkan Wars, tended to be representative of two nations involved with an internal political struggle within itself.[13]

That the fate of Tirana and Athens varied cannot be denied. According to Dr. Bernd J. Fisher, the author of *King Zog and the Struggle for Stability in Albania*, the political world of Albania in the 1920-1930's was no more than:

> *The reality of politics in those early years immediately after the war, 1914-1918, came down to what it had always been – individual personalities and raw power based ultimately on the number of guns a leader could muster...*[14]

This accurate observation makes one aware that the hallmark of the Albanian political scene of the interwar period stemmed directly from the fact that the Albanians were and are to this day prisoners of their own psycho-historical past. In Athens, the historical "Cradle of Western Democracy", it must be noted that the desire of Hellas to bring northern Epirus (southern Albania), Thrace, the conquered lands of Turkey in Europe, the religious center of Eastern Orthodoxy-Constantinople, the Pontos and Smyrna regions in Asia Minor, the Dodecanese islands and Cyprus under the political jurisdiction of Greece could not be turned aside when the Ottoman Turk entered the Great

---

13. Peter Sugar, *Eastern European Nationalism In The Twentieth Century* (Washington, D.C. American University Press, 1995) pp. 184-190
14. Bernd J. Fisher, *King Zog and the Struggle For Stability In Albania* (Boulder, Colorado, East European Monographs, 1984) p. 26

War on the side of the Central Powers in November, 1914. For Venizelos, this decision by the Ottoman Turks provided the means to transform the "Megali Idea" from an elusive goal into a political reality. Thus, in 1917, Greece entered the conflict in support of the Entente Powers.[15]

Throughout the twenty year interwar period, 1919-1939, the political flip side of Hellenism for the Greek was Enois-Union as Athens sought to transform an unquenchable illusion into a diplomatic reality. The emergence of an inner force, equivalent to that which served as the catalyst which drove the Americans to conquer a continent – The Manifest Destiny, arose in Greece. Following the Great War of 1914-1918, it gave birth to the "Great Idea-Megali Idea", as in the past. As popular gusts of emotional winds swept across the Land of Hellas, the criterion of moderation was swept aside and replaced by the potentially unchecked force of hubris. In so doing, it appears, from the benefit of hindsight, that the Ancient Gods on Mount Olympus elected to punish the Greeks as they sought to bring under their political jurisdiction all Greek settlements in the Balkans, Asia Minor, the islands of Eastern Mediterranean, together with Constantinople, the seat of the Patriarch of the Eastern Orthodox Church.

Given that a nation-state tends to believe in a manner which is consistent with what one has come to anticipate, then the individual actions of man and nations are reinforced by its positive or negative images. It is at this historical moment that the political environment served to define for the people and the government of Greece an opportunity that had to be taken advantage of. One must be aware that Greek-Turkish relations possessed a very high degree of negativism since the conquest of Greece and subsequent period of protracted occupation by the Ottoman Turks. In addition, the Greeks once again confronted the Turks in the Balkan Wars of 1912-1913 and World War I. Furthermore, the positive circumstances did combine with the national Greek cultural ideology and the existing attitudinal predisposition of the people, government, and the military command of Greece to propel them to the ultimate disaster that awaited them on the Anatolian plains by the forces of Mustafa Kemal, an Albanian from

---

15. Peter Sugar, *Op. Cit.* pp. 177-184

the Ottoman city of Thessaloniki. This tragic defeat shattered the vision of redeeming Hellenism across the sea as 1.25 million Greek Orthodox Christians, together with the honored remain of their forefathers, moved to Greece as refugees in 1922.[16]

From the national tragedy of 1922 to 1936, the legacy of bitterness gave birth to Venizelist and anti-Venizelist's political feud. It must be noted that Venizelos was not in favor of the ill fated offensive military plans which were supported by the King of Greece. Thus, following the conflict, Venizelos turned his attention to the internal problems of the nation and to the evolution of a unified and stable Greece. At this time the activities of the Greek Communist Party supported the quest for a Macedonian political entity and in 1935 the KKE called for equality for all minorities in Keeping with Moscow's desire to establish a popular front against the Fascist tide. By 1936, after a period of prolonged, political disunity and gridlock, the king on August 4, 1936, dissolved Parliament, instituted martial law, and the strong man of Greece was now General Metaxas.

On October 28, 1940, the Sawdust Caesar's military formations crossed the Albanian-Greek border following a declaration of war and rushed headlong not to the anticipated glorious victory, but to a crushing defeat. The Greek military forces undertook their offensive operations which were to result in the liberation of the Albanian cities of Gjirokaster and Korce, and the Italian military withdrawal to the Albanian port city of Vlora. On November 22, 1940, a statement was made that the Greeks were fighting not only their country, but also for the other people of the Balkans, as well as the liberation of Albania following the fall of the Albanian city of Korce. The political significance of the statement is not lost to the Albanian for they were quick to realize that liberation did not mean independence. As Italian military force clung to the port city of Vlore, the people of Greece celebrated the defacto political conquest of "Northern Epirus", an unstated objective which in reality was the internationally acknowledged and lawful region of "Southern Albania".[17]

---

16. Nikos Kazantzakis, *The Fratricides* (New York, Simon and Schuster Inc. 1964) p. 156

17. Nicholas J. Costa, *Op. Cit.* p. 38

With a negative military situation confronting Benito Mussolini in Albania and a coup taking place in the Yugoslav capital city of Belgrade, following the signing of the Tripartite Pact by Premier Cvetknovic and Foreign Minister Cincar-Markovic, and an awareness that British troops would soon be landing in Greece, Adolph Hitler had no choice but to pull Italian chestnuts out of the Grecian fire. However, he delayed his plans for the invasion of Russia and punished the Yugoslavs despite the fact that General Dusan Simovic offered to sign a nonaggression pact with Germany. On Palm Sunday, April 6, 1941, the German 12th Army struck and a week later, German and Hungarian military units entered the shattered and burning city of Belgrade. The Greeks, who had humiliated the Italians, were beaten by General List's 12th Army which consisted of 15 divisions, as were the British military units that were sent from Libya. Britain now stood alone.[18]

A study of the protracted and yet tragic history of the international relations of Albania makes the political analyst aware that the nation's power elite responds to what they believe to be as opposed to reality. Thus, in the Albania of the decade of the 1920's and that of the 1930's, transpiring political events at both the domestic and international level, did not augur well for the future of this political entity. Given that feelings projected by a neighboring nation-state towards another is a perceptional by-product, it is not surprising that following Albania's emergence on the world stage, one's view of this Islamic nation in a Christian Europe ran from a powerful distortion to nonexistence. Yet, at this critical moment in history of Albania, both the Kingdom of Yugoslavia and the government of the Kingdom of Italy, now a Fascist dictatorship headed by Benito Mussolini, extended their hand of friendship as each sought to enhance their security and to gain geopolitical, diplomatic and strategic advantages at Albanian's expense.

Students of international relations learn at an early phase of their studies that the domestic policy of a nation plays the formative role in the determination of a country's foreign policy. The epic, heroic and tragic story of the "Land of the Eagle" is a country forged in war where tribes, clans, and feudal lords clashed against one another and the individual became involved in blood feuds as they all battled to deter-

---

18. William L. Shirer, *The Rise and Fall of the Third Reich* (New York, Simon and Schuster Publishers 1960) p. 286

mine who would rule in their village, administrative area or nation. And when they were not fighting against one another, they were defending their homes and lands against outside intruders. Since time immemorial, fighting has been a way of life for the people of Albania, who possess a rage to live and a ruthless, abiding taste for reality. This unaccepted orphan country on the world's international stage has been kicked around, threatened and influenced by Greeks, Slavs, Turks and Italians as well as brutalized, invaded, looted, occupied and divided, as evident by the historical fact that as many Albanians reside in total in Serbia and in western Macedonia as the number of people who currently constitute the total population of Albania. Its geographic location, in spite of the sophisticated advancement in weapon technology, together with its abundance in natural resources, has always whetted the appetite of its more powerful neighbors: Greece, Serbia, Montenegro and Italy. Furthermore, this predicament of history tends to envelop the Albanian in a protracted crisis environment which threatens not only the nation's survival, but also the Albanian's existence as an Albanian. On many counts the lone "Son of the Eagle" has always lived in spite of his surroundings encased within an Albanian environment. Thus, when Albania emerged as a new member of our Global Village in 1912, the Albania emerged as a new member of our Global Village in 1912, the Albanian and his country found themselves at one and the same time in Europe, but not a part of Europe.

Throughout the decade of the 1920's and that of the 1930's, Albania's political situation was precarious. The surrounding nation-states of Yugoslavia, Greece and Italy desired to acquire either outright or defacto, control of the land and the people of Albania. Furthermore, they distrusted each other and considered their respective foreign policy interests in relation to Albania at least partly incompatible in their quest for power over the "Land of the Eagle". The decades of the 1920's and the 1930's were to witness Ahmed Zog's advancement in the rough and tumble of Albanian politics from the status of the Prime Minister in 1924 to that of the president in 1925 and in the year, 1928, to the station of King of all of the Albanians. A pragmatic and utilitarian practitioner of the policy of "Real Politik", he turned to Italy and the Fascist government of Benito Mussolini in the mid 1920's. Given the internal political environment confronting him and the governmental demands as well as a minimalist Gross Domestic Product, he was left with no other political alternative.

The dramatic restructuring of the power relationships among the nations of the Balkan peninsula throughout the decade of the 1920's made it impractical for Zog in his position of president to maintain his former ties with Yugoslavia. Aware of the basis for the close relationship between Paris and Belgrade, Ahmed Zog came to the logical conclusion that France would not place its relationship with Yugoslavia in jeopardy in order to assist the Albanians in their ongoing dispute over the Kosovo issue. An additional reason as to why the Belgrade-Tirana connection could not be maintained may be attributed to the potential projection and reinforcement of the negative image that Ahmed Zog had once again abandoned his Albanian brethren across the border as he did in 1924 when he granted Yugoslavia the lands which included Lake Ohrid, the church of St. Naum, and additional Albanian territory, in return for Yugoslav assistance in his quest to bring down the government of Fan S. Noli. Such a politically repugnant, counter-productive image would result in an internal conflict with the irredentism group led by Hasan Prishtina and Bajram Curri, let alone with Zog's other opponents.

The barriers to the formation of a Tirana-Athens bond made it impossible for Ahmed Zog to turn to Greece for the financial support required by the government of Albania. The major obstruction to the development of normal relations between the countries in the decade of the 1920's and which exists to this day is the issue of "Northern Epirus". Before the government of Greece would enter into any agreement with Albania, it would first require that Tirana cede that Albanian territory which is inhabited by Albanians of the Eastern Orthodox faith and in which the cities of Korce, Argyokaster, and Sarande are located. Such a request would automatically by turned down by the government of Albania. Furthermore, Greece, which like its northern neighbor had entered the postwar era in a state of economic distress, had as its primary goal the settlement of the dispute which existed between Athens and Belgrade regarding the port city of Salonika.

The marriage of convenience having radically altered the domestic and the international political landscape with the signing of the 1927 Treaty of Tirana, made it possible for Benito Mussolini to propel Italian interests into a position of dominance over Albanian internal and foreign affairs. Yet, what is ironic in the game of deception which was taking place between King Zog and the Sawdust Caesar is to be found in the fact that ordinary deception requires a conscious and forceful will to fool others and self-deception requires an unconscious will to fool one's self. In that nations and their respective leaders are accountable for its self-deception as well as for its deceptions, the question arises in this "Great Game" of who, in the final analysis, is deceiving whom? Or are they boxing with one's own shadows?

At this moment in the political and international arena of diplomatic interaction of the nations of Europe and America, the gravest events in the Land of the Eagle were in the offering. Tragically for the world, the fact is that what transpired in Albania was inconsequential except for the nations of Greece, Yugoslavia and Italy. Perhaps this may be attributed to the fact that the Sawdust Caesar's defacto takeover failed to correspond to the accepted image of what a great event should be. We have been conditioned into thinking that great and significant events take the form of such actions as the blowing up of the USS Maine in Havana Harbor in 1898, the killing of Archduke Francis Ferdinand in Sarajevo on June 28, 1914, St. Vitus' day, Vidovdan – two events that were to result in military confrontations. As a result of political hindsight, the conflict between Italy and Albania was, in fact, two nations entering into a boxing ring and beginning to beat up one another. By the time round one was coming to a close, it became a contest of weakness, a contest where the winner must be the one who knocks himself out first. However, it must be noted that Italy has always been obsessed by Albania which symbolically represented a small corner of the world and a national concern of the Kingdom of Italy for which the government of King Victor Emmanuel consciously felt responsible.

Given the protracted historical link between the two countries, it is no wonder that the fascist dictator of Italy, Benito Mussolini, considered Albania as a birthright (hegemony over all Albania). Furthermore, given the evolving Italian governmental mind-set, it appears that the "Power Elite" within the Fascist Grand Council reached a point through a complex process of mental gymnastics where an offer from Tirana became transmuted into an Italian right. Thus, it demonstrates, at the very least, the degree to which King Zog and his advisors and Benito Mussolini along with Count Ciano were doomed not only to mutual incomprehension but also to a military conflict situation. As the storm clouds gathered over Europe, the ancient vendettas among the various "Tribes with Flags" in the Balkan peninsula, brought on by the historical protracted irredentists' urge, made it a political necessity to coexist. However, it was a subconscious type of coexistence without conviction or real hope. Thus, the existing insatiable quest for the annexation of the lost historical lands created a diplomatic hot potato that was to result, prior to the outbreak of World War II in Europe as of September, 1939, in an attempt to transform that opportunity into a political and diplomatic reality.

This may be attributed to the fact that there exists between man and the mind's eye a delicate relationship. This coupling results within the individual an innate quest to desire that which he has viewed. This self-created inner desire is never satisfied. It is this internal torment, born of the quest for more and more, that remains indispensable for the understanding of the uncontrolled passions of men at war and statesmen alike. In relation to the protracted Italo-Albanian conflict situation, one must recall the words stated by Signor Tittoni before the members of the Italian Parliament on May 4, 1904. At this time, in unmistakable words, he summed up the true reason for Italy's unending interest in the Land of the Eagle.

> *Albania in itself is not of great importance. Its real value consists of its ports and of its coast, the possession of which for either Austro-Hungary or for Italy would signify incontestable supremacy in the Adriatic.[19]*

Unknowingly, time was running out for the citizens of Albania and the inhabitants of the Balkans, for Europe's political and diplomatic events were rapidly approaching their conclusion. The more politically astute packed their families and bags and left the country as did Albania's King Zog with the nation's gold reserve when he fled to Athens, Constantinople, Cairo, Paris and London. An all-out war was just over the horizon.

As previously noted, the Land of the Eagle-Albania became a legitimate member of the community of nations on November 28, 1912. However, the first six years were truly a time of troubles with its neighbors coveting Albania's lands. Tragically, the nation's greatest enemy was that which involved the Albanian in a national Danse Macabre against his fellow Albanian.

---

19. Hamilton Fish Armstrong, *The New Balkans* (New York Harper and Brothers Publishers 1926) p. 78

CHAPTER SIX

DEADLY ENTANGLEMENTS

The human condition of military conflict which swept across the Balkan peninsula and which was to embrace the totality of the Global Village became the force that provided the leftist-oriented ideological revolutionary forces an opportunity to sweep away the old institutions and relations that anchored man to the Old Order and the norms of the status quo. No one can deny that villages were destroyed and cast asunder in the Wars of National Liberation in the Land of the Eagle-Albania, the Land of the South Slavs-Yugoslavia and in Hellas-Greece. Nor can one deny that the principle of violence was to reign supreme as man became degraded and uprooted and the age-old ties of kinship were fragmented. Brother fought brother to the death and fathers put their sons to the sword. The civil war became the necessary precondition for the rise of the political left from a position of impotence as a political nonentity to one of power as rulers of their respective nation-states. Of this socio-political transformation, the supporters of the leftist-oriented ideology and followers of Marx and Lenin were to become the masters of their country. The sentiment of many British Liaison Officers who served with the partisans tended to reflect the conclusion rendered by H.W. Tilman, who had served in Albania.

> For my part, I returned convinced that our policy of giving financial and material support to the L.N.C. was just and expedient... The fact remains that the partisans of the L.N.C. fought, suffered and died for their professed aims and by so doing helped us.
> The resolution they showed through many months of hardship and disappointment, the will to win, their faith in them-

*selves and in their cause, all seemed to me to establish their
claim to leadership and to manifest that in them lay the best
hope for Albania's future.*[1]

Yet, it must be pointed out, on the basis of my own experience, that
it is difficult to spend a year in combat against the enemy and exclude
the preference for those who fought on the same side as you.

In the Balkans and the world over, events lead a double life. The
appearance of events within the context of a military in spite of the
field of paradoxes which engulfs them. It is this contradiction between
reality and appearance that Balkan politics had reached since the close
of World War I on November 11, 1918. The ambiguities brought on by
the Axis conquest were endless: the people of the southwestern tier of
the Balkans, following the invasion and rapid conquest their country,
now found themselves confused and demoralized. The Italians who
invaded Greece in October, 1940, now in the month of November, 1940,
found themselves confronted with a potential forceful evacuation of
the Albanian port of Vlore as the Greek military offensive possessed
the power to push the Italians out of Albania into the Adriatic Sea. In
April of 1941, with the German invasion of Yugoslavia and Greece,
the Italians became the mythical conquerors and masters of Greece.
The Albanians, who were militarily subdued by the "New Roman Legions" of the Sawdust Caesar in April, 1939, as their king fled into the
limbo of exile with the nation's gold reserves, were divided about the
issue of the war and the Italian occupation of their country. The Yugoslavs, at this historical moment, neither trusted nor believed, given the
rapid disintegration and defeat of their military units and the prevailing
emergence of the vehement anti-Serb attitude in Croatia together with
the massacre of the Serbian Eastern Orthodox population by the Ustase
under the leadership of Ante Pavelic. Considering such negative experiences, the population of the Kingdom of the South Slavs accepted
and expected the worst of everybody and everything.

As the protracted night of barbarism extended itself, the people of
the Balkans became aware that the major political parties of yesteryear were truly bankrupt and offered no alternative that would com-

---

1. H.W. Tilman, *When Men and Mountains Meet* (London, Cambridge University
Press 1946) pp. 152-153

mand the total confidence of the people in the form of a new leader, a new philosophy, or a new ideology. Thus, at this time, the only group (of whom they knew little) that represented a major break with the past and a major radical, socio-political, structural transformation was the communist. It is they who, according to Milovan Djilas, went forward into the ranks of the younger generation of the tradition-directed clans to create an awareness of-what was, what is and what would be – in simple meaningful terms.[2] In so doing the communist-led partisan movements in Albania, Greece and the Kingdom of Yugoslavia were able to carry into the irregular combat situation a unified and dedicated segment of a society that was willing to offer up as human sacrifice its sons and daughters to the unquenchable desire for blood by the God-of-War, Mars, for a new tomorrow.

The Balkans of the Thirty Year War, 1914-1945, demonstrated that the distance between the dreams of mankind and the "Reign of Terror" that was imposed upon the civilian population of numerous villages, remains to this day due to the rise in the level of brutality and the diminishing and shattering of that line which in past wars separated the civilian population from the combatant. As the irregular conflict situation engulfed their lands and the conqueror's reaction turned into an officially sanctioned policy of public executions, deportations to concentration camps and forced labor installations, the level of anxiety was raised as the conqueror became the executioner of the innocent. In addition, the inhabitants learned to identify and fear the fanatic who would commit any crime in the name of his cause. They also learned to be frightened of the individual who, through his negative actions, projected an attitude of indifference and would kill indiscriminately because he truly enjoyed the ultimate power rendered him as an active participant in the killing process.

In the savage and cursed lands of the nations of the Balkan peasant, a geo-political region drenched in the blood of the forefathers of the inhabitants of this detestable domain, the victorious forces of the Axis powers collided with the resistance in the mountain fastness of Albania, Greece and Yugoslavia. In the Land of the Eagle-Albania, resistance began at the individual level. To the peasant-warrior who had

---

2. Milovan Djilas, Person Interview, Belgrade, Yugoslavia

quietly endured the yoke of subjugation and had borne the scars of personal and national humiliation, the oncoming struggle represented not only the beginning of the end of a period of feudalistic servitude as well as the end of Italian and German occupation, but it also meant the reestablishment of Albania as a free, independent state, preferably within the boundaries as established by the Fascist government of the Kingdom of Italy. To the young intellectuals, the ensuing conflict marked the dawning of a new era which was to be characterized by a clean break with the old forces of resignation, injustice and disintegration of the Albania of the feudal lords and the Albania of the peasantry and the entry of the "Land of the Eagle" into Europe.

To the young communist idealist, who had lived as a marginal man in a state of moral isolation and extreme, potential, physical elimination, his sacrifices and failures with the onset of the war of national liberation now became worthwhile. To this person and that hard-core, minute element of young, dedicated, professional revolutionaries, the developing period of revolution by frontal assault served to verify their vision as representatives of that avant-garde revolutionary movement that would mold their country's destiny and would justify the sacrifices which they made on behalf of an idea. To that element which viewed the emergence of the Army of National Liberation as a tool of the Cominturn and who had entered into various degrees of accommodation with the forces of occupation in an attempt to offset and destroy the Partisan Movements, there could be no turning back. Accepting the full consequences of their actions together with the political ramifications, they believed that history would be the ultimate judge. If they succeeded, then success would serve as its own justification. If they failed, then the future historians of their native land would condemn them. In the final analysis, the emergence of the resistance movements in Albania, whether Balli Kombetar (Republican and anti-communist), L.N.C. (National Liberation Committee – communist-led resistance movement), or the Legality Party (sought the restoration of King Zog), was the result of an action-reaction cycle. The full fury of the various groups was not directed at all times against the Fascist and the Nazi occupation force, but against one another in the quest for the ultimate power in determining the destiny of the Land of the Eagle-Albania.

The reaction of the citizens of Albania to the conquest and the occupation of their country was in part determined by the policies of the Italian government from April 7, 1939 to 1943 and the German military forces of occupation from 1943 until the end of the Nazi presence in late 1944. The northern Catholic tribes, not desiring to sacrifice an opportunity, prestige, positions of influence and to safeguard their homes and their families, reconciled themselves to their new overlords with a minimal degree of resistance. Most of the Islamic segment of the national population, following the initial shock of defeat, found itself confronted by a crisis of conscience. They could accept outright the Fascist occupation of their country and in so doing, maintain the old society and way of life in which they were psychologically secure. They could elect, as did their forefathers, the road of national resistance. The vision of resistance and its ultimate by-product – the physical destruction of the land and its people – appeared in the dark days of 1941 as suicidal. Thus, they elected (for now) to accept the Italian occupation with the traditional sense of fatalism as expressed in the rationale, "Eshtu est shkrojtur" (thus, it is written).

The Beys of feudal lords who controlled tracts of land together with their dependent population were frustrated and confused by the rapid turn of events. Suffering from a sense of personal betrayal, as a result of the flight of their king, Ahmed Zog, which left them leaderless, and aware of the dominant military position of the Axis powers on the European content, they viewed the specter of national resistance as quixotic. The only segment of society which indicated, on the basis of an emotional reaction, a willingness to challenge the forces of the status quo and move the nation forward in hopes of regaining its soul, was the minute segment of the intelligentsia which possessed a socialist orientation or a Marxist perspective. The intelligentsia and certain elements within the urban population were determined, regardless of its diverse ideological orientation, to overcome the national humiliation by whatever means possible. Within a minuscule group of the urban population, the potential conflict situation and the occupation were considered to be an opportunity to establish a revolutionary base from which would evolve a socio-political and economic transformation of the Land of the Eagle-Albania along Marxist-Leninist lines.

If the masses had failed to act or react to the ultimate eventuality of depredation, prison camps and torture, it was more the fault of the traditional leaders who had remained in the country and stood paralyzed and resigned before the onrush first of the New Romans of Benito Mussolini's Fascist legions in 1939; the Greeks in 1940; and in 1943, the Wehrmacht, than the people themselves. One must recall that at this time Albania possessed a feudalistic ethos and in the northern regions of the country a tribal social structure. Each social entity bound the tradition-directed individual to the dictates of the feudal lord in the south and to the head of the clan in the north. That the spirit of resistance did exist cannot be denied as indicated, in a most dramatic manner, by the ill-fated assassination attempt on the life of King Victor Emmanuel III in May, 1939, by Vasil Leci. Yet, for the majority, it must be noted that what the French philosopher, Albert Camus, stated concerning rebellion and revolution had not as yet taken place among the Albanian people: "The desire for revolution is burn when the sense of revolution passes into the mind, when feeling becomes an idea, when spontaneous elan culminates in concerted action."[3]

Were one to return to the Balkans and especially to Albania in 1940-1941, one would find that certain psychological and political conditions were in place which became from April, 1939, to the Peza Conference of 1942, barriers not only to resistance, but also to the creation of a united, national, resistance movement. First, there was the tremendous, psychological advantage enjoyed by the invader who in 1941-1942, stood at the pinnacle of success. The string of military victories in the West, together with the fall of France in May, 1940, followed by the withdrawal of the British Expeditionary Forces from the beaches of Dunkirk at the end of the month of May, 1940; the series of American defeats in the Pacific following the bombing of Pearl Harbor by Japanese naval and air units; and the initial, massively successful German offensive operations following the invasion of the Soviet Union on June 22, 1941, projected to the lone, Balkan peasant with his outmoded Turkish long rifle, an image of Axis military superiority which served to reinforce the atmosphere of resignation and despair.

---

3. Albert Camus, *Resistance Rebellion and Death* (New York, Alfred A. Knopf, 1961) p. 1

The second, major obstacle existed in the failure of the government of Great Britain to declare itself, in spite of Greek reaction, not only on the future status of the exiled king who now resided in London as a private citizen and not as a representative of a government in exile, but also to define the position of the Foreign Office in relation to the issue concerning the post-war boundaries of Albania. Furthermore, there was no agreement in relation to the ethnically enclosed Albanian state which emerged following the German defeat of Yugoslavia and Greece in 1940.

The third barrier was to be found within the weaknesses of the organizational structure of the various, independent groups, the atmosphere of distrust due to the personal animosities and the political orientation of the emerging factions. One must recall that in 1943, the intricate relationships which particularized the attitudinal predisposition of the leaders of the various resistance movements, served to become a force in being which could not be removed through compromise or transcended by the various British liaison officers attached to Security Office Executive. Whereas Balli Kombetar, which proclaimed itself to be republican and liberal, could not accept on ideological grounds the pro-monarchist philosophy of Abas Kupi and vice versa, neither could the two accept the revolutionary goals and the discipline as required by the followers of Marx and Lenin as personified by Enver Hoxha. Nor could the leadership of the pro-communist forces establish the basis for a policy of sincere unity with the supporters of Gani and Said Kreziu, who were engaging the occupation forces in the Kossovo-Metohija region of the German-Italian created "Greater Albanian Ethnic State". The Kossovars' adherence to the concept of an "Ethnic Albania" placed them at odds with Enver Hoxha's pro-communist resistance movement and the pro-Yugoslav Kosmet Partisans of Fadil Hoxha who were a part of the overall Yugoslav resistance movement led by Josip Broz-Tito. Furthermore, the anti-Zogist stance of the Kreziu brothers, together with their advocacy of a policy of protracted military confrontation against the Italo-German forces of occupation, served to erode the fragile base upon which their guarded relations with Balli Kombetar and Abas Kupi's Legality Movement rested.

The fourth barrier was to be found within the person of the peasant himself. This worker, farmer and tradition-directed plebeian could not accept as yet the call for resistance and revolution whether the appeal came from the pro-communist groups, the supporters of the exiled king, or the agrarian reformers who adhered to a republican and nationalist orientation. The vision of resistance, together with the quest for a radicalism of the masses, was quickly viewed as a threat against the foundation upon which the peasant's traditional society existed with its normative order, cultural myths and its cherished ethos.

The fifth restraint which worked against the heeding of the call for resistance against the occupying forces was the adherence by the Italians and the Germans to a policy of reprisals that were both swift and ruthless in its execution. Such a negative reaction on the part of the occupation authorities not only neutralized a major segment of the population, but also reinforced the conservative nature of the leaders of Balli Koambetar and the Legality Movement. The sixth obstacle which had to be transcended if the people were to take up arms was the propaganda barrier. Axis successes on the battlefield in Europe, Asia and Africa served to reinforce the "wait and see" attitude of a segment of the population and numerous anti-communist resistance leaders. In addition, it served to encourage the tendency, once it became obvious that there would be no cross-Adriatic invasion, to enter into various degrees of accommodation with the occupation authorities in an effort to avert a communist political, economic and social revolution and preserve the unity of the ethnically enclosed Albanian nation which emerged with the blessings of the Axis powers. Moreover, the oppressive occupation policy which could have served to neutralize the psychological and the political barriers, was not present in the initial and the immediate phases of the occupation. Beyond the essential administrative demands of occupational supervision and control, the Albanians enjoyed during the Italian phase of control a high degree of internal autonomy. However, with the arrival of the German military in 1943, the occupation became a heavy burden on the nation's soul.

Unlike Albania both Greece and Yugoslavia immediately following the capitulation of each country, were to find themselves caught up in total war with the totality of society being transformed into a blood-soaked battlefield. History shows the observer that resistance evolves from a psycho-social base brought on by the activities of the occupation forces in the form of terror, reprisal killings and hostage taking. In addition, deportations of the people to Germany as forced labor gives birth to revenge. Furthermore, in both Hellas-Greece and in the Kingdom of the South Slavs-Yugoslavia, as in Albania, ELAS-the Greek People's Liberation Army emerged and was determined to monopolize the resistance and absorb or discredit EDES-the Greek National Democratic League. EDES was a conservative resistance movement led by Napoleon Zervas. In Yugoslavia the student of the conflict situation will find that Tito's Liberation Front – AVNOJ, possessed the same set of political and military objectives in the quest to acquire control over the Yugoslav nation-state and transform the country along lines dictated by the Marxist-Leninist formula.

Following the signing of the final surrender document on April 23, 1941, in Salonika by General Tsolakoglu, military units of Field Marshal List's 12th Army with men, cars, trucks and motorcycles of the 6th Armored Division entered the capital city of Athens via Vasilssous Sofias Avenue. As this force drove by the embassy of the United States of America towards Syntagma Square where rests the tomb of the Unknown Soldier, people gathered along the side streets and behind the shuttered windows of their homes and their apartments to catch a glimpse of the Detachments of the Leibstandarte, Adolph Hitler and SS units in light green, brown and black camouflage tunics as they marched by in a most impressive manner. With the announcement of the capture of the capital city of Athens and the surrender of the city to General von Stumme by the mayors of Athens and Piraeus, the prefect of Attica and the commander of the Greek Army garrison at the "Parthenon" coffee house in a northern suburb of the city, the war that both Hitler and Greece hoped to avoid came to an end.[5]

On March 25, 1941, the representatives of the Yugoslav Cevtkovic government, following Bulgaria's adherence to the Tripartite Pact on March 1, 1941, and the placement of 350,000 German troops in Bulgaria, signed on the dotted line and became members of the Tripartite

---

4. Nicholas J. Costa, *Albania: A European Enigma* (New York, East European Monographs Columbia University Press, 1995) pp. 41-49
5. Mark Mazower, *Inside Hitler's Greece: The Experience Of The Occupation 1941-1945* (New Haven, Yale University Press, 1993) p. 5

Pact.[6] On the 27th of March, 1941, the Cevtkovic government fell as a result of a coup d'etat and Winston Churchill stated, "Now, Yugoslavia has found its soul". Following this dramatic event by a small group of Serbian officers, Winston Churchill on March 22, 1941, forwarded a telegram to the Yugoslav Premier Cvetkovic that called to his attention the following points:

> *1. The combined determination of England and the USA to defend the cause of freedom.*
> *2. The abundance of natural resources and means to carry on to a successful conclusion.*
> *3. Yugoslavia should not adopt the course of action followed by Bulgaria – the negative consequences would be irreparable.*
> *4. That Yugoslavia and Turkey together with Greece should form a united front against Germany.*[7]

Tragically, what was desired and what in fact took place did not meet the request submitted by the Prime Minister.

On April 6, 1941, Adolph Hitler's "Operation Punishment" took place in spite of the assurances given the German government, for Hitler was determined to wipe the Land of the South Slavs of the face of the earth. Furthermore, the German Fuhrer, Adolph Hitler, also drew up plans to pull Italian chestnuts out of the Grecian fire in Albania following Mussolini's request for aid to launch "Operation Marita" – the invasion of Greece. On April 6, 1941, the German Luftwaffe (Air Force) was methodically engaged in bombing Yugoslavia's capital city of Belgrade and every town and village time and time again. The Wehmacht (German Army) advanced throughout the country to establish its military presence and control. Within a two week period, all of Yugoslavia's fighting force, due to a faulty defensive strategy, was defeated. According to Vukmanovic-Tempo, the psychological shock was disastrous as people fled the cities. King Peter and the representatives of the government went into the limbo of exile to form a government-in-exile in London.

---

6. John R. Lumpe, *Yugoslavia As History* (London, Cambridge University Press 1996) p. 196
7. Winston Churchill, *The Grand Alliance* (Boston, Houghton Mifflin Company, 1950) p. 160

Linking up with the Italians in Albania, the German military forces under the command of Field Marshal List took the major port city of Salonika in northern Greece and by April 26, 1941, continued to drive towards Athens as both Greek and British units retreated before the German onslaught. On April 27, 1941, at 8 : 10 a.m. two armored cars of the Sixth Armoured Division entered the capital city of Athens. Shortly thereafter, the cry, "Swastika over the Acropolis", could be heard. The Balkan peninsula had now become a part of the Third Reich.

The dismemberment process which followed the Germanic conquest was to result in Slovenia being annexed by Germany. Italy acquired a part of Slovenian territory and most of the Adriatic coastal area and the off-shore islands. Hungary gained control of various territories in Slovenia and Croatia, plus the communities of Backa and Baranya in Voyvodina. Italian occupied Albania was awarded all of the Albanian lands in Serbia and Macedonia as well as in Montenegro. The Bulgarians acquired that sphere which they believed was historically theirs – Macedonia. There also emerged the two puppet states of Croatia and Serbia with a different occupational status.

The outbreak of resistance beyond individual acts of defiance in a well organized manner throughout the southwestern tier of the Balkan peninsula by various pro-communists in their "War of National Liberation" may be attributed to the very same reason that Mao Tse-tung gave to Edgar Snow during the dark days of the Japanese occupation of his native land.

> *The defeat of Japan takes precedence over social revolution because it was necessary first to defeat foreign imperialism and win independence; only then could the struggle for socialism succeed.*
>
> *For a people being deprived of its freedom, the revolutionary task is not immediate socialism, but the struggle for the independence of China.*
>
> *We cannot even discuss Communism if we are robbed of a country in which to practice it. If China wins its independence, the world revolution will progress very rapidly.*[8]

---

8. Barbara W. Tuchman, *Stilwell and the American Experience In China* (New York, The Macmilan Company, 1970) p. 159

Resistance in the Kingdom of Yugoslavia began even before then Germanic victory over the Land of the South Slavs and Greece. The swiftness of the German advance and its shattering impact upon the Yugoslav army made it possible for many scattered and isolated units to go home with their weapons, hide or melt into the forest with their weapons as they journeyed inland to join the Ravna Gora Cetnik forces under the command of Colonel Draza Mihailovic. It must be pointed out that the internal political situation within the Cetnik held territory was highly complex due to internal divisions. On the one hand, the leader of the Cetnik movement in April, 1941, was Kosta Pecanac, who entered into a relationship and understanding with the puppet Prime Minister of Serbia, General Nedic. On the other hand, the situation was complicated to a greater degree due to the fact that various groups of Serbian irregulars came into being. According to a former POW who escaped from a prisoner-of-war train, then existed among the Cetniks "utter confession, backbiting, antagonism and bloody hostility".[9]

It was not until the second week of September, 1941, that a weak radio message was received in Malta and relayed to London. It was from Mihailovic informing his government and King that his organized Cetniks would, as their fathers and forefathers had done against the Ottoman Turks, continue resistance. From this point on, Draza Mihailovic was to be caught in a personal transformational process that would take him from a person to a mythical figure and finally to a prisoner of the victorious forces of Tito's partisans. At his trial in September, 1944, on the charge of treason, he was to state in a three page typewritten statement the following significant, last paragraph.

I wanted nothing for myself. The French Revolution gave the world the Rights of Man; the Russian Revolution also gave us something new, but I did not wish to start today where they started in 1917. I never wanted old Yugoslavia, but I had a difficult legacy. I am a soldier who sought to organize resistance to the Axis for our own country and for the whole Balkan peninsula. I am sorry that anyone should think I have been disloyal to

9. Walter R. Roberts, *Tito, Mihailovic and the Allies 1941* (New Jersey, Rutgers University Press 1973) p. 21

the government, but documents exist concerning that. I was caught in the whirlpool of events and the movement for a new Slav unity which I have long favored. Believing that the world would follow the course of the Russian Revolution, I was caught among the changes in the Western democracies. They are for out people good, so are the Russians. I had against me a rival organization, the Communist party, which seeks its aims without compromise. I was surrounded by every imaginable intelligence service, British, American, Russian and German – all the intelligence services in the world. I believed I was on the right road and invited any foreign journalist or Red Army Mission to visit me and see everything. But a merciless fate threw me into this maelstrom. I wanted much I began much but the gale of the world carried away me and my work. I ask the court to judge what I have said according to its true value.[10]

Draza Mihailovic, dressed in his old uniform tunic of the Royal Army of the Kingdom of Yugoslavia, stood at rigid attention with a sense of dignity while his sentence of death by a firing squad was read out. Of the sentence, Tito, according to Fitzroy Maclean, was said to have stated that symbolically, "Mihailovic had been a sentence on international reaction".[11]

The major personalities who were to emerge in this Balkan drama with its moments of glory and pathos from Joseph Broz-Tito and Draza Mihailovic in Yugoslavia; Enver Hoxha, Abas Kupi, and Abas Ermenji in Albania; George Siantos, Nikos Zachariades, Aris Velouchiotis (nom de guerre of Thanasis Klaras), Napoleon Zervas in Greece; and the various men who served in occupied Europe and specifically in Albania, Greece and Yugoslavia as members of SOE-Security Office Executive-together with their exploits, all had to pass through the stages of glorification, pulverization and reevaluation. Furthermore, a self-defeating political, diplomatic, ideological and nationalistic ferocity accompanied them like a curse and like a hyena of conquest, grew

---

10. Fitzroy Maclean, *The Heretic: The Life and Times of Joseph Broz-Tito* (New York, Harper Brothers Publisher 1957) pp. 283-285
11. Fitzroy Maclean, *Ibid* p. 285

more and more ravenous by the frenzy of battle as it fed upon the bodies of their country men and the burned-out villages of their country. They had one purpose from the very beginning: to destroy the enemy and in the process of the parallel war, the men of Security Office Executive became the casualties.

One cannot help but recall a situation when President Wilson, a strong advocate of the League of Nations, once stated to a friend, "It's a terrible thing to look over your shoulder when you are trying to lead – and find no one there". In many confrontations with the enemy, British Liaison Officers found just such a situation confronting them. In one of the battles for Vithkuq, Major David Smiley and Lt. Colonel "Billy" McClean make references in their memoirs to the fact that such did take place as indicated in Sir Julian Amery's publication *Sons of the Eagle*. Also, Colonel David Smiley recalls the following episode in his book *Albanian Assignment*.

> *About this time I heard that the Italians were in Voskopoje, so I walked the few miles to see what was happening... On our arrival we found the whole town in flames, the Italians having withdrawn after setting it on fire for what was alleged to be the 15th time in its history. The Italians had met no opposition and the partisans were there but had withdrawn without firing a shot. When I met Vincani in the town, I asked him why the partisans had not fought; he replied that his battalion was "doing a flanking movement to cut them off", which I did not believe. It was obvious that they had run away, and I became somewhat offensive, telling him that his battalion was not a battalion but a guerrilla band, and a damned bad one at that, and that the sooner he stopped trying to be a general instead of a guerrilla leader, the better...[12]*

The multiplicity of primary documents and the memoirs of various S.O.E. officers and men who served in the wild, mountainous, backwater regions of Albania in 1943, possessed a series of major handi-

---

12. Julian Amery, *Sons of the Eagle* (London, Macmillan and Company LTD. 1948) p. 285

caps. None of these young men had an awareness of the folkways, mores, language of the people, let alone the uniqueness of the customs and traditions of the Albanian tribes and clans. They were to find themselves wrapped in the web of uncertainty as they sought to remain objective in their analytical reports to Headquarters Command. Their quest to establish a united resistance movement consisting of pro-communist and anti-communist forces was blocked by the Albanians whose only interest was to eliminate not the German, but one another as a potential post-war political rival. Yet, in spite of the adverse conditions confronting them, such men as MacLean, Smiley, Neil, Simcox, and Tilman carried on in the face of attitudinal changes and setbacks.

Peter Kemp, who first served with MacLean and Smiley eventually was to find himself in northern Albania assigned to the Stepmother Mission. Tragically, this more than capable and astute son of England was forced out of the activities which were transpiring due to pressure placed upon the British Foreign Office by Joseph Broz-Tito. Major "Tony" Neel, who was assigned to Slender Mission, worked with Abas Kupi in a region north of Tirana. Major Anthony Quayle was in charge of "Seaview", which was located south of Vlore on the Karaboun peninsula and in between communist and Balli Kombetar zone of operation and conflict. Of his experiences at "Seaview", both Major Quayle in his study *Eight Hours From England* and Major Reginald Hibbert in his study of the involvement of the British in Albania in 1943, entitled *Albania's National Liberation Struggle – The Bitter Victory*, calls to one's attention the following data:

> *1. Major Gerry Fields of the Sapling Mission who was in charge of Seaview due to German drives against partisans and the protracted conflict between partisan and Balli Kombetar units became allergic to both that he would not permit Albanians near him in his poverty surrounded base.*
>
> *2. Constant conflict among Germans, Balli and Partisans facilitated German control of the coastal area.*
>
> *3. Officers attached to Balli would be viewed by the officers attached to Partisans as neo-Fascists and those attached to L.N.C. would be considered nothing more than the cunning and the bloody agents of world Bolshevism.*

4. Various members in dealing with the Partisan or the Balli forgot that while only self-interest or a choice between two evils drags a great nation into war, the same rule might hold true for a mountain village in Albania.

Thus, as one scrutinized and reflects upon the readings of the documents, one cannot help but conclude that there appeared to be in Albania, as opposed to Greece and Yugoslavia, a tendency to follow a policy of delay, insisting that they (the various resistance groups be they Communist, Balli Kombetar or pro-Zogist Legalitite of Abas Kupi) were preparing to fight but with NO intention of engaging the enemy. Given this widespread propensity among the various tribes with ideological flags, one can only ask – did they ever truly prepare to fight? Tragically, one could conclude that they preferred not to do so unless pressed to engage the enemy as a result of military circumstances confronting them at a given moment.

One must recall the words of the military leader of Balli Kombar during an interview session in the city of Paris, France.

That the Germans would be beaten and that the forces of occupation would, in the final analysis, be forced to withdraw from Albania. This departure would not come about because of the military power and overall strategy of the Allied Command.[13]

Given this awareness of all contending resistance groups, one can understand the quest for more and more arms and other military supplies. Of the military situation and the multiplicity of positions taken in relation to the issue of victory or defeat, the following statements were made by Skender Mucho, an anti-communist leader within the ranks of Balli Kombetar, and Major Anthony Quayle at Seaview in 1944 prior to his receiving a communication from Cairo marked "Top Priority".

"... I was an anti-Zogist since Zog was a tyrant... I was condemned to death by Zog but my sentence was commuted to life imprisonment."

---

13. Nicholas J. Costa, *Op. Cit.* p. 100

"When the Italians invaded the country, I was set free. Then I went into the mountains and fought against the invaders."

"You are not fighting Germans now?"

"No, I am fighting with them."

His frankness took me somewhat aback.

"You are surprised to hear me say that?"

He leaned forward. "I will tell you the reason. Our war is not your war. For us Albanians that is a great pity, but it is true." I asked him to explain what he meant. "One day", said, "the Allies will defeat the Germans. That is certain.

One day the Germans will either be driven from the Balkans or they will leave on their own accord. Then will begin our troubles – the real troubles for Yugoslavia, Albania and Greece."

"Why?" I asked, not out of ingenuousness, but because I wanted him to give the answer.

"Because we shall then be left with the communist in our midst, with the terrorist and the anarchist, and for us those are worse enemies than the Germans. Albania is a very small country and a very long way from England and America. Are you going to take a part in our affairs once the war against German is over?"... "You know quite well you are not. We shall be left to settle our own disputes."

"Then", I said, "why not settle them when the war does end, and not do so now in the middle of it?"

"Because", he said, "the communist movement under the guise of a patriotic movement will then be too strong. Then every man will have a pistol pushed into his ribs and be ordered to salute with the clinched fist. Sooner than that I will use the Germans who are now in Albania as a weapon with which to destroy the communist."

..."As soon as the Partisans are destroyed, we shall turn on the Germans and fight them."

"And you think you will destroy the Partisans?"

"As I think you well know, Major, there is now a very big drive against the Partisans – not only against the 5th Brigade, but over the whole of southern Albania. The drive is going well

– very well. You, if I may say so, are in a position of a man who must make a bet. Whom are you going to back – the Partisans or the Balli? It would be useless for me to try to influence you at this state, and I would not expect you to believe my prophecies, but in three or in four weeks' time I hope you will recall what I now say: the Partisan movement is on the eve of destruction."[14]

The apocalyptic expectation was not to be. Love of the fatherland divides people, feeds national hatreds and from time to time may even dress the earth and a national movement in mourning, but at this historical moment, the death knell – the bell – did not toll for the partisan resistance. Possessing a consciousness of historical destiny, like the phoenix of Greek mythology, they rose from the ashes of military disaster to once again confront the German and Italian forces of occupation together with their native allies in the protracted battle for their nation's soul. What the supporters of Balli Kombetar and the followers of Abas Kupi failed to realize is that they were caught within a reality which they did not accept as the true reality confronting them and which truly was beyond their control. Yet, they held to the delusion that the communists were finished and limited in their power and influence to the Korce-Gjirokaster administrative region.

Furthermore, one must recall that in the nation-states of Albania, Greece and Yugoslavia of 1943-1944, with political concerns pervading everything and with an internal background of emotions dominating all individuals and all parties, the complexities of the existing situation defied reason. Following the informal verification of the fact that the forces of the resistance should not look forward to an Allied invasion of the Balkans, illusion and reality were to clash. All of the resistance groups were now to become the lead actors in the tragic drama which in the words of Tyutchiev can only be labeled, "The Conspiracy of Hell". Prisoners of their respective illusions, they could not disengage, for the study of the history of the nations of the Balkans tends to demonstrate that disputes can only be resolved by taking up arms.

---

14. Anthony Quayle, *Eight Hours From England* (New York, Doubleday and Company, 1946) pp. 124-127

Here there exists a culture of violence wrapped within a blanket of virulent nationalism as demonstrated by the historical Yugoslav-Albanian conflict relating to the issue of Kossovo and the Greek-Albanian clash concerning Northern Epirus, let alone the Yugoslav-Greek and Bulgarian controversy pertaining to the Macedonian question. The coming struggle in the configuration of a civil war in a symbolic sense is representative of the clash of two spiritual entities, of two worlds which fell themselves radical enemies. They proceed from different ideologies and different principles, yet they maintain common folkways, mores and remain tradition-directed people. In 1943-1944, the Communist and the non-Communist were politically representative of two entirely separate or opposite trends who were engaged in an undeclared war throught World War II as each sought to establish its version of the Pilgrim's "City on the Hill".

Pan-Slavism, a movement whose origins go back to the 18th century, is a mixed bag possessing elements of supra-nationalism sprinkled with a dash of imperialism. In the aftermath of the Russian Revolution of 1917, it underwent a political transformation from that of a creed to that Marxist-Leninist political program which became a challenge to the Western domination of the Global Village's socio-political and economic entities. Thus, the civil wars which emerged in the Land of the Eagle-Albania, the Land of the South Slavs-Yugoslavia and in Hellas-Greece in 1943-1944 were part of this movement.

One of the most insightful and revealing assessments as to why revolt and revolution took place in Hellas-Greece is provided in a report from an Italian official to Benito Mussolini dated January 12, 1942.

The reasoning which pushes the Greek towards revolt is simple enough and straightforward. It tells him: "Come what may you cannot live. Your sons are condemned to die of hunger. All that is left to you is to revolt, kill and be killed honorably. All Europe, suffering like you, will follow your example and the country will have new heroes."[15]

---

15. Brigadier "Trotsky" Davies, *Illyrian Venture* (London, The Bodley Head, 1952) p. 78

Foreign Minister Ciano reckoned that, "anything is possible, from epidemics to ferocious revolts on the part of a people who know they have nothing to lose".[16]

The people of Greece who were the innocent victims of a prolonged period of starvation throughout the famine of 1941 with a cost of 250,000 lives, according to estimates given by the International Red Cross, were to react by engaging in individual and isolated acts of defiance. The negative Italo-German graffiti that could be found on the sidewalks, walls and monuments ran the total spectrum from the defiant warning "5 minutes to 12" to that which applied to the Blackmarketeers following the rumor that an invasion was imminent, "Telegram for General Alexander. Please delay your arrival. We are being ruined." The replay followed, "For the Blackmarketeers of Piraeus. Can't Stop. Sell." One must also recall the attitudinal change among a growing segment of the population as a result of the poetry of Angelos Sikelianos of which the following is very significant.

> *The swallows of death threaten to bring you*
> *Oh Greece, a new spring, and from the grave a gigantic birth*
> *Vainly is the guard of the Romans on watch around you.*
> *Soon you will rise up in a new Twenty One** [17]

Following the death of Greece's most honored poet, Kostas Palmas, on the 27th of February 1942, the individual citizen of Athens, Piraeus, Patras and Salonika, together with the citizens of the other major communities, found themselves reading a variety of newspapers and pamphlets. Such clandestine, published materials were circulated from one person to another and those who were unable to read were made aware of the message by word of mouth. As all of Greece became involved in the silent process, the major attitudinal transformation that quietly emerged gave birth to the reemergence of a national awakening that was projected within the form of a defiant spirit of nationalism through massive demonstrations. Of the developing situation, General Pieche stated in a submitted report:

---

16. Mark Mazower, *Op. Cit.* p. 89
17. Mark Mazower, *Op. Cit.* p. 93-94

> *The Greek situation is continuously worsening.*
>
> *Enemy propaganda... is developing with great intensity, as-*
> *suming a tone of extreme violence and making itself available*
> *in all possible ways from endless radio broadcasts to graffiti,*
> *from the preaching of the most tenacious voices to the circula-*
> *tion of anti-Axis pamphlets and fliers, communist and national-*
> *ist, exciting the people to revolt... Intense propaganda contin-*
> *ues to be scrawled on walls against civil mobilization, against*
> *the arrest of hostages, against the Axis in general, and against*
> *the Greek government itself, which is accused of excessive do-*
> *cility against the occupier and held to be principally responsi-*
> *ble for the catastrophic food situation of the country.*[18]

A combination of serve food shortages, inflation and the policies of the occupation authorities, combined with the strains of war and inept, corrupt Greek governmental officials, was to make strange bedfellows. As the tradition-directed person forcefully became an independent, political animal, one must note that in pre-war Greece, the major segment of its population consisted of people as members of a clan or an extended family who considered themselves no more than an appendage of the family or clan and who willingly accepted the dictates of such. This individual would never act in a manner that would bring dishonor to the family. In addition, he would accept the good fortune as well as the negatives which trickled down to him as a member of the collective. He would accept without any question whatsoever the authority of the family and that of the village elders. yet, his willingness to become a part of the growing resistance movement which was to shatter the political divisions of yesteryear, may be attributed to E.A.M. (Ellenikon Apelevther/ot/ikon metopon-Greek Liberation Front, The Greek Communist-led resistance alliance) which focused on those bread and butter issues which impacted greatly upon the people of Greece on a day-to-day basis.

With the active emergence of KKE – The Communist Party of Greece – on the historical stage, one is confronted by two outstanding,

---

18. Mark Mazower, *Op. Cit.* p. 116

political personalities, Georgos Siantos and Nicolas Zakhariadis. Georgos Siantos, born in 1890 in Thessaly, became Secretary-General of the Party in 1925. He first became a casualty of the internal conflicts of the 1930's at the time of Stalin's Great Purges. From 1930 to 1933, he remained within the Citadel of Communist-Moscow and was eventually reinstated to his former post until 1937, when the was arrested by the dictator of Greece, General Metaxas. Following a cycle of arrest-escape-arrest, he found himself in 1941 the Secretary-General of the KKE once again following the "Disaster of 1941". Nicolas Zakhariadis, an Asiatic Greek, was born in 1902 in Skoplye and was educated in Adrianople. A former seaman who became a graduate of the Lenin School, he was sent to Greece to reorganize the party in 1931 while Siantos was in exile. During World War II he was arrested and sent to the concentration camp at Dachau until the close of the war in 1945. He was to appear in a prominent position during Greece's second civil war.[19]

In the Land of the South Slavs-Yugoslavia, there was to appear on the illegal, political scene a dedicated, professional revolutionary and a young acolyte of Marxist-Leninist. This young man was endowed with the gift of leadership and the strength of character that would enable him to emerge in 1937 with the responsibility of restructuring the Communist Party of Yugoslavia and in 1941, AVNOJ – the Anti-Fascist Committee of the People's Liberation of Yugoslavia. Of this soldier of revolution, Josip Broz-Tito, who was committed to a belief that the leadership of a revolutionary movement, if such were to succeed, required that the movement's governing body remain in the country of its birth among its own people and in the land where the struggle was to take place. Furthermore, this Yugoslav conspirator and political realist while in his nation consisting of carefully selected cadres. In addition, he proceeded to surround himself with such dedicated professional revolutionaries such as Edvard Kardel, Ivo Ribar, Alexander Rankovic, Mosje Pijade and Milovan Djilas – all men of the proven ability and commitment to the revolutionary cause and the impending

19. Franz Borkenau, *European Communism* (New York, Harper and Brothers Publishers 1953) p. 410-411

world revolution. It must also be noted that Tito was able to make the Party independent of foreign financial assistance – thus granting him and the Party a higher degree of independence and maneuverability. It was also throughout this period of restructuring that a program of ideological education was undertaken to make both old and new recruits aware of the basic laws of social development according to Marxist doctrine and to sweep away any and all of the confusion which may have existed within men's minds as to who was the class enemy.[20]

The aggressive, diplomatic and war-like moves of Hitlerite Germany were to result in England's Neville Chamberlin and France's Edouard Daladier's failure to accept the totalitarian challenge. Following the bankruptcy of their position and policy in 1938, the shroud of death and destruction began to descend upon the European psyche. From 1938 onwards, one became aware of the fact, to a greater degree than ever before, that while history informs, myth inspires. Thus, in the fateful days preceding the outbreak of the Second World War, the people of the "Global Village" were to bear witness to the Anschluss and the union of Austria and Germany as Hitler entered Vienna in 1938. By the summer of 1938, Berlin's demands placed on Prague in relation to the Sudetenland issue had reached its apogee. Autumn brought the Prime Ministers of Great Britain and France, Chamberlain and Daladier, to Munich and the capitulation of the Western powers with Benito Mussolini being proclaimed as the "Savior of Europe".

In Spain, 1500 Yugoslavs were to fight against Fascism in the ranks of the International Brigade; of this group, 750 were killed, 300 wounded and 350 were placed in the concentration camps or holding areas near the French-Spanish frontier following the collapse of the Spanish Republic.[21] In March of 1939, Adolph Hitler's military forces took possession of the "Rump state of Czechoslovakie". In April 1939, Italy which possessed the dominant position in Albania, elected to annex the country. Moscow let it be known at the Wilhelmstrasse that the Soviet Union saw no reason why relations between Berlin and Moscow might not be normal. On the 23rd of August, a German-Soviet Non-Aggres-

---

20. Vladimir Dedijer, *Tito Speaks* (London, Weidenfield and Nicolson, 1953) pp. 111-114

sion Pact came into being. German troops marched into Poland on September 1, 1939. England and France, who had elected not to support Czechoslovakia in 1938, now elected to come to the aid of the Polish government and its people. The Second World War had begun.

CHAPTER SEVEN

FREEDOM OR DEATH

War was first to break out in the Balkan Peninsula with the Italian military invasion of Albania on the morning of Good Friday, April 7, 1939. On October 28, 1940, Italy's Roman Legions were to cross the Albanian-Greek frontier in what Rome anticipated to be a triumphant march into Athens and the absorption of Greece into the "New Roman Empire." The Italo-Greek war was to be so great an unmitigated defeat for Italian arms that German military units were required to simultaneously undertake the invasion of Yugoslavia and Greece on April 6, 1941, in order to rescue Italy's pride. In discussing the moves and the countermoves of the military, I was made aware by Vukmanovic Tempo's publicist, Zoran Jovanovic in 1978, that Hitler was determined to destroy Yugoslavia "both militarily and as a State" as a result of the coup of March 27, 1941. His desire to punish the Land of the South Slavs-Yugoslavia and to save the honor of Fascist Italy was to result in the deployment of General List's Twelfth Army and the Second Army under the command of General Von Weick. The objective was to undertake a dual strike out of Bulgaria and Austria by the two armies as the Italian Second Army struck from the south. In addition, Hungarian forces would cross into Vojvodina as Bulgarian forces would be deployed in a blocking move along its southeastern region while other Bulgarian military units would strike westward into southern Yugoslavia.[1]

Sunday, April 6, 1941, was a sunny day in Belgrade. Families with their children could be found strolling along the banks of the Sava river, swimming in the river, visiting the fortress of Kalamagden, or just enjoying a cup of Turkish coffee and a dish of ice-cream at the

---

1. Zoran Jonanovic, Personal Interview Belgrade, Yugoslavia, 1978

outdoor cafe of the Hotel Moskva. This tranquil scene was to be shattered on this day as Hitler's "Operation Punishment" took place. The German Luftwaffe began its series of bomb runs which razed the city from seven in the morning until the late afternoon hours. Belgrade was, at this historical moment, to take its place along with Guernica in Spain; Coventry in England; Rotterdam in Holland; with over two thousand deaths and an excessive number of casualties.

The decision made and the actions undertaken in Berlin, Paris, Washington, London, Rome, Belgrade, and Athens as Europe continued along its calamitous road to destruction tended to combine international murder and national suicide into a single act. Furthermore, there also appeared to exist among a major segment of the population of Italy, Germany, France, The Soviet Union, Greece, Yugoslavia, Albania and Spain, a willingness to escape from their responsibilities as imposed upon them by the concept of freedom. The desire of the lower class and to submit themselves and their nation's destiny to totalitarian rule may be attributed to the psychological impact of World War I, the economic downturn of 1929, and the quest for a new tomorrow. Given the psycho-political climate of the decade of the 1930's, they elected to engage in an act of abject submission to the all-powerful State. It is at this historical moment that many of the governments of Europe stripped themselves of the democratic attire they put on following the close of the "Great War" in exchange for an authoritarian straight-jacket with its totalitarian stripes.

Furthermore, they engaged in a type of mental gymnastics which made it possible for the peoples of Europe to accept a policy that sanctioned aggression, the establishment of holding areas for domestic, political nonconformists which would become, with the passage of time, concentration camps. In addition, there existed a tendency to accept outright and render, at the individual level, blind devotion to the leader. Given the national temperament of the Balkanite, such acts of personal chastisement or repentance, when combined with the willingness to silently renounce one's individuality to the leader, was preconditioned and reinforced as a result of the impact of the socio-political perspective of the tradition-directed collectivity of the extended family. Yet, the oral tradition among the people of the nations of the Balkan peninsula makes the student of history aware that there exists within the individual and the nation's ethos a cold pragmatism mixed with a sprinkle of romanticism and the grand illusions of the past to generate a desire to meet the invader head on as had their fathers and forefathers before them.

As Berlin talked of peace, Hitler secretly prepared of war. Europe, finding itself a prisoner of its own internal squabbles, failed to notice the rotation process at it applied to the German military that made it possible to train new recruits and transcend the limitations to train new recruits and transcend the limitations of the Treaty of Versailles. In addition, in the numerous cafes which may be found throughout the capital city of Athens, pro and anti-Venizelos supporters engaged in an emotionally charged series of words as they debated such topics as Mustafa Kemal's victory over the Greeks in 1923 (The Disaster), and the "Royalist Question and the return of King George". Also discussed were the merits of Nazi Germany and Mussolini's Fascist state where the trains ran on time, as they and the government of Greece paid minimal attention to the acute social and economic crisis that enveloped the nation of Greece.

As one turns to the Land of the South Slavs during the interwar years of 1918-1939, one becomes aware of the fact that Yugoslavia's political division revolved around the issue of centralism as opposed to decentralization. While the Croats desired a decentralized governmental structure, the Serb believed that the government should be structured as a highly centralized unit. The clash of opposing views would extract a high cost and would threaten the unity of the Yugoslav nation-state. In addition, the nationality problem pervaded all issues and thus became the midwife for additional, complex points in question such as the rise of the Ustashi Movement, and the determination of the Croats and the Albanians to acquire political independence or union with their external fatherland.

The complexities of the Yugoslav wartime epic, when dealing with its major playmarkers, confronts the historian and the observer of the Balkan theater of operations with a enigma relating to the protracted clash between myth and reality. The abundance of primary and secondary sources, relating to the events that had transpired in wartime Yugoslavia, requires the student of history in his or her quest for objectivity, to recall the fact that one is confronted with thruth's image according to the author of the message. Thus, in relation to the Partisans and the Cetniks, the War of National Liberation, the Yugoslav Civil War, and the socio-economic transformation along Marxist-Leninist lines, the historian must step lightly as he/she seeks the dual goal of creditability and objectivity.

With the close of World War I on November 11, 1918, and the acceptance by the representatives of the victorious Entente Powers of the call by President Wilson for an adherence to the principle of "self-determination of nations", there emerged on the world's steps in 1919, the Kingdom of Serbs, Croats and Slovenes. The series of complex, unsolvable, internal problems, together with the inability to resolve critical differences with the Croats, resulted in the King casting aside the pseudo-democratic facade in 1921, following an internal coup. The government which came into being in 1921, was not only a highly centralized apparatus, but it was a very authoritarian, political structure sprinkled with totalitarian control devices. On the political transformation which evolved, Dr. Aleksa Djilas, in his detailed analytical study entitled *The Contested Country – Yugoslav Unity and Communist Revolution 1919-1953*, calls to the reader's attention the following facts relating to the government of King Alexander in 1921.

1. The 1931 constitution strengthened centralism.

2. The nationality question was not admitted to exist.

3. The constitution curtailed civil liberties.

4. Only Yugoslav nationality was recognized.

5. Institutionalized non-paliamentary monarchial rule... (all ministers were appointed by the king and the government was accountable solely to him).[2]

The emergence of the Kingdom of the South Slavs was beset with numerous internal problems as Croats, Macedonians, Hungarians, and the Albanians sought a recognition of their rights, independence, or the union with their fatherland. This is truly understandable when one considers the fact that one half of Albania's population was assigned to the

---

2. Aleksa Djilas, *The Contested Country-Yugoslav Unity and Communist Revolution 1919-1953* (Cambridge, Harvard University Press, 1991) pp. 80-81

Kingdom of Serbs, Croats, and Slovenes; that the Internal Macedonian Revolutionary Organization was determined to secure the rectification of a political wrong; and that Greece, Bulgaria and the Kingdom of the South Slavs were involved in a bitter and highly emotional controversy over the port city of Salonika. The death of King Alexander in Marseilles, France in 1934, by an assassin's bullet resulted in his cousin, Prince Paul acquiring control of the reigns of power until and underaged King Peter became eligible to rule. With the coup d'etat of March 27, 1941, the Boy-King became the acknowledged King of Land of the South Slavs. However, Hitler's decision to invade Yugoslavia and Greece on the 6th of April, 1941, resulted in King Peter's ill-advised flight and the government's exile. German Stukas roared through the air and showered bombs on Belgrade throughout the day as the city burned and the people fled. In the Balkan's memory, is that one powerful force capable of transforming a noble act into an historical legend that is then woven into the fabric of the Yugoslav mythological epic. One must recall that the myth is representative of a mixture of truths and non-truths which possesses a recurring theme or character type that appeals to a nation's consciousness by embodying the nation's cultural traits, ideals and deep national emotions – such a myth became a part of the Serbian epic. Thus, the decision to leave the country and its people in their hour of peril was not in keeping with the mores and folkways of the peoples of Yugoslavia. One must recall that King Peter's grandfather had (throughout World War I) remained with his people and the army in its strategic withdrawal across a totally hostile Land of the Eagle-Albania, in order to continue the struggle on the Salonika front. This epic withdrawal of the 300,000 man force was to result in the loss of 150,000 troops as both they and King Peter passed into the noble and glorious legends of the Land of the South Slavs.[3]

The decision to leave Yugoslavia was to result in the Prime Minister of England sending a telegram to the British Minister in Belgrade which reflected Winston Churchill's attitude relating not only to the flight of the king and the government, but also to the inner qualities of Churchill's personality structure.

---

3. Milovan Djilas, Personal Interview Belgrad, Yugoslavia, 1980

> *We do not see why the King or Government should leave the country, which is vast, mountainous, and full of armed men. German tanks can no doubt move along the roads and tracks, but to conquer the Serbian armies they must bring up infantry. Then will be the chance to kill them. Surely the young King and the Ministers should play their part in this.[4]*

To the Yugoslav who gave of himself/herself totally to the fight against the conqueror of his country, one can conclude that he/she was cast into battle as a result of a deep sense of wounded self-esteem, bitterness over and unjustly lost war and the traditional inner-feeling among the Serbs that it was, in their hearts and minds, an unfinished war which they, themselves, would finish. Unfortunately, in the emerging war against the invader and the conqueror of the country, there emerged a protracted conflict within and among families and clans as such applied to the two major opposing resistance movements – the Cetniks and the Partisans.

In the course of the warfare against the Italian and the German invaders of the Land of the South Slavs-Yugoslavia and the political struggle for ultimate power, the conflict situation gave birth to an explosive situation. The existing set of unique circumstances with its inflammatory, political mix was to result in the old socio-political and economic landscape being blown to bits and the bewildered, tradition-directed people being divided into two diametrically opposing ideological camps. That Mihailovic adhered (as did Tito) to two different concepts of resistance cannot be denied. Nor can it be denied that General Draza Mihailovic held to the prerequisite laid down by Major General Sir Colin Gubbins, who stated:

> *The problem and the plan was to encourage and enable the peoples of the occupied countries to harass the German war effort at very possible point by sabotage, subversion, go-slow practices, coup the main raids, etc., and at the same time to build secret forces therein, organized armed and trained **to take part only when the final assault begins...**[5]*

4. Walter R. Roberts, *Tito, Mihailovic And The Allies, 1941-1945* (New Jersey, Rutgers University Press, 1973) p. 17
5. G.H. Cookridge, *Set Europe Ablaze* (New York, Thomas Y. Crowell 1967) p. 7

The men and the leadership of the numerous formations within the AVNOJ, Anti-Fascist Committee of the People's Liberation of Yugo-slavia, the war provided the Communist Party of Yugoslavia with the means to shatter the Old Order and carry out a triple revolution which did consist of a War of National Liberation, Civil War and a Socio-Economic Revolution.

The emerging War of National Liberation in the nation-states of Albania, Greece and Yugoslavia tended to reaffirm the prevailing be-lief that the military forces of Fascist Italy were truly a "Paper Tiger" too weak to threaten and too weak to maintain itself as an effective military power. Sadly, it also demonstrated and reminded the peasant once again that wars are not only harsh and bloody, but that the destiny of men at war, particularly a civil war, is determined by an unexpected and unpredictable reality made meaner by the highly emotional confla-gration which pits father against son, brother against brother, and clan against clan in the mountain fastness of Yugoslavia, Albania and Greece. Furthermore, the Italo-German conflict did unleash the age-old sup-pressed animosities. People who at one time lived side by side and who found themselves attending each other's family weddings, baptisms and Islamic feast days and celebrations, now found themselves engaged in a highly emotional bloodbath. It was as if the Gods themselves re-quired that the Christian, Moslem, and Catholic kill again and again, not showing any mercy toward one's neighbor and becoming totally involved in the national blood-bath. In his book entitled *Wartime*, Milovan Djilas, while discussing certain negative experiences of the raging civil war, calls one's attention to the following:

> *Even more horrible and inconceivable was the killing of kins-men and hurling of their bodies into ravines... In Hercegovina it was still more horrible and ugly: Communist sons confirmed their devotion by killing their own fathers, and there was dancing and singing around the bodies... All too lightly the Communists de-stroyed the inherited, primeval customs – as if they had new and immutable ones to replace them with... While in Montenegro the killing process occurred without the killing of the young and old, or the raping of women: ancestral norms restrained ideologies.[6]*

6. Milovan Djilas, *Wartime* (New York, Harcourt, Brace and Javanovich, 1977) p. 149

Throughout World War II, the Land of the South Slavs-Yugoslavia was a scene of epic proportions as the Communist Party under the direction of Joseph Broz-Tito moved from the status of anti-war protesters in 1939; to that of the most capable and effective resistance movement throughout occupied Europe. War was no longer the imperialist venture of 1939; it now (June 22, 1941) became the war of national liberation. In Greece, prior to April 6, 1941, the pro-German government of the dictator of the country, General Ioannis Metaxas, confronted both monarchist and constitutionalist with a series of domestic policy decisions which, when combined with the transpiring national and international political events, were to confront the sons and daughters of Hellas with problems that were not only unsolvable and tragic, but equal to that of a Passion play.

Within the oral and the written literature of the people of the Balkan peninsula, one can find a variation of an old Serbian fairy tale which involves the story of a evil wizard who stalks the village but can be defeated only by finding the hidden source of his power and destroying it. Symbolically, the resistance movement was representative of those young, dedicated men and women within the ranks of the resistance movement who were involved in the protracted conflict as they first sought to find the enemy's source of power and then proceeded to destroy it and drive the wizard from their lands. In the course of the conflict against the Italo-German occupation armies and their collaborators, everything but warfare and the struggle to maintain the security of the family was barren and senseless. As youth and life, together with its flip side, death, became absorbed in the game of kill and be killed, there emerged the real and mythical histories of the nation as its sons and daughters killed not to destroy life, but to enlarge, perpetuate and enhance life. As the hero in any myth, they, through their actions, became the givers of immortality. They killed in the service of regeneration.

The transformation of Yugoslavia into one massive killing field became at one and the same time a condemnation of that blind battle that was underway in Europe at a time in which everything had lost its meaning. To the citizens of the Land of the South Slavs who stood at death's door following the massive demonstrations which swept the country on March 27, 1941, with its cry of "Better death than the pact", they knew that shortly they and their country would be entering the valley of death. On April 6, 1941, that which they sensed would take place, did take place. On this day at 7:30 a.m., they entered the valley of death which became a land of humiliation and indifference, silent betrayals, bitter experiences, hostage taking, prison sentences, torture and executions together with the stripping away of one's dignity. Thus, forward they went with their traditional sense of fatalism as mere pawns in the hands of the hands of the gods who resided on Mount Olympus, aware that their fate and that of their country was linked in one eternal embrace. In addition, the enduring belief existed in spite of the ravages of the absurdities of war that "MAN is the force which ultimately cancels all tyrants and all would-be gods".

The internal struggle to expel the Germanic wizard from their native land became the responsibility of such men as that which since 1941 had constituted the hard core element of professional revolutionaries within the Partisan movement. Of Josip Broz-Tito, who stood head and shoulders above his fellow revolutionaries, it has been stated that:

> *He brought to the war of resistance against the Germans the same qualities which stood him in good stead in the past: leadership, courage, realism, ruthless determination and singleness of purpose, resourcefulness, adaptability and plain common sense. He imposed upon the party; he endowed it with the oracle: the party line. Where there were important decisions to be taken, whether political or military, he took them; took them calmly and collectedly, however precarious the situation. He possessed and could inspire in others an absolute devotion to their common cause, an utter disregard for the dangers and difficulties which beset them. And, most important of all, by throwing together Serbs, Croats, Slovenes and the rest of them in fight against the common enemy, he had caused them to forget their old internecine feuds and thus achieve within his own ranks an entirely new sense of national unity.[7]*

7. Fitzroy Maclean, *The Heretic* (New York, Harper and Brothers Publishers, 1957) pp. 194-199

Tito's dedicated, professional, hard-core revolutionaries possessed a similar adherence to the ideals and goals established by their ideological commitment. Yet, the set of circumstances that confronted them in the "killing fields" of Yugoslavia, together with their sacrifices, was to result in the acceptance of a Yugoslav identity based on the slogan "Brotherhood and Unity", and the establishment of a civic apparatus of power in the liberated areas as they carried out their "Revolution by Frontal Assault". All of them were dedicated whether a school teacher like Edo Karkelj, the movement's Marxist dialectical theoretician, or the son of a peasant from Serbia like Marko Rankovic, who became the head of the party's internal structure and that of intelligence and the secret police. In addition, within this collectivity of professional, dedicated revolutionaries which composed the movement's "Power Elite", one also finds Milovan Djilas, revolutionary, wartime leader, philosopher, writer, Yugoslav dissident and former vice-president of Yugoslavia, who in 1941, led his Montegrians in the initial uprising against the Italian occupation forces in Montenegro. An additional member of the inner council was Svetozar Vukmanovic-Tempo, who was Tito's loyal and dedicated workhorse and Tito's representative in Bosnia, Albania and Greece. Also, he was a strong advocate and supporter of the quest to establish a unified Balkan command structure and a Balkan federation.

Others, who in a symbolic manner, represented the heart and the soul of the partisan movement were such individuals as Koca Popovic, poet and philosopher and the son of a millionaire who in his capacity of a commander consistently found himself in "Harms Way". One would also find a young lady who served as Tito's English language interpreter at the meeting between Tito and the Prime Minister of Great Britain at Caserta, Italy. This young woman, the daughter of Nomcilo Nincic, Foreign Minister of the Royal Yugoslav government in exile, was to become the center of attention when, following her father's inquiry concerning her whereabouts, received from the head of the British Military Mission, Brig. F.W.D. Deakin, the following reply, "Reference your signal. Stop. She is in my bed."[8]

---

8. F.W.D. Deakin, *The Embattled Mountain* (New York, Oxford University Press, 1971) p. 113

The ensuing, protracted, tri-dimensional conflict situation confronting Tito's forces (Ustashe, Chetniks and Italo-German military units) required on the part of the occupation forces, to undertake certain steps that were to culminate in the battle order identified by the Germans as "Operation Weiss" and by the Partisans as the Fourth Enemy Offensive. This vital military encounter under the command of Colonel General von Lohr, the German Commander-in-Chief for Southeastern Europe, was to be an all-out drive whose objective consisted of bringing about the total annihilation of the partisan formations.

The oral folk history of the inhabitants of the land of Serbs, Croats, Slovenes, Montenegrins, Macedonians, Albanians, Bosnians, and its mix of Italians, Germans, and Hungarians is given the gift of life through its native songs, dances, poems and literature. Such gifts are no more than philosophy expressed in images as it applies to one's daily life and to the trials and tribulations of the people of Yugoslavia. Confronted by a political-oriented crisis of conscience and a perennial conflict of values, Yugoslavia, with its proud and fiercely independent inhabitants, elected in 1941 to confront the Nazi and the Fascist together with their allies in a War of National Liberation that could only result in freedom or death. As 1942 drew to a close, one must recall that a review of the military context reveled that 1942 was the decisive moment or as Sir Winston Churchill was to state, "The Turning of the Tide", the world over. Field Marshall Rommel's drive into Egypt was stopped at the battle of El Alamein. The American forces landed at several points in North Africa. In the Pacific the American naval forces first fought the Japanese to withdraw at the battle of the Coral Sea and won at the battle of Midway. The Americans inflicted such defeats from which Japan never truly recovered. Furthermore, American pilots flying off the aircraft carrier, USS Hornet, which President Roosevelt christened the Shangrila, bombed Tokyo. The United States Marines stormed ashore at Guadalcanal. Yes, the beginning of the end was upon us.

With the destruction of the myth of German invincibility, Tito elected to present to the people of Yugoslavia the "Bihac Manifesto" whose six points consisted of the following:

1. The liberation of the country from the invaders and the achievement of independence and true democratic rights for all the people of Yugoslavia.

2. The inviolability of private property and the providing of every possibility for individual initiative in industry, trade and agriculture.

3. No radical changes whatsoever in the social life and activities of the people except for the replacement of reactionary village authorities and gendarmes who may have gone over to the service of the invaders by popularly elected representatives truly democratic and popular in character. All the important questions of social life and State organization will be settled by the people themselves through representatives who will be properly elected by the people after the end of the war.

4. The National Liberation Movement which is fighting for the freedom of the people and for their social and democratic rights renounces any kind of coercion or lawlessness.

5. Officers who join the National Liberation Army are assured of their rank and a position commensurate with one's abilities.

6. The National Liberation Movement fully recognizes the national rights of Croatia, Slovenia, Serbia, Macedonia and all other regions. It is a movement which is as much Croatian as it Slovene and Serbian. It guarantees that the national rights of all of the peoples of Yugoslavia will be preserved.[9]

The Bihac Manifesto served not only to clarify Tito's position on matters of concern for the general population, but it also served as a national recruitment message based on the principle of "Brotherhood and Unity".

Yet, while proclamations played a vital role in the protracted struggle for the "hearts and minds" of the citizens of Yugoslavia, the military phase of the war with all of its brutality and sacrifice remained to be fought. The fate of Tito's Yugoslav military units in the mountain-

---

9. Stephen Clissold, *Whirlwind* (New York, Philosophical Library, 1949) pp. 113-114

ous regions varied as Tito brought his forces out through great hardships following engagements with the Germans, Italians, Ustase or Cetniks, in good order, time and time again. Yet, in the closing months of 1942 and in the beginning of 1943, the partisans were heading into a collapsing and very critical situation as the Axis military and their Yugoslav allies, Cetniks, Ustase and followers of the Serbian Fascist Ljotic, were preparing themselves for participation in "Operation Weiss". The Fourth Enemy Offensive under the command of Colonel General von Lohr, the German Commander-in-Chief of all Southeast Europe, was to commence on January 20, 1943. This military undertaking was to be a major offensive movement whose objective was to shatter and to annihilate Tito and his military units not only as a Yugoslav Army of National Liberation, but also as a contending political power.

The Italo-German quest was to encircle and isolate and destroy Tito's partisan forces which were outnumbered by a 5:1 ratio. The enemy force consisted of the 7th S.S. Division, the Prinz Eugene Division, the 369th Infantry Division, the 714th Infantry Division and the 717th Infantry Division. Also involved in this effort to eliminate the partisan units were the Italian Lombardia Division, the "Re" Division, the Sassari Division and the Muse Division. In addition, Tito's military formations were also confronted by a force of 8,500 Chetniks and a large number of Ustashe. Thus, the total number of Italo-German military forces involved in "Operation Weiss" was 100,000 as opposed to the partisan force of 20,000 effectives plus 4,000 wounded.[10]

The struggle for a breakout and for military and political survival was to result in a high casualty rate among both partisans and Germans killed to the last man in isolated firefights. Many an ex-veteran of this ordeal made me aware of the fact that one could find parts of bodies plastered against rocks and trees and many were blown to pieces minus heads, arms, legs as men lay in ditches with eyes open and flies walking on the bloated bodies of men, women, children and the aged. Others, I was told, found death by exhaustion or exposure to the elements. Yet, in spite of the responsibility of command and the conflict confronting Tito and his Yugoslav Army of National Liberation, many

---

10. Stephen Clissold, *Ibid* p. 136

within its ranks suffering with typhus and undernourishment, they broke through the "Iron Ring of Encirclement" at its weakest point. They had survived politically and military.

This major battle marked the turning point in the guerrilla war. In addition, it made the people of the Land of the Serbs, Croats, Slovenes, Montenegrins, Macedonians, Albanians, Bosnians, Hungarians – the mosaic of the land of South Slavs – aware that their military force was a reality. Furthermore, it made it plain to the citizen that with the close of the war, a new Yugoslavia would emerge from the ashes of the defeat of 1941 based on "Brotherhood and Unity". In the protracted, tri-dimensional guerrilla warfare which raged among the partisans, Cetniks and the occupation forces and their allies, the military units of Tito's formations had again and again come near to annihilation. Yet, in spite of their high casualty rates, it was their dogged determination, initiative, daring, recklessness, iron discipline, self-sacrifice, and their devotion to the cause that enabled the partisan to survive and to confront the enemy another day. Furthermore, the rigors of combat served to energize the people; also, their belief in *Ustanak* made it possible for them and the nation to adjust and to transcend the kaleidoscopic fortunes of querrilla warfare.

Following Operation Weiss, the war was to take on a new dynamic and renewed appetite of its own as the German military forces under the command of Field Marshal Maximilian von Weich were first regrouped, reinforced and resupplied to form the Second Panzer Army. With a military force in readiness consisting of over 200,000 men, together with proper armour and air power, plus a Bulgarian force and native allies, von Weich's force now totaling 360,000 prepared to launch "Operation Schwarz" on May 15, 1943. This operation was to be symbolically a "Tidal Wave" constantly supplied by air, highly mobile, and with command of the high ground. It was to sweep the Axis forces forward towards their objective – the destruction of Tito's Army of National Liberation. Yet, in spite of the enemy's 6 to 1 advantage, this struggle to destroy the Partisans was to fail as Tito's forces in suicidal actions sought to break the Iron Ring as they crossed to Sujeska river. That savage assaults were carried out cannot be denied as demonstrated by the actions of Sava Kovacevic's Montenegrins. Operation Schwarz was to end on the 16th of June, 1943, with a total of 5,697 partisans killed in action according to German sources.[11]

On September 9, 1943, the German Sixth Offensive designated Operation Kugelblitz confronted Tito's forces. Its objective was to sweep to partisan and the Cetnik military units from the positions taken following the surrender and the withdrawal of Italy from the war on September 8, 1943. It must be noted that the arrangements for the Italian surrender was such a closely guarded secret that SOE operatives in the field were not notified of what was taking place until, like the citizens of our global village, it was heard over the radio broadcasts of BBC. As news of Italy's capitulation reached the Germans, Partisans and the Chetniks, all vied with one another to rush into the power vacuum in order to acquire the arms and military equipment, let alone the stores of 10 Italian divisions which consisted of a total of approximately 300,000 men. Furthermore, as the Germans were seeking the destruction of their ex-allies, the Italians were seeking favorable surrender terms from their former enemies or entering the fight against the Germans as did the Venezia Division. In addition, it must be noted that while Tito welcomed the news of the surrender of Italy, his resentment of not being forewarned prior to the actual announcement, was expressed in the following words:

> *For days in advance your High Command has known the date and the circumstances of the capitulation. I have had no time to make the necessary troop dispositions for the taking over of the Italian arms and war supplies which are my army's life-blood. How can you wonder that the people of Yugoslavia find it hard to believe that their heroic struggle for national liberation means anything to you British? Not only have you failed to send us anything but the most meager of supplies; you have now prevented us from helping ourselves to what the Italians can provide.*
>
> *You have left us on the same footing as the Germans, the Chetniks and the Ustase – to see who can get to the Italians first. It is fortunate indeed that we have learnt to depend on ourselves and ourselves alone to take what is our due.[12]*

---

11. F.W.D. Deakin, *Op. Cit.* p. 31
12. Stephen Clissold, *Op. Cit.* p. 159

Although bitter, Tito now realized that the time had come to reap the revolutionary harvest whose seeds were first planted in 1941. Yet, battles were yet to be fought as Tito's troops confronted the German military units in Operation Kugelblitz (Operation Thunderbolt) and Operation Rasselsprung (Operation Knight's Move). On October 20, 1944, he entered the capital city of Belgrade together with Soviet military units. Throughout the war, Joseph Broz-Tito stood as an alternative to King and monarchy and as a patriotic Yugoslav as opposed to a blind communist ideologue. On March 7, 1945, following a national election, he emerged as the president of the government of a third Yugoslav nation-state. The war had been fought; the war had been won and the next battle lay ahead.

CHAPTER EIGHT

THE HOUNDS OF WAR

An analysis of the history of the political process in the Balkans demonstrates that nations, like individuals, suffer as they too forge their will to survive as a free and independent political entity. A scrutiny of the factual data, together with a multi-dimensional examination of the forces at play within the nations of the southwestern quadrant of the Balkan Peninsula (Albania, Greece and Yugoslavia) and its kaleidoscopic mixture of legends, myths, folkways, and norms, serves to create an awareness that the inhabitants of the "cursed land" have always survived the ravages of history and the barbarian. In addition, the realities of the political process, together with its built-in absurdities and its unpredictable action-reaction patterns, demonstrate beyond any question that destiny is without appeal. This ingrained presupposition in one's adherence to the axiom of the prevailing and the pervasive, negative, political power and influence of fatalism is reinforced time and time again whenever any political movement breaks upon the scene that possesses the power of translating ideas into an active and effective action program. Throughout the history of the various nation-states of the Land of the Eagle, the Land of the South Slavs, and Hellas, such attempts to transform a political dream into a reality have been beaten back by the State, which as the defender of Marxist-Leninist or that of the status quo of the past, has once again misused its power. Given the nihilistic political environment with its logic of destruction which was sweeping across Europe and the lands of Southeastern Europe of the decade of the 1930's, the people of the Balkans stumbled against the absurdity of the common threat that was personified in the policies of Benito Mussolini and Adolph Hitler.

The Land of the Eagle – Albania – was the region's first nation to adopt overtly the postulates of the Sawdust Caesar's "Fascist catechism" as early as 1926 because of the economic penetration of the country and the dominant role of the Italian government in the internal affairs of the Albanian nation-state. This Islamic country in a Christian Europe consisting of one million illiterate peasants in the pre-1939 days with its Ottoman and Byzantine cultural ethos, together with its fragile governmental infra-structure, had King Ahmed Zog I, who preferred to place his personal set of ambitions above the interests of his country. Yet, there were times when the king did seek to redress the existing imbalances in the relationship between Rome and Tirana. Tragically, at this time, one must recall that with the political tenets of Fascism overtly being adhered to across the land, Italy acquired an indirect control over the levers of the political power and Albania's military forces. In so doing, it created an environment whereby an appeal did no result in a human response, but only in a bribe from the Sawdust Caesar to Ahmed Zog.[1]

Europe at this historical moment was a Europe in political flux and a continent where totalitarianism became customary. It was a land where hate, lies, and deviousness reigned supreme and the offering of a bribe was in keeping with the political norms of the day. For approximately five decades, Albania had been a closed society following the close of World War II – the Tibet of Europe. The few foreigners permitted to vision the Land of the Eagle were unknowingly confined to a carefully structured itinerary complete with secret police guides. Not surprisingly, they would return to their homelands with positive images of Albania. Their seduction was complete and they spoke not of the ills, but of that which never had existed as they were growing up in Albania: i.e. indoor plumbing, a guaranteed yearly income, a no-cost access to medical service, free admission to schools of higher learning, electricity in the homes, and a deep sense of psychological and economic security providing one adhered to the political norms of society and law and order. They spoke not of Albania as a prison without walls, but of the Land of the Eagle as a happy, revolutionary nation with its hope and Hoxhian idealism. Yet, none could deny that there existed two Albanias: one, the official Land of the

---

1. Nicholas J. Costa, *Albania: A European Enigma* (New York, East European Monographs, Columbia University Press, 1995) p.p. 33

Eagle with its sloganeering, monthly student service work brigades, and with its Great Helmsman, Enver Hoxha, leading the masses to the Marxist-Leninist version of the "Elysian Fields" of Greek mythology. The other Albania existed with its traditional, positive human quotient. And yet, an atmosphere of fear and apprehension pervaded throughout the country which increased in everyone an anxiety that was not illusionary. Thus, Albania was to remain consciously frozen in historical immobility. In a country where tradition weighs heavily, the xenophobic tendency is reinforced throughout the communist phase of the nation's history by the sense of hubris, the preachings of the Communist Party of self-reliance, and an awareness among the people that for the first time in their history, the Albanians were free and politically and economically independent. True, the leadership has been described as consisting of "a group of bastards" by the emigre, but one must note as stated by a professor at the university, "At least they are our bastards... Albanian bastards".[2]

"The period since the founding of the Party of Labor of Albania (PLA) is the most brilliant in the age-long history of the Albanian people... Achievements have been attained thanks to the correct line pursued by the Party of Labor of Albania", so states the introductory paragraph of the 1969 publication of the *History of the Party of Labor of Albania*.[3] In the early 1920's, the Fascist government of Benito Mussolini undertook a program that first called for the economic penetration of the Land of the Eagle – Albania, and then for the transformation of Albania into an Italian protectorate. The Albania of the decade of the 1920's was to endure, according to Dr. Bernd Fischer of Indiana University, "numerous heads of government"[4] in a nation-state which possessed an internal tribal split between the Ghegs north of the Shkumbi River and the Tosks of the southern districts. One would also find a tri-dimensional religious division between the followers of Allah in the majority with its internal units consisting of Orthodox, Sunni and Bektashe. This religious category was followed

2. Personal Interview with an Albanian Professor who desired to remain anonymous, Tirana, Albania May 23, 1986
3. *History of the Party of Labor* (Tirana, Institute of Marxist-Leninist Studies, 1969) p. 5
4. Bernd J. Fisher, *King Zog and the Struggle For Stability* (New York, East European Monographs Columbia University Press, 1984) p. 41

by the members of the Eastern Orthodox Christian faith, who made up approximately 12% of the population and a compact minority of an estimated 8% of Roman Catholics in the northwestern region, adjacent to the city of Shkodra and northward into the Albanian communities in Montenegro of Ulcinj, Tuzi, Hot-Grude, and the mixed Eastern Orthodox-Roman Catholic community of Podgorica. Yet, in spite of such potential barriers and throughout this transitional phase of the nation's political environment, there began to evolve a minimal degree of worker consciousness as people began to ask the one fundamental question that always results in change and conflict, "What Is and What Ought To Be?"

There emerged in the 1920's, as a consequence of such questioning, the birth of the Workers League in Gjirokastra in 1925, the Perparimi (Progress) Association of Tailors in Tirana in 1927, and the League of Tailors in Korce in 1927.[5] The movement towards the development of a national union organization was stunted by the fact that numerous Albanians from the southern part of the nation elected to join the ranks of Europeans who immigrated to America, Canada and to Australia. Thus, such nations as the United States of America were to serve as a safety valve to the emergence of a revolutionary generation of Albanians who would be anti-Zogist and involved in the growth of a trade union movement.[6]

The internal political development in Albania, combined with the world-wide economic downturn of 1929, were to play a vital role in the evolution of organized communist cells in southern Albania and especially in the city of Korce. This city, the intellectual center of Albania with its strong revolutionary tradition, was in 1929 to produce the first communist group which by 1933 was to bring into being the Albanian Labor Association PUNA, whose chairperson was the dedicated communist revolutionary from Korce, Pilo Peristeri. This young man, a member of the National football (soccer) team, would maintain contact with not only the various communist cells throughout the country as he traveled from city to city, but he was also able to update the internal political exiles who were scattered throughout Al-

---

5. Mrs. James V. Costa, Personal Interview Southbridge, Massachusells
6. *History of the Party of Labor Op. Cit.* p. 35

bania and make them aware of the party line, according to this teammate, Vasil Karoli.[7]

Prior to the founding of the convention of the Comintern which was convened in Moscow in 1919, and from which Albanian revolutionaries sought to acquire a degree of guidance, there existed among and within the ranks of the Communist International Movement, a critical theoretical issue that was to result in a bitter quarrel between the supporters of Lenin's position and the remaining representatives. Lenin had put forth his "Fascist Theory of Elites" which called for the unorganized masses to follow a small revolutionary elite. The traditional, ideological Marxist Purists held to the position that the impact of economic forces would make the revolution and transform a capitalist society into a socialist society. Lenin did not truly believe that the revolution could be achieved unless the masses submitted themselves to the guidance of a classless elite. The ensuing internal conflict between the "Purists" and the "Revisionists" among the supporters of Lenin was to result in the breakup of the representatives into various factions and the eventual acceptance of Lenin's position in 1919, and in 1920, Zinoviev's "21 Conditions" at the Second World Congress.[8]

In the rough and tumble world of the International Communist Movement, such individual Albanians as Ali Kelmendi and Kocho Tashko requested and received guidance and instructions for the strengthening of the communist political web in Albania according to a report submitted to the Comintern on December 14, 1936. Furthermore, they were instructed to identify and remove all deviationists and opportunists, let alone Bukharinists and Trotskyites such as Zef Mali, Niko Xoxi, and Arestidh Qendro. The miniscule communist cells in the cities of Korce, Tirana, Vlore, Elbassan, Gjirokaster and Berat sought to extend the political web through their participation in anti-Zogist demonstrations as individual and separate entities and by penetrating the student body of the secondary school system. As communists, they possessed an advantage for unlike other political groups, they did not collaborate with any pro-king, pro-Italian, pro-German or pro-Greek political grouping. In addition, they created an awareness

---

7. Vasili Karoli, Personal Interview Port Charlotte. Florida, July, 1986
8. Alfred G. Meyer, *Leninism* (Cambridge, Harvard University Press, 1957) pp. 37-59

through their actions and publications that they were the representatives of the wave of the political future of Albania, defenders f socialism and the supporters of Marxist-Leninist and Stalinist objectives. The work of such men as Ali Kelmendi, who died in Paris on February 11, 1939, did not at this time result in the formation of a Communist Party, but it did result in the birth of an idea which would come to full fruition on November 8, 1941, when a decision was reached to merge the various groups towards the goal of establishing a communist party.[9]

Furthermore, it must be noted that within the protracted decade of the 1920's and 1930's, the supporters of the revolution were exemplified by two powerful image-projecting words – energy and purpose. In addition, while the impact of Yugoslav policy and military assistance was great throughout the war years, it must be noted that the Albanins possess from birth a strong sense of national identity and thus they fought as free revolutionaries in their homeland and in Yugoslavia rather than as servants of Tito. In spite of a post-war schizophrenic quality as seeing one's self as both an Albanian and Yugoslav patriot one day and the next day as an Albanian and Soviet defender of Stalinism, and eventually pose as an Albanian and Chinese Marxist-Leninist purist, they remained at all times Shqpitars – Albanians.

As the 1920's gave way to the 1930's, the economic penetration of Albania by the Fascist government of Benito Mussolini transformed Albania into an Italian colony as the revisionist bloc of Japan, Italy, and Germany – a nation hell-bent on acquiring hegemony over Europe – had made it crystal clear that in relation to its neighbors, its own economic resources and military preparedness were superior to that which they possessed. While it is true prior to the outbreak of World War II on September 1, 1939, France had the superior military force, they were immobilized by their adherence to the defensive strategy of trench warfare, which emerged following the close of World War I. Nazi Germany, on the other hand, was wed to a highly mobile, offensive strategy which became familiar to Europeans and Americans alike as "Blitzkreig Warfare". The world became a more military and diplomatic competitive place as France sought to establish major

---

9. Alli Hadri, *Ali Keljmendi 1900-1939* (Preshtina, Academie De Sciences Et Arts De Kossova, 1984) pp. 39-40

defensive political and military coalitions. In the meantime, capitalist Europe sought to isolate the "Red Bacilli of Communism" which was considered by European governments as the number one threat as opposed to Fascist Italy and Nazi Germany. In the 1930's, Europe's relative weaknesses were more apparent to the decision makers and policy formulators in London, Paris, Rome, Berlin and Tokyo that to the man on the street. Here, one must recall that the nation of France during the "Great War" of 1914-1918 was bled white and Great Britain had lost a generation in the trenches. The eclipse of France as a major power was unknowingly insured as was the weakening of Great Britain.

The Albania of the decades prior to the outbreak of World War II lay in the hands of clan-based feudal lords whose power gravitated toward those individuals who possessed resources in the form of men and arms, let alone connections. One such individual was Ahmed Zog of the Mati Tribe.[10] From a geo-political perspective, the one feature of Albania, the "Land of the Eagle," which immediately strikes the observer or the student is the political fragmentation of this technologically backward and economically underdeveloped nation-state. Albania has always been politically and socially fragmented. Its basic political and social unit had been small, localized and isolated. To a great degree, this may be attributed to its fractured landscape with its mountainous topography which separated the population into isolated villages. The impact of geography upon the people and the nation made it very difficult for the establishment of unified control even by a powerful warlord. It further served to minimize in the minds of the Albanians the belief that their country could not be overrun by an external invading force. This variegated, political landscape encouraged the growth and the tendency to maintain a decentralized political system in place with local fiefdoms, highland clans and tenant farmers which, prior to and even following its conquest by the Ottoman Turks, remained a patchwork quilt until the arrival of Ahmed Zog.

At this historical moment, Eurpe's protracted competitive interaction as she confronted many internal challenges brought on by the multitude of "Tribes With Flags" that had been smitten by the disease of nationalism, made it possible for the Albanians to deliberately elect (with

---

10. Bernd J. Fischer, *Op. Cit.* p. 26

few exceptions) to cut itself off from the rest of the world and to turn in on itself until it declared its independence on November 28, 1912.

The expulsion of the Ottoman Turk by force of arms from Europe following the close of the Balkan Wars of 1911 and 1912, was to result in an interlocking diplomatic and military campaign for the Teutonic tribes of Germany. With the close of World War I on November 11,1918, Fascist predominance confronted Europe with its second phase of its Thirty Year War, 1914-1945. The weakness of Europe's resolve to meet the Nazi and Fascist challenge of the decade of the 1930's was demonstrated by its loss of nerve when confronted by Germany's series of challenges in the form of the Nazi takeover of the Rhineland in 1936; the establishment of a German-Austrian union of "Rump Czechoslovakia" in 1939. The broad outlines of the unfolding course of World War II makes one aware that of the four major European Powers – France, Great Britain, Germany and Italy – which entered the war at the beginning on September 1, 1939, only England saw it through from start to finish. Both Germany and Italy were the vanquished powers. Nazi Germany, more so than Fascist Italy, who in 1943 withdrew from the conflict, was at the mercy of the victorious forces. Throughout the European conflict of 1939-1945, the diplomatic and political pace of change was significant, for on June 22, 1941, the military forces of Hitlerite Germany crossed the Polish-Russian border with 190 divisions to undertake the invasion of the Union of Socialist Republics, its former ally.

On December 7, 1941, the Empire of Japan unleashed a series of naval air bombardments against the United States and British air and naval installations throughout the Pacific and destroyed the American fleet, with the exception of the aircraft carrier force which was at sea. In addition, Japanese military units were to undertake offensive operations that would result within the first six months with the fall of the American possessions of the Philippine Islands, Guam, and Wake Island. Furthermore, it resulted in the total sweeping away of the "White Man's" possessions in Asia. In so doing, it gave to the Japanese a greater degree of validity to their proclamation – "Asia for the Asiatics". The two peripheral nation-states – the Union of Soviet Socialist Republics and the United States of America – were to enter the war in 1941 and to emerge in 1945 as the world's major powers in the post World War II era.

Of all the changes which were taking place in the global power balances throughout the war years, one must recall that Albania, Yugoslavia, and Greece were occupied by Italo-German forces by 1941. British Liaison units as members of S.O.E. were functioning at full strength as of 1943 and by 1943 the wars of national liberation in the Balkans – in Winston Churchill's words – "Set Europe Ablaze". The most significant political and military change in Europe following in Italo-German conquest and the occupation of the Balkan peninsula in 1941, was the emergence of the wars of national liberation and the outbreak of civil wars as the communist forces sought to move into the political power vacuum following the shattering of the pre-war state. According to Milovan Djilas, it is the disintegration of the pre-war nation-state that made it possible for the communist parties to acquire control of the levers of political power and bring forth communist revolutions in Yugoslavia and Albania, but not in Greece due to British military intervention.[11]

In the year of 1943, German military forces involved in the occupation of Adolph Hitler's "Fortress Europea" consisted of approximately five to six million combat effectives. While German sources make references to the figure that 3.9 million troopers were involved in the fighting along the Eastern front, a German reserve unit consisting of 177,000 was in Finland. In Scandinavia, the German garrison force of 486,000 occupied Norway and Denmark. The French, who were beaten in 1940, were confronted with a German military presence that consisted of 1,370,000 troops. The total German occupation force assigned to Yugoslavia, Albania and Greece, together with the islands in the eastern end of the Mediterranean Sea, totaled 612,000 men while 412,000 men were stationed in Italy.[12]

In 1940, the men of Special Operations Executive, SOE stood alone with their country, England, against the combined power of the Axis forces in the dark days following the fall of France in 1940. Of the men who were called to meet the German challenge head-on, one was a young officer stationed in Malta named Oakley-Hill, who had served

11. Milovan Djilas, Personal Interview Belgrade, Yugoslavia 1984
12. Paul Kennedy, *The Rise and Fall of the Great Powers* (New York, Random House Publishers, 1987) pp. 35

in Albania in the 1920's as an officer in King Zog's Gendarmeire. Upon his arrival in Cairo aboard the HMS Glasgow at the time when the Italian fleet at Tarento suffered major losses at the hands of British naval units, Oakley-Hill received a briefing in Cairo and quickly rushed off to Greece. From Athens, he journeyed by train to the Yugoslav frontier station at Djevdjeli where he caught the Yugoslav train to Belgrade in order to establish contact with the "D" Organization and to enter the shadowy world of espionage. Of the organization, Julian Amery in his book, *Sons of the Eagle*, related that this group was involved in carrying out "subversion" in enemy occupied countries. This would require sabotage operations, fomenting insurrectionary actions, and any type of action that would result in a negative experience for the enemy.[13] Oakley-Hill's entry into the world of "Subversive Espionage" was to result in the establishment of contacts while in Belgrade with various Albanian personalities of stature and influence. Furthermore, individuals such as Gani Bey Kreyziu provided intelligence and significant contacts with the power elite of the various clans both in Kosovo and across the border. In addition, the extension of a social-political web into northern Albania, Montenegro, and the various Albania communities in Macedonia was to be a valuable source of potential recruitment of an armed military unit capable of undertaking operations against the Italian forces in Albania.

According to Julian Amery, this 1000 man "Force In Readiness" possessed the unofficial support of the government of Yugoslavia, but lacked sufficient weapons which would render the Kosovars sufficient firepower to confront the Italian military forces in Albania. That there existed a need for supplies of war materials in substantial numbers cannot be denied. As previously noted, England was in need of such and thus only a limited degree of war materials and other types of equipment could be allocated to SOE – Special Operations Executive. However, this need was to be satisfied following the victory of British forces under the command of General Sir Archibald Wavell, who routed General Graziani's military force of 10 divisions while taking 130,000 prisoners and driving the Italian forces back 500 miles across the desert

---

13. Julian Amery, S*ons of the Eagle* (London, Macmillan and Company, LTD. 1948) p. 25

sands of North Africa. An appeal in Cairo by Major Oakley-Hill resulted in an agreement to forward for shipment from Greece several
hundred rifles and guns. His return and the news of the forthcoming
shipment of weapons were well received by Major Julian Amery and
the men at "D" Section in Belgrade and Gani Kryezzi. Of this con-
signment, Major Oakley-Hill states:

> *This quantity could about fill a closed freight truck, and ever*
> *though it would be sealed and consigned to the embassy, to pass*
> *it through Belgrade would be pretty well impossible. Gani vir-*
> *tually controlled Jakova, where the Major and the stationmaster*
> *were Gani men, so the plan was conceived by having the truck*
> *diverted at Jevdjeli on the western line which passed through*
> *Jakova and reconsigning it to the stationmaster there. For this*
> *it would necessary to bribe the stationmaster at Jevdjeli, and I*
> *would have to do this and give him authority from our embassy*
> *for the reconsignment. Gani's men could then keep this truck*
> *quiet for short time, while the contents were gradually removed*
> *to the Kreyeziu house... I went to Jevdjeli and saw the*
> *stationmaster, made my desires known and gave him a large*
> *wad of dinar notes, which spoke more clearly than I did. I gave*
> *him also the details of the consignment note, which did not re-*
> *veal the contents of the cases. He agreed to the plan and I re-*
> *turned to Belgrade.[14]*

The date of Major Oakley-Hill's return to the Yugoslav capitol
was shortly before April 6, 1941, the day which marked the beginning
of "Operation Punishment", the Germanic invasion of Yugoslavia and
Greece.

Prior to the invasion, in order to meet the contingency of a military
penetration, Yugoslav troops moved southward towards Albania in
order to strike at the Italians who were in Shkodra. They moved their
military units towards Bulgaria and Romania from which they anticipated a military intrusion into Yugoslavia. In the meantime, Gani
Kreyziu had brought together a strong, highly mobile force which on

---

14. Oakley Hill, Personal letter to the author, September 18.

the 6th of April, 1941, the second anniversary of Mussolini's invasion of Albania, Major Oakley-Hill, Gani Kreyziu, Abas Kupi, Mustapha Gjinishi and numerous clan chieftains from Dibra and Kosovo crossed into the Land of the Eagle-Albania and headed for Tropoja which was in the hands of Krasniqi and Gashi clans of the Maleija e Gjakoves or the Gjakova Higlands.

The Germanic invasion of Yugoslavia and its strike at Greece on the 6th of April created a critical situation for Oakley-Hill, for it placed him, together with the "Strike Force", in a most precarious position. While the Germans had all of the advantages, Oakley-Hill and Gani Kreyziu possessed an absolute firmness of intent to confront the Italians, who were just hanging on to the Albanian port of Vlora against a determined Greek military force with a two front war as they continued on towards their objective. The moment of euphoria which swept through the men as they journeyed the warrior's path of old, proved to be exceedingly brief. Unbeknown to the invading force of Albanians, because of the conquest of Yugoslavia and Greece, they were chasing an illusion and marching nowhere. According to Major Oakley-Hill, their initial objective was:

> *To enter Albania as a small group and find shelter with the highland chiefs. We would then sound the local feelings and try to initiate sabotage and local minor actions. If the situation was ripe and circumstances were suitable, we would work towards a general rising which, with a neutral Yugoslavia at our backs, was far from impossible.*[15]

Human history is a times a history of man and mankind involved in a quest to achieve the unachievable – or as stated, "To dream the impossible dream". Spurred on by the desire to confront the Italian military forces, their journey to nowhere was to take them from Kolgecaj to the community of has where they were satisfactorily received. It was here that Major Oakley-Hill was made aware by the citizens of Has of the Germanic invasion of Yugoslavia and Greece. With the German invasion and conquest of the Land of the South Slavs, a deep sense of anxiety and panic swept through their ranks for the reality of

---

15. Oakley Hill, *Ibid*

the situation was that they were truly isolated with no neutral base behind them. Electing to push forward, they followed the Valbone River Ford opposite Geghysen. It is here that they caught up with a Yugoslav military unit and together they moved through the Kolshi Pass to the village of Nikaj, to Salce, and then through the Agri Pass into Shala and Shoshi. It is at this point that the Yugoslav command elected, following their brief stay at Kodra Shengjergi-Saint George's Hill, to break away, join their forces to the east, and then head for Yugoslavia.

Undaunted by the negativistic, radical turn of events, the Kosovars continued on through the Shtegui i Dhenvet (Sheeptrack Pass) and into the Boga valley and the village of Boga. Of his stay at Boga, Major Oakley-Hill states:

> *I learned from Gani that the people would not support him. They said that owing to news of our invasion having reached the Italians, 600 troops were on their way from Shkodra. They wanted us to get out as soon as possible. So we were forced to turn back to the village of Thethi.*[16]

Given that the entire far north was now aware of their presence and the fact that the prevailing attitudinal disposition of the people was that the Germans has won the war, the psycho-political environment was now marked by a high degree of anxiety, confusion and bewilderment. It had been the hope of Gani and his command that they could remain in the mountains and carry out hit and run raids against the occupation forces. Unfortunately, the attitudinal transformation among the villagers made the desire to continue the fight impossible. This fatal blow was to result in their decision to return to Jakova.

From this moment, major Oakley-Hill, had to confront the reality that Gani could not, as previously promised, hide him for two years. As difficult as it was for Major Oakley-Hill to accept this reality, it was even more so for Gani who had given his "Besa" or word of honor. One must be aware of the fact that this highland chieftain, a tradition-directed person, was honor bound to keep his word unless released from its obligation by the individual to whom one's word is given. The quest to confront the Italian military occupation forces with a

---

16. Oakley Hill, *Ibid*

two-front war now became a determined effort to escape the precarious situation which confronted them by returning to Jakova and for
the Major to work his way out of Yugoslavia and to reach, if possible,
Istanbul. As it turned out, fate had turned its back on both Major Oakley-
Hill and the Kreyzius. The Italians took the Kreyzius prisoner and
sent them to the concentration camp in Italy from which they were to
escape in 1943. Major Oakley-Hill was first to make his way to Skopje
in Macedonia where he procured a passport and an unsigned Turkish
document which enabled him to travel to Belgrade an seek the aid of
the French consulate, but to no avail. Following an automobile ride to
the Turkish Embassy in Belgrade, Major Oakley-Hill, unable to pro-
cure the required signature on the grounds that he possessed a stolen
passport, now turned to the Americans.

Initially, he sought from the Americans transit papers by way of
Turkey to New York city where he would join his relatives. This request would require him to remain in occupied Belgrade for three
months providing his request to acquire admission into the United States
was approved. Confronted with this potential delay, together with the
possibility that he would not be granted permission to enter the United
States of America, he elected to return to the American embassy and
to identify himself. In an interview at Charring Cross in November,
1973, in the city of London, Major Oakley-Hill while reflecting upon
his ordeal, was to recall that:

> *When the movement collapsed such men as Lazar Fundo,*
> *Mustapha Gjinishi and the Krieziu brothers were eventually to*
> *find themselves in the Italian concentration camp at Ventotteno.*
> *For myself, possessing a knowledge of the Albanian language*
> *and disguised as an Albanian refugee, I attempted to get out of*
> *Yugoslavia by seeking the assistance of the United Stated Lega-*
> *tion. I had hoped to pose as an Albanian in the employ of the*
> *American Legation who was in transit along with the Legation*
> *bag and baggage, to Istanbul.*[17]

---

17. Oakley Hill, *Ibid*

Furthermore, he made aware of the fact that while the representative of the government of the United States and he had met in Tirane, the young man's reaction was puzzling. Thus, Major Oakley-Hill then proceeded to recall:

> *According to the American, anyone would be sure to pick me off the train and then he would get 10 years in the penitentiary for helping a British officer to escape. It may be that he too thought the Germans had already won the war. After reflection he said he had two suggestions: the first was to give me a pass to Croatia; it was relatively free of Gremans and the Croats had their own organization, separate from the Serbs. (I am glad I did not fall for this one, in view of the later developments in Yugoslavia.) His other suggestion was that he should get in touch with one of the senior members of the German legation whom he knew well and tell him that he had a British officer there whom he knew personally and who wished to give himself up honorably.[18]*

Lacking any contacts and traveling in civilian clothes, for it was impossible to travel in an occupied country in anything else, and aware that at this moment a resistance group did not exist, he was forced to accept the offer to surrender to the German legation representative. That this proud officer of His Majesty's Military was totally disappointed in the Americans is an understatement.

While the journey to nowhere marked the beginning of resistance to the enemy in the dark days of 1941, it must be pointed out that a number of communist political cells had been established in numerous communities of southern Albania. Individuals involved in the formation of such were to acquire valuable experience in subversive work in which they had become proficient by the very nature of their precarious existence under the regime of King Ahmed Zog I. To the youth of Albania, who had been suffocated in a network of family, tribal or clan obligations and the struggle for economic survival, the revolution of 1917 which had taken place in Russia was for the revolutionaries of

---

18. Oakley Hill, *Ibid*

yesteryear, representative of the victory of the spirit of all manking. Thus, social revolving, in order to succeed in the "Land of the Eagle-Albania", had to be led by political revolution if the traditional society was to be dissolved and a Marxist-Leninist society was to evolve from the ashes of the old. This transformation is understandable given that among the followers of Leninism, the present is the original of the future. Unfortunately, the Marxist-Leninist future could not be attained for the membership of the numerous pro-communist political units. Many may have accepted the message of revolution which source was the Kremlin but not the doctrinal epistle in total.

The nation of Albania had a miniscule exposure to the defining of historical, cultural, and political phenomena of Western Europe's civilization – Renaissance, Reformation and the period of the Enlightment. Its Byzantine imprint on its Ottoman Islamic soul shaped a society and gave birth to a cultural ethos which, while unique, had no resemblance to that which existed in Western European culture. Albania's failure to be an active participant and benefactor of the Renaissance, Reformation and the Enlightenment, due to the fact that it was an integral part of the Ottoman Empire was to result in it being ill-prepared to meet the political and economic challenges of 20th century Europe. To many Albanians and to the observer of the Balkan political scene, Italy, the nation-state of Yugoslavia (consisting of Serbia and Montenegro), and the country of Greece remained committed to the dual goals of subverting Albania politically and dividing it territorially. History exists as the key witness to these charges. Since the emergence of the Albanian nation-state as an independent, political entity in 1912, as a member of the Global Village, its neighboring states have always adopted an antagonistic predisposition towards the Land of the Eagle-Albania and a negativistic perception toward the Albanian or the Shqiptar. This innate antagonism among the Albanian, Greek, Serb, Montenegrin, and the Italian has, since time immemorial, been driven by domestic politics. However, what must be noted is that the transpiring historical events between these respective "Tribes With Flags" tended to reflect the changing power relationships within the European political scene and especially in Tirana, Athens, Belgrade and Rome.

By 1942, the political and military moves and countermoves of the conflict situation in the southwestern tier of the Balkan Peninsula escalated to a point in 1943, that was representative of a reality which confronted the Albanian, Greek, and Yugoslav with a series of illusions and delusions that were beyond their control as they became, along with the "New Romans" and the "Teutonic Knights of Nazi Germany", the major playmakers in the Balkan Danse Macabre. As the Germanic invasion of Yugoslavia and Greece progressed, the "Killing Fields" of the Balkan peninsula were to produce torrents of blood as the Fascist Croatian Ustase murdered 250,000 Serbian Christians of the Eastern Orthodox faith, and as the Bosnian Muslims decimated the ranks of the Christian population, let alone the Hungarians in Vojvodina and the Bulgars in Macedonia, who also contributed to the murder of the innocent.[19]

Despite such happenings throughout the dark days, it must be noted that the politic opinion of the people of Greece always remained, in spite of the strategic withdrawal of British military units, pro-British in their sentiments. This is demonstrated by the following diary entry:

> *No one who passed through the city with Barrowclough's brigade will ever forget it. Nor will we ever think of the Greek people without the warmest recollections of the morning – 25 April, 1941. Trucks and men showed plainly the marks of the 12 hours of battle and the 160 mile march through the night. We were nearly the last British troops they would see, and the Germans might be on our heels; yet cheering, clapping crowds lined the streets and they pressed about our cars, so almost to hold us up.*
>
> *Girls and men leaped upon the running board to kiss or shake hands with the grimy, weary gunners. They threw flowers besides us, crying, "Come back – you must come back again – Goodby – Good luck and God bless you".[20]*

The hounds of war, which in 1939 and 1940, were unleashed by the Italo-German masters on the body politik of the Albanian, Greek, and Serb, was representative of a cauldron of destruction and death as

19. Len Deighton, *Blood, Tears and Folly Vol. I* (New York, Harper Paperbacks, 1994) pp. 337-338
20. Len Deighton, *Ibid* p. 340

the Balkanite prepared to give away all of this tomorrows for their sons and daughters today. Now that the war, with all of its savagery was upon the peasants, the leaders of the various guerilla movements came forth to accept the task to confront the conqueror with a war of national liberation. Of such men, Joseph Broz-Tito, the leader of the partisan forces in the Land of the Serbs, Croats and Slovenes, was admired by many, feared by his adversaries, and very popular among the rank and file within the partisan movement. Enver Hoxha of Albanian was an astute student and applicator of the principle of Realpolitik, which enabled him to be aware of the political situation and undertake the required adjustments so that it would assure the satisfaction of his personal and ultimate needs. In the words of John Halliday, the author of *The Artful Albanian – The Memoirs of Enver Hoxha*, he was a "charming, ruthless Balkan wheeler dealer who saw himself as the embattled keeper of the faith". Peter Prifti, an Albanologist, confronts the observer of the Albanian political scene with the image of Enver Hoxha, "... holding the shore of the dictatorship of the proletariat in one hand and the western lamp of learning in the other".[21] Other observers of Enver Hoxha make reference to his role-playing ability, linguistic competence, his tenacity, perseverance, and ruthlessness.

No one can deny that the psycho-historical and political trajectory within the wars of national liberation following the conquest of the Land of the Eagle-Albania, the Land of the South Slav-Yugoslavia, and Hellas-Greece, evolved gradually and drew from the experiences of the national traditions of the past. nor can one dismiss the fact that it was only with the quest of the communist forces throughout their military confrontation with the Italo-German conquerors of their native countries and the outbreak of civil wars, that brought about the legitimacy of their revolutionary objectives. Throughout the war, the partisan forces became the symbol of the nation's resolution to destroy the invader. True, there did exist other resistance groups such as Balli Kombetar and Legaliteti, but tragically, as the war progressed, many within the ranks of the anti-communist forces elected to sup with the devil. Such action, together with the communists' inability to fully trust anyone, an instinctive response bred into them by ideology, was to result in the following directive:

---

21. Stephen Fisher-Galati, *The Communist Parties Of Eastern Europe* (New York, Columbia University Press 1979) p. 18

> *Through clever denunciation and secret work, we must seek*
> *to discredit the National Front (Balli Kombetar) before the peo-*
> *ple to detach the people from it and to unite them with us... to*
> *present it as striving for division and as instigator of fratricidal*
> *fighting, and to make the people see that the policy of the Na-*
> *tional Front will lead us to armed conflict, to make it (so look)*
> *that the whole people will revolt because of it, and in this way*
> *the historical responsibility for the disunity of the Albanian peo-*
> *ple and for the armed conflict will fall on the National Front.*[22]

The political significance of the above quotation is to be found in the fact, in spite of the travails, apprehensions, doubts, anxieties and the illusions that cluttered the political environment, that the communists' quest for total power over the Land of the Eagle and the perpetuation of their own power was the primary and intense consideration of the pro-communist, hard-core, professional revolutionaries, according to Sotir Shipska, an original member of the "Club of 41".[23] Since the advent of the communist challenge, a confrontation in the words of Dr. Robert Strausz-Hupe which represents "a method of conflict in space over a sustained period of time" when transformed from theory to reality, becomes, according to Mao Tse-tung, the strategy of protracted conflict. He defines this in the following:

> *The strategy of protracted conflict postpones the decisive*
> *battle and calibrates its challenges to a calculus of risks – until*
> *the balance of power has shifted overwhelmingly to the side of*
> *the revolutionary forces.*[24]

From the denunciation of the Mukaji Agreement in the following words on September 9th, 1943:

> *You know the agreement with the National From has been to*
> *the detriment of the National Liberation Movement and to the*
> *party itself, and as such it has been disapproved by the Central*
> *committee...*

---

22. Stavro Skendi, "Albania Within The Slav Orbit Advent to Power of the Communist Party" *Political Science Quarterly, LXIII* (June, 1948), p. 244
23. Sotir Shipska, Personal Interview Korce, Albania (July 6, 1969)
24. Robert Strausz-Hupe, William R. Kinter; James E. Dougherty and Alvin J. Cottrell, *Protracted Conflict* (New York: Harper Brothers Publications, 1959) pp. 2, 7

> *Therefore, we must work with the following directives: to discredit Balli before the people, ... to introduce Balli to the people as the source of civil war... and to prepare the people for war against Balli.*[25]

to the issuance of the Shpati Circular of November 3rd, 1943, the set of instructions demonstrates that the Albanian leadership followed to the letter the theory of Mao's Protracted Conflict. Thus, the historian of the Albanian wartime experience will find the following statement.

> *The Shapti Circular of November 3, 1943, instructed the Party's District Committees that any resistance group outside the National Liberation Movement should be fought without mercy. It ordered that the people should be made to believe that the reaction (i.e. non-communist elements) is a tool in the hands of the enemy and that our war against it is not a war of ideologies; that we fight it, first because it wants to bring back the pre-1939 regime which was against the people... that the campaign of the Reaction for unity is all demagoguery; that unity is possible only within the National Liberation Front; that the Reaction is fully responsible for the terror and the Civil War; and that the National Liberation Movement has brought order and discipline to the liberated areas, whereas Reaction has always pillaged and plundered.*[26]

In the war and policy are no more but two sides of the same coin, an analysis of the conflict situation in Albania demonstrates that Enver Hoxha and company fell back upon the usage of the indirect approach, deception and distraction in the early years. However, on the other hand, the pro-communist forces had acquired the necessary means of sweeping their rivals from the field of battle and had gained the monopoly of initiative. Once this was achieved, they applied the revolutionary technique which Dr. Hugh Seton Watson has identified as "Revolution by Frontal Assault".

---

25. Stavro Skendi, *Albania* (New York, Frederick A. Praeger Inc., 1957), p. 128
26. Stavro Skendi, *Ibid* p. 129.

CHAPTER NINE

DEATH IN THE SOUL

Lenin, who held to the view that military and political mechanisms are interchangeable in the execution of the world-wide strategic plan of protracted conflict and gradual political revolutionary challenge and transformation, underscored in his personal copy of Clausewitz's text entitled *On War*, the following passages:

> *If War belongs to policy, it will naturally take its character from thence. If policy is great and powerful so also will be the War, and this may be carried to the point at which War attains to its absolute from. It is only through this kind of view that War recovers unity; only by it can we see all Wars as things of one kind and only thus can we attain the true and perfect basis and point of view from which great plans may be traced out and determined upon.*
>
> *There is upon the whole nothing more important in life than to find out the right point of view from which things should be looked at an judged of and then to keep to that point, for we can only apprehend the mass of events in the unity from standpoint...*[1]

The seeds for conflict have always been and are currently present in the Balkans. The mini-power and the multi-ethno-cultural ethos of the various nation-states with their hidden agendas, proves that cultural commonalties do not erode the barriers to conflict in the foreseeable future. To this day, as in the past, the old rivalries guarantee that the Balkans will remain a geo-political "Powder Keg" with a long, smoldering fuse that, when lit, possesses the power to once again bring Europe to the abyss as it did in 1914.

---

1. Byron Dexter, "Clausewitz and Soviet Strategy, *"Foreign Affairs"* Vol. XXIX, October, 1950, pp. 49-50

As our community of nations prepares to enter the 21st century and that which President George Bush referred to as the "New World Order", one cannot but ask – were there any gains after two World Wars, the Cold War, and the demise of the Union of Soviet Socialist Republics? If so, they are difficult to discern. After all, the student of history must recall that the events prior to the outbreak of Europe's second Thirty Year War 1914-1945, combined to establish an explosive mix whereby the European nations, following the "Sarajevo Incident" on June 28, 1914, did not know how not to go to war. The significant impact of World War I – "The war to end all wars" – upon the combatant is best to be found in Erich Maria Remarque's anti-war novel *All Quiet on the Western Front*. Of the war, which in the words of Sir Winston Churchill, "... roared on till it finally burned itself out", remarque is to recall:[2]

> *It is autumn. There are not many of the old hands left. I am the last of the seven fellows from our class.*
> *Everyone talks of peace and armistice. All wait.*
> *If it again proves an illusion, then they will break up; hope is high, it cannot be taken away again without an upheaval. If there is not peace, then there will be revolution. I have fourteen days' rest because I have swallowed a bit of gas; in a little garden I sit the whole day long in the sun. The armistice, I believe it now too.*
> *Here my thoughts stop and will go no further. All that meets me, all that floods over me are but feelings – greed of life, love of home, yearnings of the blood, intoxication of deliverance.*
> *But no aims.*
> *Had we returned home in 1916, out of the suffering and strength of our experiences we might have unleashed a storm. Now, if we go back, we will be weary, broken, burnt out, rootless and without hope. We will not be able to find our way any more.*
> *And men will not understand us – for the generation that grew up before us, though it has passed these years with us here, already had a home and a calling; now it will return to its old occupation, and the war will be forgotten – and the generation that has grown up after us will be strange to us and push us*

2. Winston Churchill, *The World Crisis, 1915* (New York, Simon and Schuster, 1929) pp. 1-2

aside. We will be superfluous even to ourselves, some others will merely submit, and most will be bewildered; the years will pass by and in the end we shall fall into ruin.

Here the trees show gay and golden, the berries of the mountain ash stand red among the leaves, country roads run white out to the skyline, and the canteens hum like beehives with rumors of peace.

I stand up.

I am very quiet. Let the months and years come, they bring me nothing, they can bring me nothing. I am so alone and so without hope that I can confront them without fear. The life that has borne me through these years is still in my hands and eyes.

Whether I have subdued it I know not. But so long as it is there it will seek its own way out, heedless of the will that is within me.[3]

The essence of war and its impact upon the warrior, be it World War I, World War II, the Korean War, the war in Vietnam, or the Gulf War, is clearly laid before the reader as he quietly states unto himself, "Why, that wasn't just World War I... That was any war".[4] Yet, the importance of the passages by this young German G.I. is to be found in the fact that it projects in words a pattern of development of the future with the emerging strength of totalitarianism and its accompanying decay of democracy during the inter-war period of 1919-1939.

In that the illusion which confronts man is of one's own making, the facts supporting such cannot be altered. Thus, man seeks to define the scenario, decide what part all nations play and then, through one's individual actions, transform the illusion into reality. Germany today, as in the decade of the 1920's, because of the monetary assistance of the United States of America, became the most prosperous and politically powerful nation in Europe. One must recall that once again, as during the interwar period, the Americans would not permit any attempt on the part of any European nation to retard the recovery of Germany. It is true that World War I and the Second World War, to-

---

3. Erich Maria Remarque, *All Quiet On The Western Front* (Boston: Little Brown and Company, 1929)
4. George Kennan, *American Diplomacy – 1900-1950* (London: The New American Libary, 1952) p. 6

gether with the interwar period, have ceased to be "today" and have become "yesteryear". Yet, the observer must be aware of the fact that the crisis situations which confronted the European in the decade of the 1930's run parallel to those which a citizen of our "Global Village" views on the evening television news programs and reads about every evening on the Internet.

The close of World War I, with the signing of the Treaty of Versailles, found Europe enfeebled and adopting a defensive posture whether towards a possible resurgent Germany, as demonstrated by the emergence of the French Security System; the ideological expansionism of Communism, as indicated by the establishment of the Condon Sanitaire; and that of the preponderant, multi-dimensional power of the United States of America. America's escape from reality and into the world of illusion began following President Woodrow Wilson's quest for the acceptance of the League of France, England, and Italy, to bring about the full recovery of Germany. Tragically, the United States of America elected to repudiate its own creation and not to ratify the Treaty of Versailles. It is at this psycho-historical moment in the political environment of Europe that the government of the United States of America elected to chase an illusion and retreat to "Fortress America" and adhere to a policy of isolationism as applied to international affairs.

That the interwar years of 1919-1939 had identifiable crisis situations cannot be denied. Nor can one not acknowledge that the citizen of the post World War II generation of our Global Village has also been confronted by world crisis situations and wars that led from President Eisenhower's policy of "Massive Retaliation" to President John F. Kennedy's foreign policy program of "Flexible Response". Yet, as the reader returns to the interwar years, it cannot be denied that the people of Europe held their collective breath as a limited German military force crossed the Rhine on March 7, 1936, into the demilitarized Rhineland as a paralyzed France, encased in an environment of defeatism, stood aside as Germany annexed its own territory. One must also recall that nationalism triumphed over ideology in 1935 as the people of the Saar overwhelmingly elected by a vote of 477,000 to

48,000[5] to return to the bosom of Adolph Hitler's Third Reich. It now appears that Germany's Fuehrer may have come to the conclusion that the appeal to German nationalism was irresistible in those foreign lands – Austria, Czechoslovakia, and Poland – where the German ethnic minority constituted a compact majority of the population. One must recall that the prevailing attitude among the citizens of Europe as applied to the acquisition of former German territory is best to be found in Lord Lothian's statement, "After all, the Germans are only going into their own back garden".[6] Thus, while falling back upon this false rationalization to justify the lack of a meaningful political and psychological response, the leaders of France and England, through their lack of reaction, only legalized Hitler's illegalities. Thus, the interwar years of 1919-1939 ran their predestined course under the shadow of high anxiety and misapprehension. Once again, as in 1914, the British had nightmares of being dragged into a war, but this time for Czechoslovakia and Poland.

The total power of the magnetic force of the illusion upon the power elite of a nation's quest to achieve that which is unachievable is to be found in the following statement by Adolph Hitler as the Anglo-American military on the Western front confronted 26 German divisions and covered 150 miles a day, while our Russian allies confronted 170 German divisions and could only advance 25 miles a day on the Eastern front.

> *The following must also be considered gentlemen. In all history there has never been a coalition composed of such heterogeneous partners with such totally divergent views and objectives as that of our enemies. The states which are now our enemies are the greatest opposites which exist on earth; ultracapitalist states on one side and ultra-Marxist states on the other; on one side a dying empire-Britain; on the other side a colony, the United States, waiting to claim its inheritance. These are states whose objectives diverge daily... And anyone who, if I may use the phrase, sits like a spider in his web and follows these developments, can see how hour by hour these antitheses are increasing. If we can deal it a couple of heavy blows, this*

---

5. William L. Schirer, *The Rise and Fall of the Third Reich* (New York, Simon and Schuster, 1960) p. 238
6. William L. Schirer, *Ibid* p. 293

*artificially constructed common front may collapse with a mighty
thunderclap at any moment. Each of the partners in this coalition has entered it in the hope of achieving thereby his political
objectives... either to cheat the others out of something or to get
something out of it: the United States' objective is to be England's heir. Russia's objective is to capture the Balkans, to capture the Straits, to capture Persian oil, to capture Iran, to capture the Persian Gulf; England's objective is to maintain her
position in the Mediterranean. In other words, one day – it can
happen any moment, for on the other side history is being made
merely by mortal men – this coalition may dissolve...*[7]

Hitler's logic, based upon a false premise, was not to be achieved
though Reich Marshall Herman Goering had previously declared on
January 27, 1945, "... they would be getting a telegram in the next few
days" following Hitler's statement. While it is true that points of con-
tention could be identified among the Allies, the disintegration pre-
dicted by Adolph Hitler did not take place. To the very end, the German Fuehrer held to an illusion that was not to be.

The pendulum of history and of war, the pendulum of politics and
of diplomacy time and time again swung past the Balkan Peninsula
from one extreme to another. With such an environment one would
find those who knew where they were going and those who did not
have a clue as to where they were going. Thus, throughout the occupation, the Albanian peasant was obliged to choose among the alternative leaderships offered to him. He could elect to become a collaborator, a follower of the pro-communist resistance forces of Enver Hoxha,
or he could join Abas Kupi's Legalititi Movement and be a strong
supporter of King Zog. His final two choices consisted of joining the
ranks of Balli Kombetar and becoming a Social Democrat or seeking
and adhering to a policy of non-involvement. Individually, he was
unaware that these alternatives were not exhaustive and only dimly
aware that they were mutually exclusive. However, what must be recognized and accepted is the fact that he could have joined the movement that was dominated by the communist though he was not communist; he might easily have joined the German sponsored Skanderbeg

---

7. Gabriel Kolko, *The Politics of War – The World and United St Foreign Policy,
1943-1945* (New York, Random House, 1968) pp. 371-372

Division though he was not pro-German. His fated choice did not rest in his own hands, but in the chances which put him into contact with the resistance. Throughout the war years, the Albanian's destiny was decides for him by chance and by forces over which he had no control, but which he accepted with a deep sense of resignation as expressed in the following words, "Eshtu esht skrojtur" – thus, it is written.

For the citizens of the Land of the Eagle, the quick-witted but largely uneducated peasants from Kplik, Boga and Kukes of northern Albania, to the villages of Gurri Barde and Dibra in the central highlands and southward to Vithkuq, Shengjerg and Konispol in the southern most regions of Albania, resistance meant the loss of their livelihood, the burning of their homes, the looting of their properties, the psychological and/or physical death of family members as they were deported to a forced labor camp or concentration camp. They endured it all as long as they believed the cause to be a good one, but none of which they would have inflicted upon themselves without prompting. Generally speaking, the rank and file of the guerrilla movement in Albania included the indigenous peasantry; the leadership and the guidelines were provided from elsewhere either directly or indirectly. Furthermore, in the Land of the Eagle, politics are to a greater degree then people realize, the national pastime. Given this variable, when combined with a person's quick wit and emotionally motivated series of stubborn judgments, one can understand and appreciate why ideological conflicts pervaded Albanian society and became a barrier to compromise. Thus, the political opposition could be swept aside, absorbed, neutralized, and totally shattered. The motivating force behind all decisions and actions of the pro-communist revolutionaries led by Enver Hoxha is to be found in the indisputable fact that the conflict was viewed not as a war between national groups, but one between ideologies. Anyone who was not either with or a supporter of the National Army of Liberation was viewed ipso facto as a traitor to one's country and its people.

The task confronting the young, dedicated, professional revolutionaries of the Albania of the war years was to create an Albanian state regardless of its ideological foundation. Those who were involved in the tri-dimensional struggle for Albania's political soul had to give it stability, the required cohesion and self-respect that characterizes an independent state. Without such elements within its emerging body politik, the Land of the Eagle-Albania could not be a state in the twen-

tieth century European meaning of the term. Albania had to enter 20th
century Europe first and until this took place, the government remained
no more that King Zog's toy. Given the political realities which confronted the communist revolutionaries of yesteryear, Enver Hoxha
sought to achieve for his country in a few years what had taken Europe several centuries. Thus, at this critical time, he may be compared
to the doctor whose only cure for a headache was decapitation.

As the multitude of German mechanized military units and infantry formations shattered and crushed the opposing military of the nations of Southeastern Europe, a type of stunned paralysis descended
upon the enemy occupied countries of Albania, Yugoslavia and Greece.
Despite the catastrophe and the sting of defeat, the initial sense of
lethargy, together with the feeling that the war was over and that Germany had truly won the war, began to evaporates as the people of the
Balkans began to react to the indignities and the abuses bestowed upon
them by the occupation forces. One must recall that once the German
forces had established themselves in vital areas, partitioned certain
geo-political regions to their allies, with the exception of the Land of
the South Slavs-Yugoslavia, the responsibility for occupation and pacification fell to the Italian military.

Despite such, there began by 1942, to evolve a gradual and an emerging attitudinal transformation, a by-product of an age-old tradition of
guerrilla warfare against their neighbors and 500 years of Ottoman
rule and oppression whose vivid memories were deeply ingrained in
the psyche of every man, woman and child as a result of the oral tradition. In addition, this attitudinal transformation, from a deep sense of
lethargy to revolutionary confrontation, was reinforced by old patriotic ballards such as those sung in the liberation struggle against the
Turk, as well as tales of daring by members of one's family. Yet, what
must not be forgotten is that when they retreated in defeat before Hitler's Teutonic Knights and Mussolini's Roman Legions, they kept their
weapons on their journey home. However, the most important motivating factor is to be found in the fact that they had previously defeated the Italians in the early part of 1941. Now, Italians were strut-
ting through the streets of the towns and villages from Riyeka and
Cetinje in Yugoslavia to Shkodra, Korce and Saranda in Albania, and
Patra to Athens in Greece, while seeking to lord it over the proud and
defiant Serb, Montenegrin, Albanian, and Greek.

Given the emergence of a resistance-prone attitude, it is under-standable that the people of Yugoslavia, Albania and Greece would come to the conclusion that having defeated the Roman Legions of Benito Mussolini in the initial days of 1941, the same would reoccur in 1942. Yes, war did bring about a rapid disintegration and defeat of military formations of Yugoslavia, Albania and Greece in a limited number of days. Yet, one must be aware of the significant variable for it also brought liberty to the anti-government intellectuals, liberals, social democrats and communist inmates who in the general confu-sion were turned free following the invasion. Thus, such dedicated, professional, revolutionaries as Athanasios Klaras – "Ares" – a name one associates with the Greek god of war, was able to gain his free-dom following his arrest by Metaxas and escape to the Pindus moun-tains to for a major resistance force. Such men were destined to play a major role in the subsequent political events and history of the nations in the southwestern region of the Balkan peninsula.

The capitulation of Yugoslav military was to result in 200,000 Ser-bian officers and men becoming prisoners of war in Germany. As Nazi Panzer units with proper support forces swept across the fertile plain towards Belgrade, whose strategic position at the confluence of the Sava and Danube rivers has made it a vital military objective since ancient time, the followers of Ante Pavelic's Croatians engaged in the massive killing process of Serbian men, women and children – all members of Eastern Orthodox faith – as a Catholic pries witnessed the bloodbath before him. As stated earlier, the Croats were determined to "convert one third, expel one third, and to kill off one third" of the Serbian Orthodox population. So great was the slaughter of the inno-cent that Walter R. Roberts, the author of *Tito, Mihailovic and the Allies, 1941-1945*, writes:

> *The danger existed that the Serbs, the most numerous nation-ality, might become a minority in a Yugoslavia of the future.*[8]

With the benefit of political hindsight, it does appear that the in-habitants of the southwestern tier of the Balkan peninsula were con-fronted with a negative situation in which the extreme totalitarian Right was determined to apply the totality of its political power and its mili-

---

8. Gabriel Kolko, *Ibid* p. 371

tary strength in order to crush freedom at the same time that the young resistance warrior of the political Left, with the red star on his cap, sought to use it as a simultaneous liberating and restructuring force dedicated to the establishment of a Marxist-Leninist sphere of dominance. In symbolic terms, it does appear as if the God of War, Mars, confronted man in the form of Prometheus, who stole the fire from heaven and gave it to man and then was condemned to a horrible ordeal, for he, like the resistance fighter, refused to surrender his right to assist his fellow man in the battle for his nation's soul.

As Albania, together with the people of the Land of the South Slavs and Hellas, found themselves once again in a potential self-destructive, turbulent, political period, it was easy to fall into the spirit of the times. Their attraction to Communism, while the Land of the Eagle was under the totalitarian hell of Italian occupation forces, was to be found in the fact that the communists were the only effective fighting force. In addition, from an ideological perspective at this critical time, the communists offered nothing and demanded everything of one who was willing to engage the enemy in the War of National Liberation.

If hope is life reborn as one stands defenseless before the idea of death which pervades the nation, then one is condemned to silence. Yet, the resistant man confronted by this negativistic environment of despair, found that he lived with hope as he engaged in an act of rebirth and nobility. That the Italo-Germanic occupation of the Land of the South Slavs-Yugoslavia, the Land of the Eagle-Albania and Hellas-Greece brought with it a condemnation of silence, loneliness, disease and death can not be denied. Yes, they told lies in the presence of death for death had become the national backdrop whose black color was yet to fade Yet, the young men and women of Albania, Yugoslavia and Greece were engulfed by an immense solitude that was an integral part of the occupation. As their world of yesteryear melted away, taking with it its illusion, one sought to recall one's past life as he or she brought forth one's private sorrows, secret desires and happier days as they looked their destiny straight in the eye. Of this destiny, the individual finds that he or she is truly to one's self alone and a prisoner of one's negativistic anxiety-producing images. After spending endless hours in silence and solitude, he removed from within himself the death of one's soul and became an active participant within the resistance movement.

CHAPTER TEN

THE LION AND THE EAGLE

The year was 1943. In this wartime world of violence, death and absurdity, four individual members of Special Operations Executive boarded a solitary Royal Halifax bomber at the military airport at Dryna, Libya, commanded by Wing Commander Blackburn for a three hour flight to northern Greece.[1] The S.O.E. force aboard this flight included Major N.L.D. (Billy) McLean of the Royal Scots Greys, an officer with prior service in the Near East leading irregular forces in Abyssinia. One would also find Captain David Smiley of the Royal Horse Guards, who had also served in the Near East as the head of a commando unit behind Italian lines in Abyssinia.[2] In addition to the two officers, personnel included Garry Duffy, a Royal Engineer Lieutenant, who possessed an expertise in mines and demolition. The last remaining member of the group was Corporal Williamson, the wireless operator and a member of a Blackwatch Regiment. Following their journey from North Africa, they, who had parachuted in the late evening hours of April 17th into the wild mountainous and primitive region of Epirus, began their Illyrian venture. Of this initial experience, Major McLean stated:

I found the operational jump one of the most pleasant than the five training jumps...Like nearly everything one is anxious or worried about, it is much less bad than one's idea of it. This, of course, is also true of the good things one hopes to happen; they also almost always fall short of one's expectations of desires. Possibly only boredom and hate, illness and bad temper,

1. Nicholas J. Costa, *Albania: A European Enigma* (New York, East European Monographs, 1995) pp. 53-55
2. David Smiley, *Albanian Assignment* (London, Chatto and Windus, 1984)

quarrels and unsuccessful human relations are worst than one imagines.[3]

As England sought (in the words of Sir Winston Churchill, Great Britain's wartime Prime Minister) to set "Europe Ablaze" by encouraging the establishment and the growth of resistance movements throughout occupied Europe, she had first (in the words of Major General Sir Colin Gubbins, the head of Security Office Executive) to solve the problem of transcending certain physical and psychological barriers. Of such, he is to point out that:

> *The problem and the plan was to encourage and enable the peoples of the occupied countries to harass the German and the war effort at every possible point by sabotage, subversion, go-slow practices, coup de main raids, etc., and at the same time build up secret forces therein, organized, armed and trained to take their part only when the final assault begins... In its simplest terms this plan involved ultimate delivery to occupied territory of large numbers of personnel and quantities of arms and explosives. But the first problem was to make contact with those countries; to get information of the possibilities, to find out the prospects of getting local help, and an even more immediate task was to find someone suitable and willing to undertake the first hazardous trip, then train him and fit him for the job and ensure communications with him when he landed. But all contacts with occupied territories were closed when the last British forces returned to Great Britain in 1940, so the first man to go back to any country had to parachute "blind" as we say, i.e., there was no one waiting to receive him on the dropping ground, no household ready to give him shelter, conceal his kit and arrange his onward passage.*[4]

The unfolding of the Albanian drama following the arrival of Major McLean's Consensus I mission from the disputed Epirus region of the northern reaches of Greece, was to result in the minds of the Alba-

---

3. Xan Fielding, *One Man In His Time* (London, Macmillian Limited, 1990) p. 34
4. Nicholas J. Costa, *Albania: A European Enigma* (New York, Columbia University Press, 1995) p. 52

nians in their adherence to the traditional suspicion that "the British had come to raise Greek bands on Albanian soil". This negative attitudinal predisposition of the people of the "Land of the Eagle" may be attributed to the historical and political injustices of the past. As the clouds of distrustfulness began to dissipate, the Albanian people with its partisan formations, following their initial meeting with their Central Council in June, 1943 at Labinot, had agreed to discuss certain questions which not only reduced the high degree of anxiety among the Albanian leadership, but it also served, in the words of Major McLean, to result "in a proper working arrangement with the Partisans under the command of Enger Hoxha".[5] However, when attempting to establish a series of political and military understandings with the representatives of Balli Kombetar or the Nationalist Central Council, their efforts were to produce, according to Captain Smiley, "unsatisfactory results".[6] Yet, as they journeyed with partisan units and held talks with various commanders, both Major McLean and Captain Smiley became aware of the undeniable fact that the sons and the daughters of Skanderbeg had come to accept the fact that they could only conquer the sword by the sword. This attitudinal transformation may be attributed to the fact that individuals who were one day only interested in the occupation policies and practices of the collaborationist pro-Fascist government, became committed activists taking risks as the war progressed.

Furthermore, during the Italo-German occupation of Albania, there did evolve among the Shqiptars a growing awareness that it was as dangerous not to be in the resistance as to be a resistant, for they knew that one could be killed, taken away to a concentration camp or to a forced labor institution or be tortured just as well as a collaborator or an anti-Fascist activist. It is this awareness, together with the reprisal raids undertaken by the Italian and German units, which resulted in the youth of Albania joining the pro-communist guerrilla forces without being themselves followers of Marx and Lenin. Such an action-reaction cycle was to result in Major McLean's assessment that the pro-communist forces were:

5. Great Britain, Public Records Office, War Office File No. 204/94 "Memorandum On Albania"
6. David Smiley, Personal Interview, London, England, July, 1979

*The strongest and by far the best organized group in Alba-
nia as a whole, which had the largest number of both regular
and mobile troops and was the only party which was active
against the Axis.[7]*

It must be noted that England's interest in Albania, together with
probable policy adoptions prior to the first 1943 arrival of the Special
Operations Executive mission, was not limited to military matters alone.
Without necessarily wishing to stir up polemics as related to the evolving tri-angular diplomatic affair, it must be noted that the prime deter-
minant for the formulation of London's policy as pertained to its interest in Albania, was the "Land of Hellas" – Greece. An analysis of the
primary sources of the informative transference of significant data between Athens and London makes one aware of the dominant role of
Greece. Furthermore, in this important, political environment, it becomes obvious that the government of Greece became involved in a
denial of morality and history. The Greek government of Mr. Koryzis,
following the death of General Metaxas, was a prisoner of its own
historical legacy and its prejudices. On being informed of Section "D"
and MI (R) plans to foment an uprising of the Kosovars on behalf of
the situation in Albania, who together with the northern Albanian tribes,
would assist in bringing about the deciding moment as Italian forces
found themselves in a precarious military deployment at and around
the Albanian port of Vlore, the government of Greece reacted in a
negative manner. At this crucial moment, it was the desire of the government of Great Britain, following suggestions by Sir Julian Amery,
the head of the Albanian division in "D" Section in Belgrade, that
King Zog be brought into the operation, not as a direct or active participant, but as a motivating force and as a means of acquiring unity
and total support of the exiled Albanian community in Istanbul.

Following a series of communications between Athens and London, one can find the following note date 1 March 1941, submitted by
Deputy Under Secretary of State, Sir Orme Sargent:

*We have now received a further telegram from Athens No.
277, which makes is as opposed as ever to our suggestions, i.e.,
that we should give encouragement and publicity to King Zog*

---

7. Great Britain. Public Records Office, War Office File No. 204/9461 XIJ-928 p. 5

and that H.M. Government should make a declaration about Albania... in as much as we obviously cannot in this manner run counter to the Greek Government's wishes, I am sure that the right thing to do is to drop both ideas. As a matter of fact, the chances of our being able to launch an Albanian Movement are decreasing rather than improving. Such a rising is really only feasible as part of a successful Greek offensive in Albania, and the prospects of such an offensive are certainly rapidly declining.

It is to my mind quite inconceivable that we should be able to get the Albanians to rise at a time when the Greek were on the defensive or in retreat.[8]

The true sentiments of the Government of Greece, in relation to the Albanian people were expressed on a radio broadcast on June 22, 1941. It was at this time that the President of the Council of Ministers of the Greek Government in exile, identified the Albanians as being no more than "semi-savages". In addition, Mr. Tsouderous set aside the fact that during the Italian invasion of Greece on October 28, 1940, many Albanian military units who participated in the invasion force turned their weapons on the Italians and fought along the side of the Greek military. Yet, in spite of this action, the representatives of the Government of Greece continued to identify the Albanians in negative terms and describe them as being "... unmentionable followers of Italy".[9] Shortly thereafter, Mr. Tsouderous forwarded a Greek claim to the territory in which the two major cities of southern Albania existed – Korce and Gjirokaster – together with certain communities within the southern region of the Vlore Administrative District of Albania. It is this land, an integral part of Albania, which Athens has identified as "Northern Epirus".

Aware of their national heritage of resistance, the negativistic qualities of the occupation, together with King Zog's authoritarian reign with its totalitarian potential and dictatorial proclivities, let alone the pre-war corruption which pervaded Albanian society, they, the young men and women who proudly wore the Red Star with its accompany-

---

8. Reginald Hibbert, *Albania's National Liberation Struggle: The Bitter Victory* (London. Pinter Publishers, 1991) p. 32
9. Reginald Hibbert, *Ibid* p. 33

ing slogan, "Dekje Fashizmit-Liri Popullit" (Death to Fascism – Liberty to the people), continued to confront the invader and his native allies in irregular warfare. These young men, women and students were determined to change their beloved country so that what once was, would never again be. Thus, the partisans of Enver Hoxha, acknowledging the advantages of entering into liaison with the representatives of H.M. Government, became willing but cautions allies of the British Military Missions. Such caution was evident because of their pro-communist orientation and also because of England's failure to declare itself on the future status of King Zog and the sanctity of Albanian as a nation-state and its southern borders.

As one reflects upon the BLO's and their representative mission activities in this unfamiliar and complex land with its tribal and ideological divisions, such men as Major Simcox, Tilman, Quayle, Kemp. Palmer, Hibbert, Tony Neel and many other members of SOE who served in the "Land of the Eagle" along with Major McLean, Smiley, Amery, Brigadier General Davies and Lt. Colonel Arthur Nicholls, were able to accomplish much in the face of insurmountable odds. Of such men who gave of themselves, one cannot but recall the following lines from *Medea*, for it does apply to the men of Special Operations Executive:

> *You sailed away from your father's dwelling,*
> *With your heart on fire Medea!*
> *And you passed*
> *Between the rocky gates of the seas;*
> *And now you sleep on a foreign shore.*

While involved in Albanian affairs through the activities of Special Operations Executive, the Government of Great Britain and the officers and men sought vainly to subordinate their political considerations (with the exception of Greece) to the military demands of war. Yet, according to Major Anthony Quayle in his book entitled *Eight Hours From England*, men engaged in field operations would react in the following manner:

> *An officer attached to the Partisans was very apt to regard the Balli as a gang of neo-Fascist; the officer with Balli saw the*

Partisans as nothing but cunning and bloody agents of World Bolshevism.[10]

Yet, in spite of their own preferences, the men of Special Operations Executive sought to establish a united national resistance movement throughout the Land of the Eagle. In a most frustrating and anxiety prone political environment, the men of SOE sought to bring together Enver Hoxha's pro-communist partisans, the republic and anti-communist forces of Balli Kombetar, the royalist pro-Zogist movement of Legalitati under the leadership of Abas Kupi, the various clans in the greater Peshkopi-Dibra region and Gani and Said Kryeziu's Kosovars. What was desired was not to be, for an analysis of the political agenda of each group reveals the following:

> *The intricate relationships which particularized the structure of the resistance movement directly contributed to the inability of the British to achieve their objective. Whereas Balli Kombetar, which proclaimed itself to be republican and liberal, could not accept on ideological grounds the pro-monarchist philosophy of Abas Kupi and vice versa, neither could the two accept the revolutionary goals and the discipline as required by the followers of Marx and Lenin as personified by Enver Hoxha. Nor could the leadership of the pro-communist forces establish the basis for a policy of sincere unity with the supporters of Gani and Said Kryeziu who were engaging the occupation forces in the Kossovo-Methohija region of the German-Italian created "Greater Albanian Ethnic State". The Kossovars' adherence to the concept of an Ethnic Albania placed them at odds with Enver Hoxha's pro-communist resistance movement, and pro-Yugoslav Kosmet Partisans of Fadil Hoxha who were a part of the overall Yugoslav resistance movement led by Joseph Broz-Tito, and in the final analysis, the overall geo-political policy as it related to the Allied policy in the Balkans.*[11]

---

10. Anthony Quayle, *Eight Hours From England* (New York, Doubleday and Company, Inc. 1946) p. 34

11. Nicholas J. Costa, *Op. Cit.* p. 59-60

Such political orientations of each group, together with their respective hidden agendas, when combined with each unit's sense of distrustfulness, served to evolve a frustrating and tension-ridden environment as the members of SOE struggled against all odds to establish a united national resistance movement centrally directed and totally supplied by the Anglo-American command in Italy.

One must recall, as one reflects upon the men of Special Operation Executive, that they entered the Balkans and the Land of the Eagle as representatives of a sane and rational world. They evolved from a socio-political environment in which one was comfortable, for they possessed a total awareness of the folkways, mores and laws of their socio-political structure together with its nuancies, myths and traditions. Thus, day-in and day-out, they were consistently confronted with a predictable behavioral pattern. however, as they entered the socio-political environment of Albania and of the Balkan Peninsula with their minuscule degree of knowledge and lack of understanding of the customs and traditions of the people with their unwritten laws, they found themselves in an alien world confronted by people "from a different planet". Thus, many had to revert to the American equivalent of the "law of the jungle" and in so doing, they had to do violence to one's own traditional principles in order to survive and achieve the mission's objectives.

The realities of the ideological conflict which was ever present were not acknowledged overtly and could not be removed from the minds of the participants in this Albanian Danse Macabre by a couple of glasses of raki, a plate of goat's cheese and olives, together with a loaf of bread and a cup of Turkish coffee. Both Major McLean and Captain Smiley were aware of the probability that Enver Hoxha's National Liberation Army (LNC) could not be contained and that with each passing day, it was emerging as the dominant military and political power in Albania. This actuality may be ascribed to the fact that "they were consistently involved in fighting the Germans", according to Major McLean. When in London at his home a number of years ago, I raised the question, "Why did you and Consensus II place all your faith in Abas Kupi?" His reply was both simple and straightforward, "That was the only card in the deck left to us... what could we do to forestall a Communist victory without a direct invasion of Albania by Anglo-American forces?"[12]

The dominant position of His Majesty's Government in the Land of the Eagle-Albania; the Kingdom of Serbs, Croats and Slovenes-Yugoslavia; and Hellas-Greece, at this historical moment can be traced back to President Roosevelt and his staff's collective belief that the Balkans were not a proper sphere of United States' concerns. This region had been traditionally a British area of concern and involvement. This was later confirmed at the Casablanca Conference in January 1943, which first acknowledged and then fully proceeded to accept the historical fact that the eastern Mediterranean was an area of primary British interest and activity. Since the days of Queen Elizabeth and the Elizabethan Seadogs of the 16th century, the British have always been a nation of political realists while the Americans, on the other hand, have tended to oppose the use of full military power against European resistance movements. The British had no such reluctance. One need only recall that in September and October 1944, British military forces confronted the communist military arm of ELAS – The Greek Peoples Liberation Army – in the streets of Athens to prevent a communist takeover of the government of Greece.

In addition, one must also be aware that Field Marshal Alexander indicated that if required, he was ready and willing to apply the full power of the Anglo-American forces in Italy to remove Free French forces from northern Italy and Tito's Yugoslav partisans out of the port city of Trieste if ordered to take over all of Venezia Giulia. Washington's visceral reaction to the April crisis was that America refused to face and accept the political reality that potential post-war problems could be resolved with the correct show of military power within the protracted military environment.

The years, 1943 and 1944, were times of hope and difficulties. In Tirana, a woman was asked by a German officer to choose which of her three sons taken as hostages should be spared; she chose the eldest, thereby condemning the two others as the German officer had intended. In Yugoslavia, a family sought to save one remaining son by placing him alive in a coffin with proper ventilation as they journeyed

---

12. Major NLD "Billy" McLean Personal Interview London, England June, 1975

home. Tragically, they ran into a patrol who, following a series of questions by a partisan officer, permitted the group to pass. However, before the partisan unit departed from this chance meeting, they were ordered to fire their weapons at the casket. Their son was a member of this very unit who were looking for him. The commander of the unit, upon completing his task, now turned to the parents and said, "Now you may take your son home". In Greece, a young wife, while hiding in a cave with her baby during a "Death Squad" sweep of her village, held her infant tightly to her breast so the child's crying wouldn't alert the population of Greece began their individual descent into Hell. Such incidents should not shock one for in occupied Albania, Greece and Yugoslavia, under the totalitarian Nazi and Fascist occupation, one would find only murders of the innocent, executions and death, death, death. Although man is the main playmaker in the creation of history, he remains for all times the captive of history.

The facts of existence confronting Major McLean and all the members of SOE demonstrate that not only were they involved in confronting the occupation forces with a native reactionary movement, but they were drawn into the process of consensus building. After all, one must recall that they were consistently involved in a frustrating and anxiety-producing process that was riddled with mistrust and native deviousness. To bring together, in spite of their ideological differences and hidden agendas, the various adversaries who found themselves within a civil war environment, required a miracle and miracles were not to be found in wartime Albania. In spite of the odds confronting them, certain degrees of progress were achieved. The objective was to engage the enemy – to kill Germans and Italians wherever one found them. Thus, one finds Major Anthony Quayle's involvement in the following exchange with the leadership of the Fifth Brigade in the village of Gjormi in 1944.

> *Besnik's first request was no modest one. "I want 700 rifles." ... "What priority do you want given to food and clothes?" Again the smile, this time with a trace of bitterness.*
>
> *"You have seen for yourself what we look like. We have no coats, and the snow will soon be here; but arms and ammunition are our greatest need. Do not send food and clothing at the*

*expense of ammunition. If we have arms we can still fight –
even if we are a little cold and hungry; but we cannot kill Nazis
with blankets and tins of meat."*

As he was leaving he turned in the doorway.

*"You must excuse any hot words that have been spoken. Our
need is very great."*

*He took a step back into the room towards me. "There is a
reason why I do not think that you will fail us", he said quietly.
"It is because you, too, are young – and the young do not fail
each other."[13]*

According to Lord Byron, the Albanian is "faithful in peril, and
indefatigable in service". Major H.W. Tilman further states, "Albanians, like Irishmen, seem to have a natural genius for fighting and gen-
eralship".[14] Thus, from the ashes of the numerous burned out villages
and out of the negative excesses of the occupation forces and their
native allies, there began, according to Major Tilman, to coalesce within
the LNC, even prior to the Peza Conference, the desire to establish:

*A free democratic independent Albania, and they were con-
vinced that they alone could realize these aims.[15]*

This desire among the leadership and within the ranks of many
who were serving in the military arm of the LNC had made this common knowledge among the general population even prior to the Permet
Congress in 1944.

The first Anti-Fascist National Liberation Congress was held in
the town of Permet from May 24th to the 28th, 1944. The decision
agreed to at this meeting not only established the Anti-Fascist National Liberation Council (ANLC) as the major political body in the
sphere of the legislative and executive branches of government, but
rendered to it a greater degree of power than met the eye. Furthermore, it undertook legislative action that barred the return of King
Zog and proceeded to declare invalid any and all illegally established

---

13. Anthony Quayle, *Op. Cit.* pp. 67-68
14. H.W. Tilman, *When Men and Mountains Meet* (London, Cambridge University
Press, 1946) p. 113
15. H.W. Tilman, *Ibid* pp. 152-153

Albanian governments – with the execution of the government established by the representatives at the Permet Congress, be such established within Albania proper or outside of the country. In addition, it moved to annul all of the political and economic agreements entered into with foreign nation-states and enterprises by the previous government. It must be noted that this decision to subject past agreements to a review process was to result in the evolution of a barrier to the establishment of normal relations between the Tirana government and the government of the United States of America and of Great Britain.[16]

Those caught in the vortex of the civil war and the escalation of violence appeared to justify the means to their ends. One cannot but recall that those involved were so much alike while on opposing sides. They, the sons and the daughters of Skanderbeg, sprung from the same basic cultural environment while possessing the same cultural ethos of traditionally oriented past. They shared the same hopes and also possessed a love for the Land of the Eagle which in turn united them as brothers. In their own way, they knew that they were not truly each other's enemy. Tragically, the mythical Gods on Mount Olympus, who were the playmakers in this Albanian Danse Macabre, condemned each to suffer and die together for the sake of an ideological dream and a foreign Marxist-Leninist God. The rapidly deteriorating, internal, political situation in the Land of the Eagle caught the various members of the numerous Special Operation teams in an all-out Civil War for the political soul of Albania – between the forces of Balli Kombetar and the supporters of Enver Hoxha.

As the situation continued to go from bad to worse, the American representative of the Office of Strategic Services and those of Special Executive came to the same identical conclusion. On December 23, 1943, the following assessment was forwarded to command headquarters.

... The Balkans have shied from fighting either Italians or Germans. Their principle policy in their early days has been, "Let the Allies do our fighting for us". Now that the LNC has strengthened its position to a point where it looks as though it stands a fair chance of dominating the country at the end of the

---

16. H.W. Tilman, *History of the Party of Labor* (Tirana, Institute of Marxist-Leninist Studies, 1969) pp. 268-276

*war, the Balkans are becoming skittish and call in the Germans
to do their fighting for them in an attempt to wipe out the LNC
without doing any fighting themselves. Whatever happens, it
looks as though the Gentlemen Ballista, as they are called by
LNC, are determined to do no honest-to-goodness fighting. They
will do some refined sniping, and fancy assassinations, prob-
ably, and some folks will call it civil war, but they are not going
to stand up and fight. At least all the signs point that way.*[17]

The tangible wind of death which now swept across the Land of the
Eagle was the wind of civil war. A dispute over perspectives; a clash of
ideologies. Whatever the sources of the differences of the two groups,
the fundamental issue revolved around the question relating as to when
to engage the conquerors of Albania. In a submitted file #50400 entitled "Guerrilla Warfare and the Development of Balli Kombetar and
the LNC" dated 1943, the following imagery is presented.

B.K. says in effect, "Let us organize now but fight later".

Or as an additional report put it,

"We will go into action when the British land at Durazzo."

L.N.C. said in effect,

*"Let us organize now and fight now. Let us keep on fighting
as long as there is an Axis soldier on Albanian soil."*

Balli Kombetar said,

*"Let us organize now, do no fighting but husband our strength
for a supreme effort later. Fighting involves reprisals and reprisals deplete our resources in both men and materials."*

L.N.C. said,

*"We are organizing and we are fighting. The strength of our
organization increases gradually as we gain experience in organizing and in fighting. We strengthen our unity and build up*

---

17. National Archives, Office of Strategic Services File "Analysis of Balli Kombetar"
File No. 53011, Report No. J-133 p. 2 December 25,1943

a strong force which will be toughened for the final effort at the time of the landing of the Allied Armies."

L.N.C. said,

"Let us lay aside all factional differences whatever these may be, political, religious or regional and get together for the liberation of Albania. When that is accomplished, we can work out among ourselves a settlement of our internal problems.

Balli Kombetar stated,

"Let us lay aside all factional differences except that one pertaining to the return of the monarchy; unite under the banner of Balli Kombetar for the liberation of our country and when that has been accomplished, let the people decide under conditions that will assure no return of the monarchy."

Give the exchange and the represented clash of views as presented in the United States' document, one cannot help but draw the conclusion that was stated by Major Hibbert:

Hoxha's conclusion was that the emphasis must be put on conducting the armed struggle against the occupying power: this would oblige the Balli Kombetar "nationalists" either to make common cause with the LNC or to discredit themselves as collaborators with the enemy.[18]

As the members of Special Operations Executive grappled with the real and imaginary barriers to the creation of a national resistance movement, it must be noted that:

To any young Albanian who hated the Fascist Italians or the Nazi Germans, the LNC was the only organization which offered him the opportunity to fight for his country. Thus, the "Communists" have become associated in the minds of the Albanians with the struggle for national liberation.[19]

---

18. Reginald Hibbert, *Op. Cit.* p. 21
19. Major NLD "Billy" MacLean, *Op. Cit.* p. 11

Thus, by 1943, the battle for the "hearts and minds" of the people had already been won by the followers of Marx and Lenin. While it is true that the LNC and Balli Kombetar emerged on the political stage at the same time, one must accept the fact that as an effective, well organized military force, Balli Kombetar was out of its league and left much to be desired, for "it was a negative organization" according to Major McLean.[20]

When on 24 October 1943, Major McLean and Captain Smiley were evacuated from "Sea View" following the arrival at the Biza encampment of Brigadier "Trotsky" Davis, their departure from the Land of the Eagle in a collapsible type rubber dingy left much to be desired. Of this memorable parting, Captain Smiley stated:

Both officers (Sandy Glenn and an American OSS officer) had come to stay and we were delighted to see them; but our pleasure was considerably dampened when they told us that the boat, which was of the collapsible rubber type, had a large hole in its bottom and was leaking so badly that it could not possibly get us back to the MTB. McLean and I were determined to go, even if it mean swimming out to the boat; but each of us had a briefcase of documents, German maps and other items of interest to Cairo. I had in addition, several rolls of films for developing and my diary. We, therefore, decided to block the hole in the boat with a blanket and try to reach the MTB.

Shaking hands with numerous people who had come down to see us off, we were successfully launched against the swell. While I rowed as hard as I could, McLean bailed furiously. It was proving to be a losing battle for the boat was clearly filling with water quicker that McLean could bail; but we were now nearing the MTB. We reached it and flung our briefcases up onto the deck just as the small boat sank; McLean and I were only swimming for a matter of seconds before helping hands dragged us out of the water. We were hauled aboard to find that the officer in command of the boat was an old acquaintance, Lieutenant Davis Scott.[21]

20. Major NLD "Billy" MacLean, *Ibid* p. 15
21. David Smiley, *Op. Cit.* p. 96

As the two desperately sought to reach the MTB, which best can only be described as a tragi-comic scene, one cannot help but wonder if this ordeal was not in its unique way, representative of a foreshadowing of what was yet to come?

On April 20, 1944, in the geo-political region controlled by Abas Kupi and his Legalitite, pro-Zogist political party, the men of Consensus II arrived at Bixha, which is located northeast of Tirana. The Consensus II mission personnel consisted of Major McLean, Major Smiley and Captain Julian Amery, formerly of "D" Section in Belgrade, Yugoslavia, and associated with the Oakley-Hill, ill-fated intrusion into Albania in 1940. Their objective was to establish contact among the northern clans and the partisan leadership headed by Enver Hoxha to form a national and unified resistance movement against the occupation forces of Nazi Germany – and to prevent a civil war from breaking out. Yet, it must be noted and accepted that in the struggle for total political power, the quest for reconciliation between Abas Kupi and the pro-communist forces of Enver Hoxha in 1944 was not only unlikely, but also an elusive and an unachievable goal.

In the region of Ghegheria, which is located north of the Shkumbi River, its conservative and patrilineal oriented and tradition-directed people who were involved in the wartime inter-play between their tribal psycho-social, political structure and the degree of resistance to the occupation force, made it absolutely clear that to be successful in any military venture against the enemy, the resistance movement had to provide more than adequate or temporary protection for the inhabitants of the region against reprisals. Failure to meet this unwritten law automatically would result in the people's withdrawal of their support to the clan's leadership. Their past traditions and experiences had made them aware of the fact that, given the socio-political structure in place among the multitude of tribes with flags in northern Albania, it was virtually impossible to withdraw with one's total military force into the territory of another. Of this traditional reality, Major McLean stated:

It must be realized that since the failure of such a rising would place the whole structure of society in jeopardy, the Nationalist leaders are only likely to attempt it if the prospects of

success are good, or if expectations of long term benefits, or
personal remuneration seem to them to justify the risks.[22]

The major clan chieftains in the tragic drama which was to take place in northern Albania, in addition to Abas Kupi, were the leaders of the Dibra League: Muharrem Bajraktar, Gani Kreziu and his brother, Said Kreziu. There also existed in Mirdita, Gjon Markogjoni, the leader of the Catholic clans with a major force. Altogether, this aggregation was representative of a potential hard-core strike-force of 15,000 rifles. As the officers and the men of Consensus II Mission sought to bring into being unity among the various clans, the final assault on Hitler's "1,000 Year Reich or Fortress Europea" had begun. On June 6, 1944, Anglo-American armies landed in Normandy at Gold, Sword and Juno beaches while the Americans – having fought their way off the beaches at Utah and Omaha – now began their push inland. Fascist Italy, having previously removed Benito Mussolini from power and having withdrawn from the war only to see it occupied by the German military, was to bear witness to the fall of Rome on June 4, 1944, to Anglo-American forces.

On the Eastern Front – from the Baltic to the Black Sea – the Red Army of the Union of Soviet Socialist Republics, Russia, had swept the German Wehrmach from the soil of "Mother Russia, Holy Russia" beyond the Cuzon Line and into eastern Poland. In the Pacific Theater of Operations, the US. Marines in the middle of June, 1944, had stormed the beaches of an island only 1,350 miles from Tokyo. The name of the island was Saipan. The American drive across the Pacific continued as Guam was liberated and General Douglas McArthur's military forces invaded the Philippine Islands at the Gulf of Leyte on 20 October 1944. An image of a Japanese Empire in twilight began to emerge as American forces continued with their push across the Pacific to Tokyo Harbor.

In the Land of the Eagle in 1944, the distribution of both military and political power was to become an important variable in the determination of not only the success or the failure of the Consensus II

---

22. Great Britain, Public Records Office "Report On Consensus II Mission" November 28, 19

Mission, but also in the verdict as it related to Albania's future political status in the post-war world. Until their withdrawal from Albania in 1944, the German occupation force was the major military power in the country. Also, the various northern clans were riddled with a high degree of disunity and distrust of one another. The legacy of the past with its Gjarkemare-blood feuds, while possessing the potential for becoming a determining factor in the political end-game, never truly did evolve to a point where it reached its potential. At this moment, the only group which started out as a rag-tale, rabble-in-arms and by 1944, became the only national political player on the field of battle that possessed the determination to sweep the field clean of all opponents, was that which consisted of the followers of Marx and Lenin.

However, there did exist in the newly acquired Albanian populated region of Kossovo, a unit commanded by Gani Kryeziu and his brother, Said Kryeziu, which first proved its dedication to the western Allies in 1940. These two brothers, who were anti-Zog as well as anti-Italian and anti-German up to 1944, followed British policy with more consistency and understanding than any other Albanian force. Furthermore, beyond their willingness to meet and confront the enemy at any time and at any place, they, as Albanians, sought the incorporation of all Albanian regions in Kossovo and Macedonia into the Albanian nation-state. Of the remaining clans of northern Albania, the pro-zogist tribe led by Nik Sokol in the Scutari and Maltsia e Madhe region of Catholic Albania was of minimal political and military significance. However, on the flip side of the coin, one finds Captain Gjon Marko Gjoni with a potential force in readiness of over 3,000 rifles. While Catholic and pro-Zogist in his political orientation, it must be noted that, according to Colonel Smiley, "He would not join us until he saw the color of British gold".

With the primary political objective of all consisting only of acquiring total control of the government of Albania, together with establishing it jurisdiction over all of the levers of civic power, it became obvious to McLean, Smiley and Amery that in 1944, Albania stood on the very edge of the bottomless pit of civil war. With the surrender of Italian military power in the Land of the Eagle, all contending parties began to focus upon that which was consistently upon their minds... post-war civic concerns. Of this transformation, Major McLean's "Report on Consensus II" calls to one's attention the following:

> *It was in fact clear that there was no hope of establishing compromise between the two parties unless we were prepared to exert sufficient pressure to force them into agreement as we have done in the case of General Zervas and the Greek EAM... If, however, we were not prepared to apply the necessary pressure for bringing about such an agreement, then it is doubtful whether as late as 1944 there was real advantage to be gained by keeping missions with both sides.*[23]

Given the intelligence network existing within the ranks of the various BLO units attached to all parties, one can only come to the conclusion that the leadership of the Albanian Communist Party was aware of the "Great Game" that was being played. Thus, as one became acquainted with Enver Hoxha's *The Anglo-American Threat to Albania,* the following passage is noted:

> *As you know this game is being played in Greece in order to split the EAM and infiltrate reactionary elements into its ranks.*
>
> *... The Anglo-American Allies wanted the EAM to refrain from attacking the zones where Zervas operated because to have him as a reserve force. This is the aim of the British with Bazi i Canes here too, and in order to back up this argument, they have begun to bring out from the archives and transmit over the radio our articles which call for unity...*
>
> *They are holding Bazi in reserve for the future. We fight Kupi simply as a traitor and a collaborator of the Germans.*[24]

For some members of Special Operations Executive who served in the Land of the Eagle-Albania, the final assault against the opposition began on July 5, 1944. For others it began with the formation of the Communist Party of Albania. And yet, for others it began with the birth of an idea and this idea still exists within the Albania. On No-

---

23. Major NLD "Billy" MacLean, *Ibid* pp. 25-26
24. Enver Hoxha, *The Anglo-American Threat To Albania: Memoirs of the National Liberation War* (Tirana, The Institute of Marxist-Leninist Studies 1982) pp. 274-275

vember 28, 1944, after a series of strategic moves, counter revolutionaries as Midhat Frasheri, Vasil Andoni, Abas Ermenji and Abas Kupi departed for Italy and France to enter the world of political exile. As Consensus II Mission returned to Italy and assignments on different war fronts, Enver Hoxha took the salute of the various veteran brigades of the Albanian War of National Liberation in Tirana. No individual student of history or observer of the psycho-historical scene can deny that revolutions begin new epochs whose direction no one can foresee. There is always to be found a gap between theory and revolutionary reality and for Albania and the Albanians, the year, 1945, was to confront them with an ultra-extreme type of a monolithic, Stalinist-oriented, ideological revolution interlaced with the idealism of Albania's youthful generation.

The young men of Special Operations Executive, who first arrived in Albania, Greece and Yugoslavia in 1943, gathered intelligence and "set Europe ablaze" through the formation of national resistance movements which were born of necessity and the need to defeat the common enemy of Fascist Italy and authoritarian Nazi Germany. Throughout the conflict situation in the Land of the Hellas, there existed for the people only three options. They could have gone Right of Left into a pro status quo and anti-revolutionary bloc led by the United States of America or they could have gone into the revolutionary sphere of influence and power led by the Union of Soviet Socialist Republics. For the 3rd option, they could have opted for neutralism, for in 1945 a 3-zone divisional concept of the world did exist. Yet, it cannot be denied that the war, together with the civic leaders of the pre-war East European societies, made the advent of the political LEFT inevitable. In Greece it would be Great Britain who would determine the socio-economic and political destiny of the men and women of Hellas. However, in Yugoslavia and Albania, as Joseph Broz-Tito and Enver Hoxha acquired control of the reigns of civic power, they proceeded to establish a limited "democracy" whose limits and outcomes they and they alone would determine. One must recall that although it has been written and stated that "one can not stop an idea whose time has come", in Albania, Yugoslavia and Greece, since time immemorial, it has always been the military victory that defined local politics.

CHAPTER ELEVEN

PROMETHEUS OR CAESAR

No one can deny that the consequences of the emergence of the absolutist nihilistic trend which swept across the European landscape, together with its logic of destruction and the brutalization of man throughout the interwar period, was in part responsible for the rise of the totalitarian dictatorships. World War II's savage cycle of devastation and death, along with the transformation of the civilian population into expendable objects on the basis of military necessity and ideological requirements, may be attributed not only to the reject of the moral code of 20th century man, but also to the acceptance of the nihilistic formula. This climate of negation which was to reign supreme was to result in the 1937 obliteration of the town of Guernica by Nazi Germany's Condor Legion during the Spanish Civil War while experimenting with the concept of "Strategic Terror". Furthermore, it served to condone the issuance of a directive on September 16, 1941, which required that in all occupied regions under the command of Field Marshall Wilhelm Keitel, 50 to 100 civilian hostages were to be executed for every German soldier killed by members of the resistance be they Tito's Yugoslav partisans or Mihailovic's Cetniks, Zervas' anti-communist EDES formations or the Greek communist resistance alliance ELAS led by Sianto or Enver Hoxha's Marxist-Leninist oriented LNC formations together with the anti-communist Balli Kombetar and Legalite querilla forces in Albania which were led by Abas Ermenje and Abas Kupi.[1] Nor can one deny that the nihilistic criterion was an integral component of the ideological and revolutionary philosophy of Marxism-Leninist with its emphasis on class war-

---

1. Roberts, Walter R., *Tito, Mihailovic and the Allies, 1941-1945.* (Brunswick, New Jersey, Rutgers University Press, 1973) p. 31

fare. Yet in spite of such actions, 20th century man has also borne witness to one's struggle to secure his or her basic right to freedom, justice and the dignity of person in the face of military aberrations which have characterized that which the French intellectual Raymon Aron has identified as "The Century of Total War". Moreover, one cannot consign to the ever present historical dustbin, in the light of the events of 1989-1991 and of today's political reality, the words of Albert Camus, a former editor of the French resistance newspaper COMBAT, (where in the 2nd editorial published clandestinely under the title "Letters to a German Friend") stated: "Man is the force which ultimately cancels all tyrants and gods".[2]

Today, as one seeks to record the successes and the failures of Europe's post-communist man's search for a new Prometheus, one must note that the study of past historical cycles has demonstrated that human freedom and justice together with the dignity of person, can only be acquired, maintained and preserved through civic action and the evolution of a civil society. An additional requirement revealed through the study of 20th century history, is that man must not accept the principle, belief and/or the rationalization put forth by tyrants and presidents alike, which holds to the presumption that individual freedoms are secondary to the requirements of ideological demands, party interests and national security concerns. Should we and our East European brethren desire to comprehend the importance of the concept and the place of freedom as it relates to the individual and his or her relationship to the party, government or the state, one need only to recall the words of a young female revolutionary of yesterday, who prior to her murder in 1919 on the way to a German prison, stated:

> *Freedom only for the supporters of the government, only for the members of one party – however numerous they may be – is no freedom at all. Freedom is always and exclusively freedom for the one who thinks differently. Not because of any fanatical concept of "justice" but because all that is instructive, wholesome and purifying in political freedom depends on this essen-*

---

2. Camus, Albert, *Resistance, Rebellion and Death*. (New York, Alfred Knopf, 1961) p. 14

*tial characteristic, and its effectiveness vanishes when "free-
dom" becomes a special privilege.*[3]

That young "Revolutionary Socialist" was Rosa Luxemburg.

To achieve the goal of democracy, freedom and the dignity of person required that the individual emerge from one's protective physically individualized and psychologically self-contained political cocoon and transcend an attitudinal and an identification barrier which had permeated the totality of the pre 1989-1991 East European society and one's persona. Moreover, this person "in the form of a Gulliver-like figure" held down on all sides by a multitude of physical and psychological restraints, had first to shatter the emotional ties of a symbiotic relationship which existed between himself/herself and the party. This symbiosis was to bind the people and the party in a fatal psycho-political embrace that was reinforced by the element of fear. Furthermore, this emotional force would not only serve as an invisible psychological control device, but also serve to generate a siege mentality that was reinforced by the "Tyranny of Patriotism" which in turn gave birth to the evolution of a "Herd Mentality".

One may equate the behavioral pattern of the people of Enver Hoxha's totalitarian, socio-political structure with its built-in control devices, leadership principle and garrison mentality to that which one would find within a herd of farm animals. Basic to this resemblance is the transference intact of a whole set of characteristics from sheep or cattle to Albanian's tradition-directed people who until the close of World War II knew of no other norms and life patterns than their own and no other customs and traditions than that of their forefathers. One may argue that perhaps the most important characteristic of sheep and cattle, as far as the comparison between the herd and the citizens of a totalitarian state is concerned, is that in a group, sheep and cattle are generally easily led – even to slaughter. In addition, it appears that they lack a mind of their own. This characteristic of the member of the totalitarian society may be attributed to one's awareness of the normative order in place, the reinforcement of such behavior through the S-R Bond conditioning process and peer pressure. The internal psy-

---

3. Nettle, J.P., *Rosa Luxemburg*. (New York, Oxford University Press, 1969) p. 434

chological conditioning process, when combined with the external control devices of the totalitarian state, results in the individual (when separated from the herd) becoming almost totally defenseless and an easy prey to predators in the form of the secret police (Sigurimi).

When frightened, the herd can stampede and destroy everything in its way. By prudent leadership, however, a good shepherd can prevent a stampede and guide the herd with the help of one or two well-trained dogs. Given that throughout the Communist Phase of the History of Albania, there was no major uprising, it now appears that the good shepherd was Enver Hoxha who, as the leader of the Albanian Communist Party, was leading the people to the joyous pasture lands of the Marxist version of the Elysian Fields of Greek mythology. In relation to the "well trained dogs", one could associate such with the members of the Communist Party and their official and unofficial minions.

The herd possesses the potential for becoming a destructive power when unleashed as evident by East Berlin's revolutionary outbreak in 1953, the Pozan uprisings, and the Hungarian national revolution of 1956, also Alexander Dubcek's Prague Spring of 1968. Thus, the members of the herd must be trained to obey commands, be kept on a tight leash, and each member of the herd (for the sake of his personal and family's survival) must see one's self as a member of the herd who obeys the orders of the shepherd who generally knows what is best. No individual sheep should be permitted to think that it can become a shepherd. Whenever a huge population is cast in the image of a herd, there is the implication that most of the people do not know what is best for them or how to go about in meeting the nation's socioeconomic and political needs. Therefore, the people must be told by the shepherd what is best and how to go about achieving the goals established by the "Red Puritans" who seek to build their city on the hill. Yet, because the herd is conditioned to accept the shepherd's projected image, the people who constitute the herd, are simple and simple-minded people who are happiest when told what to do, when to do it, how to do it and, of course, made to do it, for they (the herd) must constantly accept the image of the reality of life as it is projected by the shepherd of the totalitarian state. Thus, as one examines the essence of the Hoxhain society of the Land of the Eagle, one finds that the herd must have faith in their shepherd, for as stated in one of the massive rallies in Hitlerite Germany by Rudolph Hess, "In your heart you know he is right". The significance of this statement is twofold: first, the sheep are not to use logic or reasoning in the election of their leader, and secondly, the sheep must blindly follow their shepherd. While the views expressed do not present an exact picture of the full realities of life in communist Albania, it does, however, reflect to some degree the spirit of Hoxha's Albania, a nation-state where the law of man reigned supreme over the rule of law.

In order for the sheep to become the master of their own destiny, they must ask of themselves two questions: What Is? and What Ought to Be? In so doing, the sheep come to recognize and come to acknowledge not only the existence of oppression, but that the shepherd has committed an intolerable transgression against certain rights which the sheep fell intuitively are theirs. At this moment, while confronted with a crisis of conscience and a conflict of values, the idea of revolt takes form in the mind of man. Thus, with the revolt taking form in the human consciousness, the sheep confront the shepherd and his minions and affirm the existence of both a value (which is represented in their very being) and a limit to the absolute freedom of the shepherd. From this point onward, not only do the sheep no longer accept what was, but now insist that their worth as a human being renders them equal to their master and endows them with the right to the dignity of a person and the measure of freedom accorded the shepherd. Having reached this stage in their revolutionary consciousness, the sheep are determined that what was will never again be.

The agony and ecstasy of the historical experience is to be found in the immense sacrifices man makes in order to obtain significant results only to see such victories swept aside by some unpredictable force. Such notable occurrence have taken place in Lithuania where the people voted the communists back into office and in Romania where the National Front for Salvation headed by Ion Iliescu, a man with impeccable Communist credentials, stole the revolution. Today, the philosophical issue confronting the people is, in the words of Albert Camus, the enduring issue which has confronted individuals, ideologues, philosophers and statesmen alike since time immemorial.

"Whom do you prefer, he that would deprive you of bread in the name of freedom and democracy or he that would take away your freedom in order to guarantee you bread?"[4]

No one can deny that the advent to political power of the oppositionist, or better yet, "the reborn-again democrat", has resulted in the sweeping away of the "Old Order" in the form of a hygienic purge. Nor can it be denied that due to the Hoxhain legacy and a 47 year old psychological conditioning process which was reinforced by the element of fear, various representatives of current competing political power centers have sought to extend, either covertly or overtly, their power and their influence. Contemporary examples of attempts to extend one's power beyond the limits imposed by the democratic constraints of the events of 1990 and 1991 are to difficult to identify. Of actions undertaken by the government, the decision relating to the continuance with the imprisonment of the leader of the Socialist Party together with the judgment to arrest the son of Enver Hoxha, are symbolically significant.

Mr. Fatos Nano, the president of the Socialist Party, was arrested on July 30, 1993 and sentenced to a 12 year prison term on the grounds that, "He was involved in the embezzlement of state property – in the form of emergency aid – to the benefit of a third party and the falsification of official documents". Ilir Hoxha, the son of the former leader of the Albanian Party of Labor, was charged and was sentenced to a one year prison term as a result of an interview which appeared in an April, 1995 issue of the magazine *Modeste*. According to the government, Ilir Hoxha, while defending his father's record, did criticize the government and as a consequence, "Incited hatred against the government".[5]

Of the government's grounds for the arrest and the incarceration of the two men, Amnesty International has concluded in a letter to Dr. Sali Berisha, dated July 31, 1995, that:

> *These two men have been imprisoned as a result of their political beliefs and our organization considers them to be prisoners of conscience.*[6]

---

4. Camus, Albert, *Op. Cit.*, p. 123
5. Amnesty International Letter. 31 July 1995. Ref. TG-EUR. 11/95.06
6. Amnesty International Letter. *Ibid.*

Furthermore, President Berisha's repressed anti-democratic and authoritarian proclivity emerged when he stated, according to Nemik Dokle and as reported in the August 11, 1995 edition of *Zeri i Popullit* (Voice of the People – the newspaper of the Socialist Party of Albania), "Socialists are the enemies of the people". This declaration is diametrically opposed to his October, 1992 statement that, "The future of democracy in Albania depends to a great extent on the development of a parliamentary tradition". Of the development of such a tradition, together with the application of the democratic system of governance by Dr. Berisha and his inner-circle, the president of the Socialist Party, Nemik Dokle, (in a personal interview) stated:

> *The Albanian people like democracy, but they do not like the way the democratic theory is being applied by the leadership of the current government which is riddled with corruption from top to bottom.*[7]

Dr. Berisha's declaration that, "Socialists are the enemies of the people", together with his position on the "Referendum Issue" which resulted in a break with Eduard Selami, tends to suggest that the president of the Republic of Albania was ill-advised or that he possesses a need to create an enemy in his personal quest to perpetuate one's hold on the reigns of power.

In a significant and yet astute manner, such post World War II existentialist philosophers as Albert Camus and Jean Paul Sartre, call to one's attention that should any political leader come to believe that "the end justifies the means", or that "the means justifies the end", in one's individual quest for ultimate power, then the rebel of yesteryear is no longer Prometheus; he is Caesar. If this is to be for the people of the Land of the Eagle, then the question confronting the sons and the daughters of Skenderbeg – according to Milovan Djilas in his study entitled *The Unperfect Society: Beyond the New Class* – remains,

> *Are men doomed to become the slave of the times in which they live, even after irrepressible and timeless effort they have climbed so high to become the masters of the times?*[8]

---

7. Tirana, Albania. August 11, 1995. Personal Interview with Mr. Nemik Dokle, the acting head of the Socialist Party
8. Djilas, Milovan, *The Unperfect Society: Beyond the New Class.* (New York, Harcourt, Brace and World Inc., 1969) p. 237

As one separates the illusion of freedom and democracy from the reality of democratic responsibility and freedom as it applies to the government and to the process of governance in the Land of the Eagle, there emerges a sensing that one is confronted with the "Myth of Sisyphus". That the people of Albania are attracted to the ideals of democracy after six decades of authoritarian and totalitarian rule, cannot be denied. However, whether the attraction and the application is to be that (in the words of Eric Fromm) "representative of a Static Adaptation", or that of a "Dynamic Adaptation" is yet to be determined. Nor can it be denied that the definition and the interpretation rendered the concepts of democracy and freedom varies from political party to political party and from urban centers (or the core city) to the agricultural regions, let alone from individual to individual as a member of an extended family or clan relationship. Moreover, the meaning of the concepts of democracy and of freedom for this tradition-directed person changes according to the degree of one's awareness and conception of himself as an independent and a separate being as opposed to being just an extended appendage of the family or that of the clan. In addition, such variations in interpretations exist because various segments of the intelligentsia and the bureaucracy, together with the former group of apparatchiks of yesteryear, one time opponents of radical change from below, today find themselves defenders of the new privileges which they appropriated to themselves. It is this differentiation brought on also by the clash of class interests, the impact of economic forces and the quest for domestic tranquillity and national security, that renders to the current, fluid, political situation its Sisyphean quality.

It appears that like the cruel King of Corinth, who in Greek mythology was condemned forever to roll a huge stone up a hill in Hades only to have it role down again in nearing the top, the current group of government policy formulators and decision-makers in Tirana finds that upon rolling the "democratic" stone up the hill, it too rolls down on nearing the summit. Thus, in a land which has had no democratic heritage nor a understanding of the concept of freedom and of the responsibilities incurred by the individual as a citizen of a democratic political entity, it is understandable why difficulties exist. In part, the reaction of the people to the frustration-producing process with its various twists and turns as the government seeks to solve the multitude of problems which plague the leadership and the people, was made known to me in the form of the following joke.

> *Two former members of the communist party were sitting at a table in the lounge of the Hotel Djati enjoying a cup of Turkish coffee. One turns to the other and asks, "Tell me, Sali, what is worse than communism?" Sali pauses for a moment and after slowly removing his cigarette, replies, "That which comes after".*

To the observer of the post-communist Albanian socio-economic and political scene, there emerges two diametrically opposite images. On the one hand, one is confronted with the representation that Albania is on the threshold of the "Take-off Stage" with its rudiments of democratic practices and institutions in place, its numerous political parties, vigorous public debate on issues, unexpected outcomes at the voting booth, and evidence of the nation's entrepreneurial advancement as evidenced by the numerous number of outdoor cafes, restaurants, kiosks, and the huge Coca-Cola plant which greets the visitor on the way to or from the airport. On the other hand, there emerges, as a result of discussions with intellectuals, representatives of the younger generation and the man on the street, an illustration which makes one aware that the economic, political and social conditions have all combined to generate a perception among the people that they function within a degenerating environment which reinforces one's personal sense of economic insecurity, personal sense of physical and psychological vulnerability and a sense of powerlessness to change the existing conditions as such relates to the present and to the future. In addition, as a result of the depressing conditions, people have elected to vote with their feet as they migrate to Western Europe, Canada and to the United States of America. Moreover, if, as a result of the social interactional process, one is confronted with the feeling that there exists a slight itch for the security of the past, one must recall that the ideology of communism generated an expression of a new feeling of freedom in the form of the philosophical tenet of historical determinism. In so doing, the theory of Karl Marx and the interpretations rendered it by the advocates of communism and the discipline and sacrifices of the dedicated professional revolutionaries contributed to the individual's sense of a new beginning and a feeling not only of an escape from democratic responsibilities, but also that of the added burdens of freedom.

This is not to state nor to imply that a return to the Hoxha-Stalinist socio-political and economic model will take place. The house which Enver built with its totalitarian features and with its highly centralized command economy is shattered. In addition, that which the man on the street longs for – the impression of stability and law and order which Hoxhaism gave to the individual in society together with a prevailing awareness of economic security which communism offered the person through the financial subsidization of the market, a national health program, and job security from cradle to grave-generates a nostalgic desire to recall the pluses and to forget the minuses. The situation which currently confronts the nation and its citizens in the period of protracted national transition and anxiety as it enters its fifth year of radical multi-dimensional structural transformation, is similar to that which confronted the people of the medieval world as it, too, was undergoing a period of marked change in the character and the function of its economic and political structure together with its cultural ethos. As in the 16th century, the citizens of Albania's transitional economic structure find that the preference for hard currency exchange within the economic interactional process at the personal level and within the market itself, let alone that of competition, has combined to transform one's personal situation into one characterized by insecurity and anxiety as the role of the man on the street becomes that of a competitor.

The attempt of the government of Dr. Sali Berisha to jump-start the economy, put into place an equitable safety net, and to evolve a politically viable, liberal and democratic structure together with an open-market oriented economic system, has to date received mixed reviews. Dr. Elez Bibera, in a study of post-communist East European States entitled *The Legacies of Communism*, calls to one's attention the fact that "Dr. Berisha seems committed to the establishment of a pluralistic democracy based on law and order... and that a comprehensive reform program is well underway".[9] However, Dr. Ray Taras, in a study entitled *East European Politics*, holds to the view that, "Presi-

---

9. Barany, Zoltan and Ivan Volgyes, *The Legacies of Communism in Eastern Europe.* (Baltimore, John Hopkins University Press, 1995) p. 265

dent Berisha's style of leadership seemed to be taking Albania to an executive-dominant system where checks and balances might become insignificant".[10] In the words of Paul Kennedy, "It is difficult to predict how the present may evolve into the future". Yet, the following assessment of the contemporary situation confronting Albania given by Ramiz Alia is significant and insightful. One must recall that it was Ramiz Alia who reacted to the demand of the hard-liners within the party to adopt the "Chinese Solution" as demonstrators were toppling the towering bronze statue of Enver Hoxha in Tirana with the following words, "Me mire te mbledhim cobra bronce se sa kufome njerzuer (It is better to pick up pieces of bronze than human corpses)". Moreover, it is this man, who through his words, actions and decisions, prevented a civil war from enveloping the country. In an interview, Ramiz Alia called to my attention the fact that "400,000 people were unemployed and that 500,000 had left Albania to become economic emigres". In a statement that was designed to underscore the significance of his remarks, he declared, "A majority percentage of our nation's competent people are either unemployed or outside of Albania with their expertise helping other countries and not their country". This is not at all surprising in view of the fact that with the advent to power of the Democratic Party, a "Hygienic Purge" was undertaken to get rid of personnel in the nation's civil service who were identified as undesirable. The alleged criteria for the identification of such persons and their subsequent removal from government service, was not qualification or expertise, but that of time of service and one's assumed prior political orientation. It is rather ironic that in the game of power politics that this should emerge as criteria for expulsion. After all, one must recall that the president of the Republic of Albania, Dr. Sali Berisha, was a member of the Communist Party. Moreover, the current Minister of Defense, Safet Zhulali, had been a communist functionary. In addition, the former premier and co-founder of the Democratic Party, Gramos Pashko, a close colleague of Dr. Berisha, was also a member of the Communist Party. In fact, with the exception of

---

10. White, Stephen and Judy Batt and Paul Lewis, *Developments in East European Politics*. (Durham, Duke University Press, 1993), pp. 172-173
11. Tirana, Albania. August 12, 1995. Personal Interview with a government official who preferred not to be identified.

the Prime Minister, Alexander Meksi, the majority of Albania's current leadership is said to have been members of the old nomenklatura.

Other significant statements made by Ramiz Alia consisted of the following, "Albania would not undergo major economic growth without first opening the factories, for one cannot maintain a nation on the proceeds of coffee houses and juice bars and without developing a modern industrial base". Furthermore, he agreed with the opinion of a segment of the population on a point to which I had called his attention: that "the government had not opened the factories for fear that the concentration of the work force would result in the worker being organized by the political opposition". In addition, while discussing the impact of greed and corruption upon Albania's general economic and political status, he was quick to equate Albania's posture to that of a "Latin American Banana Republic".[12]

The reality of contradictory truths makes it impossible to deny that the fragile Albanian economic and political system, in its own unique manner, has achieved degrees of success. In that prior existing totalitarian oriented institutions and attitudes are in a gradual process of transmutation and that examples of the democratic process (together with an open-market system) exist, cannot be denied. However, it is too simple to assume that the complexity of the Albanian socio-economic and political transformation can be reducible to a single, simplistic mold possessing the label, "Made In America".

Regardless of the historical, political and the economic circumstances surrounding the people, the nation of Albania remains today, as it has been since its emergence as an independent nation state on November 28, 1912, not only a country in a crisis, but a state in search of its future. It is the interplay of the legacy of the past, together with the challenge to liberal democracy and the protracted state of the economy, which will determine if Caesar will topple Prometheus, for in the words of J.F. Brown, the author of *The Surge to Freedom* and the study, *Hopes and Shadows: Eastern Europe After Communist* – "The longer the market economy takes to deliver the goods under de-

12. Tirana, Albania. August 14, 1995. Personal Interview with Ramiz Alia, the man who succeeded to the head of the Albanian Party of Labor upon the death of Enver Hoxha, Albania's former dictator.

mocracy, the more attractive the authoritarian alternative could become".[13] A means of acquiring an insight as such relates to the question, "What now for Albania?" may be derived by examining transpiring political events through Albania's cultural prism. It is this cultural prism, a by-product of the nation's myths, belief system, value structure and attitudinal dispositions or predispositions which will determine Albania's domestic and international perception and thus its perceived national and foreign policy options.

According to Machiavelli, "There is nothing more difficult to carry out, nor more doubtful of success, nor more dangerous to handle, than to initiate a new order of things".[14] Yet, an examination of the political trends and the political events which have transpired in the period since the advent to power of the anti-communist and pro-democratic oriented political parties through Albania's cultural prism, suggests that the chances for a truly democratic rebirth look no better today than they did in the interwar period. While no one can deny that the rudiments of democratic institutions are in place, one can question – on the basis of past decisions made and subsequently retracted and actions taken, the government and the individual's commitment to democracy. Moreover, an analysis of the governance process in Albania reveals that because f the combined 66 year authoritarian and totalitarian legacy and the conditioning process of the past, there exists the tendency to clothe the realities of arbitrary power, to one degree or another, in the protective garb of tradition and legitimacy. Thus, in the words of Dr. Merle Fainsod, "Constitutionalism becomes the facade to conceal the authoritarian tendency within the governing formula".[15]

It is hard to deny that Albania's emerging political process is yet to manifest itself in its definitive form. Furthermore, given the actions and the reactions of the representatives of that body which constitutes the "Power Elite" within the various competing political power centers, it is difficult not to conclude that they are advocated of the democratic

---

13. Brown, J.F., *Hopes and Shadows: East Europe After Communism.* (Durham, Duke University Press, 1994) p. 309
14. Schlesinger, Arthur, *The Coming of the New Deal* (Cambridge, Riverside Press, Houghton Mifflin Co., 1959) p. i
15. Fainsod, Merle. *How Russia Is Ruled.* (Cambridge, Harvard University Press, 1962) p. 311

process not by conviction but by calculation. Meanwhile, the "Re-born-again Democrats", the by-products of a negative conditioning process in the form of a totalitarian mind-set, tend to misinterpret and to manipulate the message of the fragile concept of democracy. Nor can one but wonder if they unconsciously adhere to the belief proclaimed by the pro-fascist philosopher of Action Francaise, Charles Maurras, when he stated, "There is only one way to improve democracy: destroy it".[16]

Today, as in the past, Albania remains the sum of its differences. The legacy of a half century of totalitarian rule weighs heavily upon the national psyche and upon the nation's political culture. This psycho-historical scar is reinforced by the historical fact that the people know of no instance where a leading class or a self-contained political elite or a leading personality (with the exception of Ramiz Alia) has voluntarily renounced its political privileges and its economic advantages for the sake of Albania in the post World War II era.

As the Land of the Eagle enters the fifth year of its post-communist phase of governance, democracy remains on trial. Once again, as in the past, every economic and political decision results in power shifts as the competing "Power Elites" scramble to preserve or the increase their power, influence and their privileges. In the March, 1992, national elections, the people of Albania (who were confronted with one issue) rendered to the Democratic Party the electoral victory which had initially been denied them in 1991. Now, four years later, with the crystallization of many issues, the citizens are being called upon to accept or to reject the leadership and the policy programs of the Democratic Party. The convergence of various streams of discontent has given birth to fissures within the Democratic Party: the most notable being the formation of the Democratic Party: the most notable being the formation of the Democratic Alliance. Reacting to the authoritarian tendency (as projected in statements made and decisions entered into by the political elite within the Democratic Party), such men as the ex-Vice Prime Minister and co-founder of the Democratic Party, Gramos Pashko; to ex-Minister of Defense, Perikli Teta; and Neritan Ceka, a prime mover

---

16. Nolte, Ernst, *The Three Faces of Fascism* (New York, Holt, Rinehart and Winston, 1966) p. 108.

in the events of 1991, together with Arben Jmami, have established a competing power center in an attempt to acquire political power. Their goal, according to a former supporter of President Sali Berisha (who prefers to remain anonymous), consists of "Formulating a policy of national regeneration based, in part, upon the doctrines and the principles originally advocated by the founders but which have been abandoned by the current leadership of the Democratic Party".

The emergence of a multitude of opposing political constellations has resulted in agreements being reached by individuals and political parties who seek to bring about what is perceived to be the unseating of a government which is engaged in separating freedom from justice. Thus, in Tirana's coffee houses and outdoor cafes, one can hear talk of the potential impact of the Social Democrats' decision (under the leadership of Dr. Skender Ginushi) to form an alliance with Neritan Ceka, the current president of the Democratic Alliance. Other speculative statements tend to suggest that the Socialist Party may join this emerging coalition, for it is aware that the people of Albania prefer to have a coalition government. This may be attributed, in part, to their past varied experiences under the "democratic" tutelage of President Sali Berisha. Moreover, it is also rumored that independent factions such as that which is currently emerging in its embryonic form around the former chairperson of the Democratic Party, Eduard Selami, may also join the opposition. An additional political grouping, because of its stated adherence to a nationalist-oriented program that calls for the unity of all Albanian lands and its stated commitment to the establishment of the rule of law as opposed to the rule of man, is the Party of National Unity. Headed by Jelajet Beqiri, this party consists of students, intellectuals, ex-military personnel, pensioners and former members of the nomenklature. While it does not have representation in parliament, it does have a large body of active supporters and sympathizers which cuts across the total political spectrum. According to former Albanian mission personnel to the United Nations, this political party can be said to represent Albania's "Silent Majority".

Given the national experience, together with the Byzantine mind, it appears that there exists within the body politique, the traditional desire to right old wrongs and to establish an authoritarian system of governance as a means, but with democracy as its future goal. This may be attributed to the fact that the "Reborn-again Democrats" are not reformist enough to break with the old thought patterns of the communist era and the hide-bound national traditions of the past as demonstrated by President Sali Berisha's political decision. According to the October 7, 1995 issue of *The Economist*, Dr. Berisha signed a law which in effect banned the present leaders of the Socialist Party, the Social Democrats and the senior members of the old Communist Party (with the exception of Sali Berisha, who was once himself a candidate member of the party's central committee) from participating in the parliamentary elections due next April, 1996. Moreover, he has banned such individuals from participating in any local or national election until the year, 2002. This political maneuver, when combined with past statements and actions, is representative of a democratic failure which will once again result in Caesar toppling Prometheus in the Land of the Eagle – Albania.

REFLECTIONS

REFLECTIONS

Albania, a participant in our computer inundated telecommunica-tion global network, is has been and always will be a nation in crisis and a nation in search of its political soul. Today, 1997, Albania's political life and economic well-being is adrift in cross currents of ambiguous guidelines that can neither be identified, defined nor delin-eated. While aware that competition in government inadequately con-trolled leads to anarchy, the Land of the Eagle-Albania, remains a country pervaded with scandal, corruption and political in-fighting. According to Namik Dokle, the vice-chairperson of the Socialist Party and organizational secretary, "The month of February, 1997, confronted the citizens of Albania from February 2 to February 10, 1997, with a potential all-out civil war between the forces of the political status quo headed by Dr. Sali Berisha and the supporters of the Democratic Party and those of change consisting of the Democratic Alliance and the Socialist Party together with the leadership of other opposition politi-cal parties". This delicate and conflict-prone situation was presented of Albania, as a Tosk-Gheg conflict brought on by actions undertaken by the Tosks of southern Albania, for the sought to politicize cultural differences. One must recall that Albania is divided into two distinct geo-political and psycho-historical entities by the Shkumbi River which is located south of Albania's capitol city of Tirana. Furthermore, ac-cording to Petrit Kalakiela, a member of the National Council, who was a strong advocate for the opening of all Secret Police (Sigurimi) files of all the members of the State Security and the political deputies, called to one's attention, "That Berisha's statements were to true as demonstrated by an analysis of the voting patterns and especially since the Socialist Party won in all of Tirana's nineteen electoral zone..."

Albania is today an armed camp. According to the country's leading literary figure and member of Parliament, Dritero Agolli, "There exists approximately 1 to 2 million illegally held modern day weapons in the hands of the people". In addition, he called to my attention his observation that "Far more damaging to the nation is the lack of trust among the people in their government regardless of which political party possesses political power". Of this point, a Parliamentarian who desired to remain anonymous, interjected the following, significant statement:

> *If a reasonable and workable plan is introduced along with an adherence to ethical principles of government and law and order is reestablished throughout the land – that would be a major democratic achievement. Furthermore, the process of economic restoration will need time for the building of a modern day industrial and technetronic infrastructure which is a complex process requiring major financial investments. In addition, I have observed that the government is making the same mistakes as others have made. It is a difficult situation which confronts us as we seek to climb out of the socio-political quagmire the Berisha administration left us with.*

Of the transpiring political events, the Socialist Party's political victory in the 1997 election may be attributed to the "Protest Vote" and to the fact that a total of 800,000 people did not vote in the last national election. This resulted in the ouster of President Sali Berisha, a former communist and professed democrat with authoritarian proclivities together with the representatives of the majority of the Democratic Party from the seats of civic power. In the 1997 election, the Socialist Party won 670,000 votes. Today, the Socialist Party headed by Prime Minister, Fatos Nano, and President Rexep Mejdani, while possessing a dominant position within the political process including 128 representatives in a 155 seat Parliament, find themselves confronting a deficit over 300 million dollars or 15% of the Gross Domestic Product. Furthermore, on the basis of my personal observations, the government of Fatos Nano must establish a national climate of acceptability for public order cannot be restored throughout the country without the evolution of an attitudinal of trust at the personal level by the citizens of the nation in relation to their government. The quest to establish a climate of trust can be achieved by the government of Fatos Nano by remaining on all issues – clear, simple, direct, and resolute. As the trustee for the people, the Socialist Party must not only preserve and develop the nation's industrial and economic potential, but it must also seek to establish the 21st century oriented technical infrastructure which in itself results in the establishment of a modern day technetronic society with future oriented institutions.

A glance at the political, economic and psychological mind-set today clearly indicates that the Land of the Eagle-Albania must be involved in a reappraisal not only of its national values, but of all of its governmental mechanisms. In addition, the leadership of the government must, to greater degree than that of the Berisha government, become involved in the confidence building process and in a Populist national program. Furthermore, the power elite within the Socialist Party must structure viable programs for the administration of resources and plants already in place, reestablish foreign markets and adapt existing economic organizations to the service of the people in such a manner that not only is the nation's economic independence maintained, but that no external politician can acquire control of the economic levers of power as did Benito Mussolini in the mid-1920's through a program of economic imperialism. The election of 1997 cannot be viewed – as so many cynically do in Albania – as a mere shifts from one group of exploiters only interested in personal gain to another which is also only interested in the acquisition of ill-begotten wealth. The political significance of the election of 1997 is to be found in the undisputed historical fact that it will determine the direction that

Albania will take not only as it enters the 21st century, but also if the nation moves forward as a viable and contributing member on the European political scene.

For Albania's Prime Minister, Fatos Nano, the words of Machiavelli are relevant:

There is nothing more difficult to carry out nor more doubtful of success, not more dangerous to handle than to institute a new order of things.

The above words must ring true as he seeks to bring about the required degree of reform and recovery of a nation which in March, 1997, was vanishing down a sinkhole and was no longer an organized society but a state of chaos where children brandishing grenades and automatic rifles were contributing to the continuing breakdown of civil authority. Dr. Sali Berisha admitted that "he had no national control. He had no army and no police". After interviews with the Deputy Foreign Minister, Ilir Meta; Dritero Agolli; Namik Dokle and Petrit Kalakiela and others, I became aware that the people involved in the decision-marking process realized that success in administrative matters and politic relations stands or falls in the execution of policy. According to the Deputy Foreign Minister, Ilir Meta, on the one hand in the realm of foreign policy, Albania currently seeks entry in Europe as an active member in a Balkan Federation – while on the other hand, Namik Dokle seeks to establish a climate of trust as he seeks first to acquire from the people control over all automatic weapons, heavy weapons and explosives in the government's drive to return Albania to a state of national reconciliation. Yet, as the man in street seeks to leave the country in search of employment and opportunity to improve one's standard of living – even if need be by paying $10,000 for an America visa – he reflects on the words of a former Parliamentarian, Todor Keko, who recited the following verse to his fellow legislators:

Ja na erdhi pluralizmi
Me prempteme te medha
Zoghy kendojn me cingrin
Mbreterit mbeten po ate,

whose English translation would make one aware that political pluralism now exists in Albania with great promise for the future, but while the birds may sing, the kings remain the same, for with few exceptions all are former members of the Albanian Party of Labor.

The complex, national dimension of the Yugoslav tragedy symbolically is representative of a festering sore that first appeared in 1919, and which once lanced, resulted (following the death of Joseph Broz-Tito in 1980 and the advent to political power of Slobodan Milosevic in 1987), in the shattering of an age-old dream of national unity and the disintegration of a nation-state. Of this seven decade Yugoslav epic with its slogan of bratsvo i jedinstvo (brotherhood and unity) and a central non-state source of political power, the Communist Party of Yugoslavia and the life-long, protracted struggle among the various republics as well as the two autonomous regions of Vojvodina and Kosovo over the issue of Confederation and Federalism, became by 1981, a full blown ethnic guerrilla war that touched upon all aspects of Yugoslav political, economic and social life.

That a low-intensity type of political warfare was to be found in the Yugoslav nation-state, cannot be denied. Nor can one dismiss outright the impact of the ethnic variable on governmental policy. The increase in the voices of opposition to governmental centralization, as opposed to the concept and the practice of federalism (as applied in the West) could not be permitted to be at the expense of the dominant power position of the Communist Party of Yugoslavia or Tito's personal prerogatives. One must recall that:

> *Tito was not a democrat at heart; he was always suspicious of both the intrinsic virtues of democracy and its validity as a system of political organization. He had little patience with differing views, let alone with a system that would institutionalize them. All his flair for experimentation and political dynamism was to stop at a line that would preserve and hopefully solidify his hold on power under difficult circumstances.*

It must be noted that the Balkans have yet to produce an individual statesman or rule who adhered to and applied to the principles of democracy while in office. This, in part, may by attributed to the fact that while yesteryear's revolutionaries may have desired to be democratic while far from the seats of power, they found upon the acquisition of the seat of power that the dynamics of the situation confronting them and the country made it impossible for democracy to be applied. The above phenomenon may be due to an appreciation of the realities of political power that served to make it possible for both Tito and Milosevic to accept the fact, for the good of the nation, that a little tyranny required more tyranny until each abandoned all of their individual and personal compunctions against its practice.

As the winds of war began to sweep across the plains and the mountainous regions of the Land of the South Slavs-Yugoslavia in 1989, it became obvious to the observer of the Balkan scene following the walkout of the Slovenian delegation at the Congress of the federal parties of the various individual republics, that the end of the Communist Party would take place in the immediate future and that the status of the nation-state of Yugoslavia was not only questionable but in a state of jeopardy. The year, 1990, was to be the year of decision as free multi-party elections took place in April 1990, and in May 1990, in Slovenia and Croatia respectively. The elections resulted in Milan Kucan emerging as president of Slovenia and heading the drive for independence. In Croatia, Franjo Tudjman became the first elected president of Croatia, a man who is anti-Serbian, a Croation nationalist and an individual who was to replace the old state symbols with the symbols that reminded the Serbian population of the mass murders and their zero experience under the reign of the Ustashi during World War II. Furthermore, with the Croatian media's daily call for "Croatia for Croatians Only", there took place wholesale dismissals from governmental positions, Croatian citizen of Serbian heritage. Such actions which could only be called, at this historical moment, a hygienic purge which definitely confronted the Serb not only with negative images of the past, but also with a deep foreboding of the future which served only to confirm one's worst fears.

The outbreak of the conflict situation between Slovenia and the nation of Yugoslavia began and remained a low intensity conflict. As the Slovene defense force engaged the JNA in numerous "fire fights", the war became a propaganda war as Ljubljana successfully turned world public opinion against the Serbs and the Yugoslav nation-state. However, what one must recall is the historical fact that Belgrade had written off Slovenia even before the first shot was fired. The outbreak of the Croatian conflict with its highly explosive mix, a product of the Ustashi of the past and its war-mongering rhetoric, became the force which gave birth to that which the world would come to know as "Ethnic Cleansing". In this era of intrusive mass communication and instant media coverage, the citizens of our "Global Village" were soon to be exposed to the horrors of a civil war possessing a heritage in the words of Milovan Djilas, "Of a land without justice throughout the ages". The Croatian leadership, as a result of the one-week JNA-Slovenian conflict, became aware of certain internal weaknesses which essentially consisted of the following:

> *The lack of a clear strategy and the demonstrated lack of determination to follow in full force (the) official doctrine of preserving the sovereignty and the territorial integrity of Yugoslavia as envisioned by the Yugoslav constitution.*

The ensuing, protracted period of warfare which was to grip the totality of the Yugoslav nation was also to give birth to such negative world-shattering killing fields as that which the historian, the statesmen of the world, and the innocent observer were to witness – which bore the names of Vukovar, Srebrenica, the bridge at Mostar and the Kosovo Hospital Incident at Sarajevo. Of two of the occurrences, it must be noted that in relation to the hostile fire which took place at Kosovo Hospital, General Rose informed the President of Bosnia, Aliya Izetbegovic, in a most angry tone that it was "an act to have come not from Serb controlled areas but from Muslim controlled areas".

Furthermore, in the book *Balkan Odyssey*, Sir David Owen calls to the reader's attention the following significant data:

> *A senior ballistics expert in Zagreb had studied a map of likely trajectory patterns produced by United Nations' investigators in Sarajevo and believed the angle at which the motor had hit the*

*roof at the market stall (February 5, 1994) indicated that the
firing point was to be 1100-2000 meters from impact than 2000-
3000 meters and that this would tend to indicate that the 120
m.m. motor had been fired from a Bosnian Army position.*

Today, 1997, approximately two years following the signing of the
Dayton Peace Accord, the Yugoslav danse macabre has moved from
destruction to reconciliation. The war among Slavic brothers has come
to an end, but the bitter taste – a legacy of the war – remains behind.
Yugoslavia as a viable, political entity possessing its varied ethno-
political republics, no longer may be found on a modern day map of
Europe. Today, the European map is more akin to that which existed
before the firing of the Guns of August of 1414-1918.

The essence of the Yugoslav drama with its extremes of rage and
violence, together with man's continual quest for symbolic immortality, makes all of the participants in the dance of death and the slaughter
of the innocent aware that only through conflict and killing can one
became as his grandfather and father before him, the mythological
warrior within the clan's immortalizing process. It is this force and the
fatalistic belief that blood cries for blood (as in the past) that will confront Europe in the 21st century with yet an additional Balkan nightmare. The study of the history of mankind heightens the awareness
that there exists an integral relationship between man and his dreams.
In addition, as one chases his illusion, he, together with a multitude of
internal and external variables over which he possesses no control, works
to shatter the impression that it is no more than a figment of one's
imagination. Since time immemorial, this vicious cycle of hope and
destruction has served to transform the people of the Balkan peninsula
into fatalists and its territory into, "The Land Without Justice".

As with Yugoslavia, shattered illusions played havoc with Greece.
The liberation of Athens came on Thursday, 12 October 1944, as German military units of Army Group E continued with its withdrawal of
the Wehrmacht from Greece. While Security Battalions that were left
behind clashed with EAM/ELAS units in various communities such
as Meligala, Kalamata, Pyrgos and other areas, an orderly transfer of

power took place. Yet, it must be noted that the quest for blood and vengeance did exist and take place as in the village of Kalamata on Sunday, September 17, 1944, when the former governor of Messenia and other officials were brought back from Meligala. Of what transpired, Mark Mazower stated, "As soon as they were marched into the main square, frenzied onlookers broke loose of the ELAS civil police and in ten minutes beat some of the prisoners to death and strung the others up from lamp-posts". Of the liberation on October 12th, Theotokas wrote:

> *Today we feel an enormous uncontrollable popular wave lifting us and carrying us off.*
>
> *What this mass wants exactly, no one knows, not even its most articulate members. This is not the industrial proletariat of the great European centers with concrete socio-economic demands of scientific socialism. Here we have to do with incalculable forces. The Russian Revolution is in the air, but also the French Revolution and the Paris Commune, a national liberation war and who knows what other confused elements.*

Yet, while the people shouted the EAM's slogan, "LAOKRATIA", which translates into "People Power", Moscow failed to alert the leadership of the Greek communist-led resistance alliance and the Greek People's Liberation Army about the Churchill-Stalin percentage deal of 1944, that had awarded to Great Britain the dominant voice in Greek affairs. The failure to render the above cue to the KKE's power elite bankrupted the moment for the seizure of political power as victory services took the place of an anticipated communist, political coup d'etat.

In closing, let it be known that the Europe of the interwar years, 1919-1939, caught between the mythical monsters of Scylla and Charybdis – the totalitarianism of the Political Right (Naziism and Fascism) and the Political Left (Communism) generated numerous mythological and elusive illusions. The pull of an illusion, an erroneous perception in which the individual, the collective or a nation, is deceived by its adherence to a belief or a perception, remains today as powerful a force as it was throughout the interwar years. For the people of the nations of the Balkan Peninsula, the cycle of birth and death is seethed with violence and cruelty, for the legends of the land and the family rest upon the memories of the past. The people possess a spiritual bond with one's past and it is this which makes both the nation and the individual aware of the historical fact that their transmitting permanence is maintained by the silent quest to chase after the illusionary images of unattainable goals. Thus, Albania, Greece, and Yugoslavia are destined to remain prisoners of the age-old tragedy of the Balkan past.

BIBLIOGRAPHY

BIBLIOGRAPHY

Amery, Julian, *Sons of the Eagle;* London, 1948

Armstrong, Hamilton-Fish, *The New Balkans;* New York, 1926

Barany, Zoltan, *The Legacies of Communism In Eastern Europe*; Baltimore, 1995

Borkenau, Franz, *European Communis*; New York, 1953

Brown, J.F., *Hopes and Shadows: East Europe After Communism;* Durham, 1994

Bullock, Allan, *Hitler A Study In Tyranny;* New York, 1952

Camus, Albert, *The Plague;* London, 1961

Churchill, Winston, *The Grand Alliance;* Boston, 1950

Churchill, Winston, *The World Crisis, 1915;* New York, 1929

Ciano, Glaezzo, *Count Ciano's Diary;* Perbrrrana, 1949

Clissold, Stephen, *Whirlwind;* New York, 1949

Conquest, Robert, *The Great Terror: A Reassessment;* New York, 1990

Cookridge, G.H., *Set Europe Ablize;* New York, 1967

Costa, Nicholas J., *Albania: A European Enigma;* Boulder, 1995

Crnobrnja, Mihailo, *The Yugoslav Drama;* Montreal, 1996

Davies, "Trotsky", *Illyrian Venture;* London, 1952

Deakin, F.W.D., *The Embattled Mountain;* New York, 1971

Dedijer, Vladimir, *Tito Speaks;* London, 1953

Deighton, Len, *Blood, Tears and Folly;* New York, 1994

Djilas, Aleksa, *The Contested Country-Yugoslavia Unity and Communist Revolution 1919-1953;* Cambridge, Massachusetts, 1991

Djilas, Milovan, *The Unperfect Society: Beyond the New Class;* New York, 1969 *Wartime;* New York, 1977

Fainsod, Merle, *How Russia Is Ruled;* Cambridge, Massachusetts, 1962

Fielding, Xan, *One Man In His Time;* London, 1990

Fischer, Bernd J., *King Zog and the Struggle for Stability In Albania;* Boulder, 1984

Galati, Stephen-Fischer, *The Communist Parties of Eastern Europe;* New York, 1979

Hadri, Ali, *Ali Kelmendi, 1900-1939;* Preshtina, Yugoslavia, 1984

Harowitz, David, *The Free World Colossus;* New York, 1965

Hibbert, Reginald, *Albania's National Liberation Struggle: The Bitter Victory;* London, 1991

Hoxha, Enver, *The Anglo-American Threat To Albania;* Tirana, Albania, 1982

Isaac, Jeffery C., *Arenth, Camus and Modern Rebellion;* New Haven, 1992

Kazantzakis, Nikos, *The Fratricides;* New York, 1964

Kennan, George, *American Diplomacy, 1900-1950;* London, 1952

Kennedy, Paul, *The Rise and Fall of Great Powers;* New York, 1987

Kirkpatrick, Ivone, *Mussolini: A Study In Power;* New York, 1964

Kolko, Gabriel, *The Politics of War: United States Foreign Policy 1943-1945;* New York, 1968

Koestler, Arthur, *The Yogi and the Commissar;* New York, 1946

Laqueur, Walter, *The Dream That Failed: Reflections On The Soviet Union;* New York, 1994

Lifton, Robert J., *History and Human Survival;* New York, 1961

Lumpe, John R., *Yugoslavia As History;* London, 1996

Maclean, Fitzroy, *The Heretic;* New York, 1957

Mazower, Mark, *Inside Hitler's Greece: The Experience of the Occupation 1941-1945;* New Haven, 1993

Meyer, Alfred, *Leninism;* Cambridge, Massachusetts, 1957

Nettle, J.P., *Rosa Luxemburg;* New York, 1969

Nolte, Ernst, *The Three Faces of Fascism;* New York, 1966

Owen, David, *Balkan Odyssey;* New York, 1995

Quayle, Anthony, *Eight Hours From England;* New York, 1946

Remarque, Erich, *All Quiet On The Western Front;* Boston, 1929

Roberts, Walter R., *Tito, Mihailovic and the Allies 1941-1945;* New Jersey, 1973

Rosenstone, Robert A., *Crusade Of The Left: The Lincoln Battalion In The Spanish Civil War;* New York, 1969

Schlesinger, Arthur, *The Coming of the New Deal;*
Cambridge, Massachusetts, 1959

Shirer, William, *The Rise and Fall Of The Third Reich;*
New York, 1960

Skendi, Stavro, *Albania;* New York, 1957

Smiley, David, *Albanian Assigment;* London, 1984

Sugar, Peter, *Eastern European Nationalism In The 20th Century;*
Washington, D.C. 1995

Thomas, Hugh, *The Spanish Civil War;* New York, 1960

Tilman, H.W., *When Men and Mountains Meet;* London, 1946

Tuchman, Barbara W., *Stilwell and the American Experience
In China;* New York, 1970

Watson, Hugh-Seaton, *East European Revolution;* New York, 1956

West, Richard, *Tito and the Rise and Fall of Yugoslavia;*
New York, 1994

While, Stephen, *Developments In East European Politics;*

INDEX

INDEX

K

L

M

V

Venizelos, Eleftherios 78, 79, 111
Vithkuq 37, 41, 42, 98, 151
Vukmanovic Tempo 75, 94, 109, 118

W

Watson, Hugh-Seaton 33, 35, 59, 69, 144, 204
Weick, General (German) 109
Weil, Simone 15
Wilfred Owen 9
Wilson, Woodrow President 11, 98, 112, 148
Winetrout, Kenneth 16, 18, 36, 204
Wolff, Robert Lee 47
Workers League 128

Y

Yugoslavia
29, 30, 31, 33, 34, 35, 36, 37, 39, 40, 49, 51, 52, 53, 57, 58, 59, 61, 62,
63, 64, 65, 67, 68, 69, 70, 71, 72, 73, 74, 75, 76, 80, 81, 82, 83, 85,
86, 87, 91, 92, 93, 94, 96, 97, 100, 101, 102, 103, 106, 109, 110,
111, 113, 114, 115, 116, 118, 119, 120, 122, 123, 125, 130, 133,
134, 135, 136, 137, 138, 139, 140, 141, 142, 152, 153, 154, 163,
164, 170, 174, 195, 196, 197, 198, 200, 202, 204

Z

Zakhariadis, Nicholas 65, 72, 106
Zog, Ahmed King
45, 46, 47, 52, 59, 77, 81, 82, 83, 84, 88, 89, 100, 126, 127, 131, 134,
150, 152, 158, 159, 160, 165, 194, 202
Zukov, Marshal (Russian) 61

ABOUT THE AUTHOR

Nicholas J. Costa was born in Southbridge, Massachusetts. He received degrees from American International College, Springfield, Massachusetts, Boston University and University of Connecticut. Following his service with the First Marine Division from 1950 to 1952 during the Korean War he entered the teaching profession. In 1965 he accepted a professorship at Manchester Community College in Manchester, Connecticut. In 1967 he was assigned to a position a Greater Hartford Community College, Hartford Connecticut until his retirement in 1992.

*He was a visiting professor at Easter Connecticut State College, Wesylan University and George Washington University in Washington D.C. He is the author of the numerous articles that have appeared in East European Quarterly and the analytical study entitled, **Albania A European Enigma**.*